Realist Criminology

Roger Matthews
Professor of Criminology, University of Kent, UK

First published 2014 by
PALGRAVE MACMILLAN

Palgrave Macmillan in the UK is an imprint of Macmillan Publishers Limited, registered in England, company number 785998, of Houndmills, Basingstoke, Hampshire RG21 6XS.

Palgrave Macmillan in the US is a division of St Martin's Press LLC, 175 Fifth Avenue, New York, NY 10010.

Palgrave Macmillan is the global academic imprint of the above companies and has companies and representatives throughout the world.

Palgrave® and Macmillan® are registered trademarks in the United States, the United Kingdom, Europe and other countries.

ISBN: 978–1–137–44569–8 Hardback
ISBN: 978–1–137–44570–4 Paperback

This book is printed on paper suitable for recycling and made from fully managed and sustained forest sources. Logging, pulping and manufacturing processes are expected to conform to the environmental regulations of the country of origin.

A catalogue record for this book is available from the British Library.

A catalog record for this book is available from the Library of Congress.

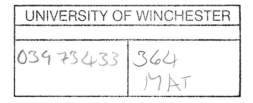

For Jock

Contents

List of Figures

Preface

This is a book of two parts. The first is largely exponential and provides a basis for engaging in a revised form of critical realism. It is mainly about what was previously known as 'left realism', which is essentially a political and social mode of analysis providing a critique and a counter to the dominant liberal-conservative consensus within criminology. It has become increasingly necessary, however, to broaden the theoretical and methodological focus of this approach if it is to be established as a critical alternative to existing perspectives.

This revised version of *Realist Criminology* draws heavily on the body of work developed over the last two decades by critical realists. This work, in addressing questions of epistemology and methodology, has made a considerable contribution to the development of a critical social science. Contributions by Roy Bhaskar, Andrew Sayer, Margaret Archer and others have produced a range of texts that have opened new areas of debate and provided new ideas about a number of unresolved issues which have long concerned social scientists. Their aim has been to develop an approach to social issues that is essentially critical and useful and also contains emancipatory themes.

One of the main arguments in the book's earlier chapters is that criminology, far from fragmenting, increasingly centres on varieties of liberalism on the one hand and administrative criminology on the other. With that in mind, the second part of the book provides examples of these approaches in order to demonstrate how they address the issues of crime and punishment and attempts to identify their respective weaknesses and limitations.

Thus, the book operates on two levels. The first, a mostly modest project, involves transposing many of the ideas and insights of critical realism into the criminological enterprise. The second level is more ambitious: it aims to fashion a fairly fundamental critique and rethink of the direction of criminology itself. The ultimate aim is to re-establish realist criminology and contribute to the development of a more critical and progressive approach to crime and punishment; an approach aimed at reducing suffering, abuse, exploitation and victimisation while improving the operation of the criminal justice system and thereby contributing to the goal of achieving greater social justice. These ideals may be lofty, but they are achievable, although they require a major rethink of how theory, methods and practice are linked.

Acknowledgements

A number of people have contributed in different ways to this book. I thank Keith Hayward, Francis Cullen and Helen Easton for their comments on different chapters. I have benefited greatly from discussions with Phil Carney and John Pitts. For their support and encouragement, I also thank all my colleagues at the University of Kent, particularly Caroline Chatwin, Johhny Ilan, Jennifer Fleetwood and Kate O'Brien.

Acknowledgements

1
The Successes and Failures of Modern Criminology

The birth of modern criminology

This history, like all histories, is highly selective. Its starting point is the 1960s and early 1970s. It was a point at which criminology emerged as a recognised subject area drawing freely on sociology, psychology, law and economics, resulting in the establishment of a multifaceted field of study which began to attract students in large numbers. Its exponential growth was fuelled by what Stuart Hall (1980) described as the 'drift into law and order society', with crime becoming firmly established as a major cause of public and political concern. Over the last thirty years criminology has become one of the fastest-growing subject areas in the social sciences.

David Garland (1997) has identified the foundations of contemporary criminology in Britain as being laid in the 1950s and 1960s by publications emanating from the University of Cambridge Institute of Criminology – particularly the work of Sir Leon Radzinowicz, on one hand, combined with a growing body of work from the Home Office, on the other. These two formative strands, Garland argues, generated a mix of pragmatic and administrative criminology. Paul Rock (1988), in contrast, attributes considerable influence to the work of Herbert Mannheim. However, in the formation of the 'new criminology', which took place in Britain in the 1970s, Radzinowicz and Manheim were not central reference points in the main criminological textbooks.

Modern criminology, in fact, was the product of four intersecting lines of force: positivistic and administrative criminologies no doubt represented two of these strands; in the UK it was also the influence of a growing body of deviancy theory – much of it imported from America – that served to create a new paradigm through the work of writers like

1

Howard Becker, Ed Lemert, Alvin Gouldner, Erving Goffman, David Matza and Robert Merton; this in turn was underpinned by a fourth strand incorporating the more general classic texts by Marx, Durkheim, and Foucault that provided the impetus for the development this new subject area (Taylor, Walton and Young 1975). The 'new' criminology was profoundly sociological, critical and political. It was more than an inflection in the historical curve of criminology. Rather, it represented a qualitative shift. As Michel Foucault (1984) has pointed out, it is not so much that certain 'founding fathers' created the subject area of 'criminology' but rather that the establishment of a particular discourse and the formation of a significant audience, along with the development of a set of institutional practices and networks, retrospectively gave various authors their notoriety.

The establishment of the National Deviancy Conference in 1968 provided an important vehicle for giving impetus to the development and promotion of this new criminology. Similarly, the formation of the European Society for the Study of Deviance and Social Control, which was established in 1973, provided a similar vehicle for a new generation of young European scholars (Cohen 1998; Ferrell, Hayward and Young 2008, ch. 2). A number of books concerned with crime and deviance began to appear that set in motion new ways of thinking about these established themes. A major contribution to the development of this emerging subject area was the publication in April 1973 of *The New Criminology* (Taylor, Walton and Young). As Alvin Gouldner pointed out in his foreword to the book, this was 'the first truly comprehensive critique that we have ever had of the totality of the past and contemporary, of European and American, studies of "crime" and "deviance"'. The book became required reading in every newly established criminology course around the country. The aim of the book was to critically review the major theories of crime and deviance and in particular to develop a critique of positivist criminology locating the problem of crime within a larger socio-economic and political framework. In pursuing this objective the Young Turks, as they were known, injected much-needed critical energy into the subject area while questioning the dominant conceptions of the normal and pathological. These Young Turks, together with the growing body of apprentice criminologists, were not based in the established centres of learning, such as the Institute of Cambridge or the London School of Economics, but were located in the new universities, many of which had been built or modernised during the 1960s.

In America the development of what we might call the 'new criminology' took a distinctly different form. John Laub (2004) and Francis

Cullen (2011), in their respective presidential addresses to the American Society of Criminology, argued that a new criminological paradigm emerged in the 1960s influenced by the work of Edwin Sutherland and Donald Cressey's *Principles of Criminology* (1960) and Travis Hirschi's *Causes of Delinquency* (1969). Both publications are seen as pioneering texts that contributed to the establishment of a new paradigm that was critical of earlier individualistic and biological accounts of the causes of crime. However, as in the UK, these publications were supplemented by the growing body of deviancy theorists. In addition, the legacy of the Chicago School, which included the work of writers like Albert Cohen (1955) on working-class subcultures, displaced some of the existing work on the social psychology of offenders with a more thoroughgoing sociological account. Cloward and Ohlin (1960) tried to refine Cohen's work and combine it with Merton's (1938) notion of 'illicit means', producing what became known as strain theory (Cressey 1979). These contributions resulted in the production of an approach to crime and control that was more sociological and theoretical and which was to be tested through the development of new empirical techniques. However, instead of being generally influenced by writers like Marx, Durkheim and Foucault the 'new criminology' in America was more likely to be influenced by writers like Spenser, Comte and Parsons (Mills 1959). There were also important cultural and political differences between Britain and America that served to shape this new sub-discipline. Developments in the UK were deeply influenced by the class struggles that occurred in Europe in the 1960s, while American sociology and criminology was, to a significant extent, shaped by civil rights movements and the legacy of the McCarthy era.

Thus, there was not a single landmark text in America along the lines of *The New Criminology*. Instead, there was a growing *critical mass* of texts alongside the rapid expansion of the American Society of Criminology, whose membership increased from 300 in 1970 to just under 2,000 in 1977 (Scarpitti 1985). In addition, the publication in 1970 of the first issue of the flagship journal of the American Society of Criminology – *Criminology: An Interdisciplinary Journal* – signalled the growing professionalisation of academic criminology in America.

Thus, on both sides of the Atlantic the new criminology grew as a hybrid subject with four main and competing strands existing in an uneasy tension. The deviancy and sociological approaches were critical of positivistic and administrative approaches, while positivists, in turn, were sceptical about what they saw as the metaphysical and 'unscientific' tendencies of new deviancy theory. As a result, the new criminology has always been in danger of imploding. On the other hand, the multifaceted nature of the sub-discipline allows it to remain fairly agnostic about disciplinary boundaries and to draw widely on a range of social science literature, making it a potentially rich and diverse subject area.

In a review of the developments in criminology, David Downes (1988) has suggested that from the early 1970s to the late 1980s three fundamental changes took place in the nature of criminological inquiry. These were first, a requirement to address the motives and meanings of crime and deviant behaviour. Second, a greater focus on social reaction and the process of social control, including the role of the media. Third, a broadening of the focus of inquiry to include occupational crime, domestic issues and the operation of the 'hidden economy'. In addition, we might add that criminological endeavours became more politically attuned in this period, with an increasing recognition that crime and justice are politically contested issues and an appreciation of the ways that politics and power serve to shape the behaviour not only of those under study but also of those undertaking research.

Over the past decade or so, however, the energy and the stimulus which the new criminologies brought to the subject area have been dampened and redirected. Conventional forms of positivistic criminology, which had been under continued attack during the 1970s and 1980s, have re-emerged in new forms. At the same time, criminology appears to have lost its focus and direction (Ericson and Carriere 1994). The demise of the National Deviancy Conference in 1973 and the incorporation of the Critical Criminology group within the American Society of Criminology during the 1980s signalled the resurgence and increasing domination of the conservative-liberal consensus in criminology. Thus, although the last thirty or forty years have seen an unprecedented expansion of academic criminology, the nature and quality of its output have been inconsistent, and the promise of the new criminology developed in the 1960s and 1970s is beginning to fade.

In this chapter the aim is to examine the development of criminology over the past forty years in order to understand something about its present state of health and, in particular, the contribution that critical realism might play in ameliorating some of the growing concerns – particularly in relation to the recent claims that criminology is becoming increasingly socially and politically irrelevant (Austin 2003). Indeed, a growing body of criminology has been described as 'so what?' criminology, which includes those publications that are theoretically thin, methodologically weak or have little or no policy relevance (Currie 2007; Matthews 2009, 2010a). In addition, Francis Cullen (2011) has identified the limitations of what he refers to as 'adolescence-limited criminology', which he argues is increasingly plagued by a sense of pessimism while offering limited explanatory power. Much criminological work is presented in a language that is opaque and impenetrable, while the subject has become very inward looking, and the debates that take place in many criminology journals are of interest to very few people outside academia (Davis 2004).

Radical and critical criminology

What became known as radical or critical criminology played a major role in the development of the new criminology on both sides of the Atlantic, although there were differences in terms of theoretical orientation and the range of issues addressed. Critical criminology turned conventional wisdoms upside down, and much that had previously been presented as truth was increasingly presented as ideology (Sykes 1974). Mental illness was identified as a 'myth'; those diagnosed as 'paranoid', it transpired, did in fact have people talking about them; sexuality was anything but natural; becoming a marijuana smoker was seen as an uncertain process which involved developing a conception of 'getting high' as pleasurable and desirable; while crime itself, it was argued, has no ontological reality (Hulsman 1986; Becker 1953; Lemert 1962; McIntosh 1968; Szasz 1970). In challenging the conventional definitions of normality, it connected with the feminist movement, gay rights campaigns and anti-racist struggles that challenged the established consensus and called for change. It also was more in tune with the changing social relations of the period, with their growing emphasis on diversity, fluidity and moral ambiguity (Bauman 1991).

Critical criminologists took delight in rejecting the main tenets of positivism, and expressed a deep scepticism towards the use of criminal statistics and widely embraced a social constructionism that claimed social reality was built up intersubjectively (Berger and Luckmann 1967). There remained, however, a deep and unresolved debate about objectivity, value freedom and the standpoint of the researcher. These issues were played out in the debate between Alvin Gouldner and Howard Becker. Becker (1966) had raised the provocative question "Whose side are we on?" arguing that there is no value-free or neutral position in social science and that researchers have to decide where their sympathies lie and from which vantage point they are going to conduct their analysis. Gouldner had written an essay in 1962 entitled 'Anti-Minotaur: The Myth of Value Free Sociology', in which he had taken issue with Max Weber's claim that social investigation ought to be value free. Gouldner had argued that the commitment to value freedom provided sociologists with a moral escape clause and led to an abandonment of public responsibility for social ills (O'Brien and Penna 2007). However, Gouldner argued in a later article, entitled 'The Sociologist as Partisan' (1968), that Becker was in danger of replacing the myth of value-free sociology with the equally untenable myth that it is impossible for social scientists to do research uncontaminated by personal and political sympathies. Gouldner maintained that it was possible for researchers to have sympathy for the underdog without privileging the 'truth' from their perspective or losing a commitment to objectivity. Although he willingly conceded that studying the world from an underdog's stand-point could bring into public view certain neglected aspects of social reality, he was critical of what he saw as the desire to take ownership of the subjects under study and become 'zookeepers of deviance', whereby social scientists want to protect or display their collection of 'exotic specimens' rather than criticise or change them.

By focusing on the underdog, criminologists attempt, he suggests, to claim the moral high ground while pointing to the apparent failure of the state. However, Gouldner argues that if there is a justification for focusing on the underdog it is not so much because we see them as victims of mismanagement but rather because of an appreciation of their suffering. In this way Gouldner helped to set the agenda for a realist criminology by countering liberal and idealist tendencies while pointing out that in the process of depathologising deviants there was a danger of romanticising them instead. Also, in line with a realist approach, he argued that a critical social science is driven by the possibility of social transformation. This objective, he suggests, is structured by two considerations. First, a critical social science is normative and involves identifying certain issues, such as those linked to oppression, suffering and discrimination. Second and relatedly, it requires the identification of ways in which these issues might be resolved. This, in turn, involves the formulation of viable alternatives rather than opting for the non-committal notion of 'the unfinished' (Mathieson 1974).

In a pivotal article published in 1975, entitled 'Working Class Criminology', Jock Young developed some of the themes outlined by Gouldner and applied them to criminology (Young 1986, 1992, 1997). This was to be the first in a series of articles that criticised the idealist tendencies amongst critical criminologists, which had also been evident to some extent in *The New Criminology*. In this article, Young argued that rather than transcending conventional positivist criminology many critical criminologists produced a mirror image. Whereas conventional criminology focused on the act, critical criminology focused on the social reaction. Whereas conventional criminologists talked in terms of consensus, critical criminologists talked in terms of conflict and division. Whereas conventional criminology depicted offenders as pathological, critical criminology presented them as normal. As Gouldner had argued, there was a tendency to replace conservative thinking with laissez-faire liberalism and full-blown romanticism. These tendencies, Young argues, were evident in the Society for the Study of Social Problems in America in the early 1960s and were developed by the National Deviancy Conference in Britain. In contrast to this brand of critical criminology, which became known as 'left idealism' but is probably better characterised as 'liberal idealism', Young calls for a greater sense of social responsibility amongst criminologists and a recognition of the personal and social consequences of different social problems. In response to the authors of *Policing the Crisis* (Hall, S. et al. 1978), who presented mugging largely as a media 'moral panic' involving a process of miscategorisation, Young argues:

> It is unrealistic to suggest that problems of crimes like mugging is merely the problem of miscategorization and concomitant moral panics. If we choose to embrace this liberal position, we leave the political arena open to conservative campaigns for law and order – for, however exaggerated and distorted the arguments the conservatives may marshal, the reality of crime in the streets *can* be the reality of human suffering and personal disaster. We have to argue, therefore, strategically, for the exercise of social control. (Young 1975: 89)

This statement marked the significant recognition that the key players in the drama of 'law and order' were the working class, who were seen as the prime constituency of the left. Therefore, as Ian Taylor was to argue some years later in *Law and Order: Arguments for Socialism* (1982), crime and punishment are issues that those on the left of the political spectrum should take seriously and that should no longer be seen as issues that can be left to the conservatives. As a result, over the next decade or so a group of critical criminologists' identifying themselves as 'left realists', began to flesh out a political and theoretical stance in opposition to the dominant liberal and conservative consensus on one hand, and the growing body of left idealists on the other (Lea and Young 1984; Kinsey, Lea and Young 1986; Jones et al. 1986; Matthews 1987).

On the other side of the Atlantic, writers like Elliott Currie were exploring similar themes (Currie 1985, 1989). Moving away from a critique of the liberal and conservative consensus in America, he addressed some of the more challenging questions related to interpersonal violence while proposing strategies for dealing with a range of individual and family problems. He also raised the issue of individual responsibility, often overlooked by liberals and left idealists, and questioned their call for the acceptance of diversity and the decriminalisation of crime. In addition, he argued that what he calls 'plain left realism' should not shrink from the responsibility of exploring how the criminal justice system could be made more effective and just. Among the major attributes of plain left realism are

> Its commitment to taking crime seriously; its insistence that crime *comes* from somewhere, and is driven by some kinds of organization more than others; its willingness to take on the difficult job of looking for workable solutions to crime that flow from its causal analysis, and its insistence that doing so is part of the duty of the criminologist – all of these will necessarily be part of the tool kit of scholars who want to seriously explore the most destructive of crimes, and who see their reduction as a social and moral imperative. (Currie 2010: 121)

The task of engaging with crime, Currie argues, requires a deepening and broadening of our analysis, identifying its roots and how it can be combated, while simultaneously embracing social democratic principles in the pursuit of social justice.

These observations raise the question of what is 'critical' about critical criminology. The vast majority of criminological approaches, whether tagged 'liberal', 'conservative' or 'radical', routinely engage in critiques of other positions and of state policies on crime and punishment. So-called critical criminology is no different in this respect. Nor does self-styled critical criminology have any monopoly of engaging in ideology critique in an attempt to identify illusions and misconceptions. Nor is it alone in proposing alternative policies and practices. What distinguishes critical criminology from other 'mainstream' criminologies is the problematisation of the concept of crime and the attempt to identify and understand the broader social, political, historical and economic processes that 'create' and shape different forms of crime. Most importantly, the distinctiveness of critical criminology lies in its normative orientation involving a concern with the alleviation of suffering, abuse, exploitation, discrimination, forms of oppression and the pursuit of social justice. It is these values that provide its unique vantage point and allow it to engage in 'progressive' reform. It is the commitment to these and related objectives that provides the raison d'être of critical realism (Sayer 1997). The difference between progressive versions of critical criminology and critical realism is how these objectives are to be realised. Many of these concerns also featured in the second wave of feminism (1970s), which provided the initial impetus for the establishment of feminist criminology.

The impact of feminist criminology

Although there is some uncertainty about exactly what is meant by 'feminist criminology', there can be little doubt that the impact of feminism on criminology has provided one of the most productive and progressive inputs on the subject over the last two or three decades. A steady stream of criminological literature emerged in the 1970s underpinned by the second wave of feminism and which challenged mainstream criminology at every level (Adler 1975; Chesney-Lind 1973; Brownmiller 1975; Smart 1976). Overall, there are five main contributions which feminists have made to the study of crime and punishment: a thoroughgoing critique of conventional criminological theory; an appreciation of the nature and impact of victimisation; a reconsideration of methodologies; a deeper understanding of the nature of power and gender relations; and a commitment to engaging in social reform and policy development (Gelsthorpe 1997).

The most significant feminist contribution to criminological theory remains Eileen Leonard's often overlooked classic *Women, Crime and Society* (1983), which provides a thoroughgoing critique of the major theoretical approaches to crime and punishment. Theoretical criminology, Leonard argues, was produced predominantly by men for men until the 1970s. This male-centred criminology, she maintained, was simply not up to the analytic task of explaining female patterns of crime. She pointed out that within criminology the major theories did not provide explanations of human behaviour, as they claimed, but rather a particular account of *male* behaviour. These one-sided, often sexist, accounts systematically fail to explain both the generally low crime rate amongst women and how women are treated by the criminal justice system. A critical examination of criminological theory, whether differential association, subcultural theory, strain theory or even Marxist theories, reveals that these approaches at best provide limited explanations of female crime and at worst ignore the significance of gender altogether.

One of the major contributions by feminist criminologists is the identification of the nature and extent of the victimisation of women. It is evident that the various forms of violence inflicted against women, including rape and domestic violence, have been underreported and underresearched (Mooney 2000; DeKeseredy 2011). It is also the case that while the victimisation of men tends to be located in the public sphere, the victimisation of women is spread across both the public and private domains (Crawford et al. 1990). In fact, whether at home or at work, engaging in leisure activities or walking the streets, women experience a more extensive, and frequently more damaging, level of victimisation than that of men. Thus, the research on women's victimisation raises issues not only about the incidence and prevalence of victimisation but also about impact.

Feminists have begun to detail the extent of violence that many women encounter. It is claimed that in Britain, for example, one in four women will be sexually assaulted at some point in their lives and two women a week are killed by violent partners (Fawcett Society 2004; Silvestri and Crowther-Dowey 2008). Although it is generally argued that official statistics and victimisation surveys underestimate the true extent of rape, it is estimated that in England and Wales around 47,000 women are victims of rape or attempted rape each year and that there are around 190,000 recorded incidents (Myhill and Allen 2002). These studies, like other feminist and realist contributions, point out the unequal nature of victimisation and its social and geographical concentration amongst the poor and the vulnerable (Young 1988).

Investigating these forms of female victimisation, as well as women's experience of crime and punishment, has called for the reconsideration of research methods. Feminist researchers have questioned the value of highly quantitative forms of research and positivistic methods in general. In contrast, they have emphasised the need to understand meanings and social relations and argued that social scientific investigation is primarily interpretative. Therefore, there is a preference for qualitative methods that are designed to gain a deeper understanding and to have practical relevance.

It is also no accident that feminist social scientists engage with the issue of power. The widespread victimisation of women is seen as a function of unequal power relations (MacKinnon 1997). In a similar vein, the relatively low level of female crime is seen as a function of the particular forms of regulation and discipline directed towards women.

The examination of power has been directly influenced by the work of Michel Foucault, although some feminists have also been critical of what is seen as the masculinist bias in his work (Fraser 1981,1989; McNay 1992).

Given that many of the contributions by feminist criminologists have tended to focus on a particular problematic, it follows that much of this work has been aimed at developing viable policies and practices, particularly as they relate to the position of women. Such an approach involves not only rethinking current policies but also re-examining prevailing assumptions and perspectives. In relation to rape, for example, not only does it focus on the ways in which rape cases are handled, but it also involves an examination of the key notions of consent and the ways in which the female victim is constructed (Christie 1977, 1986). Consequently, the skewed and distorted perceptions that have historically guided legislation on rape in different countries have been consistently challenged and revised (Munro and Kelly 2009).

Despite these important contributions to social scientific and criminological investigations, which have deeply influenced the development of realist criminology, feminist criminology has lost much of its impetus in recent years, particularly in relation to its alignment with postmodernism and standpoint theory. One of the most influential critiques of the modernist project is Carol Smart's (1990) rejection of 'malestream' criminology. Smart berates criminology for what she sees as its adoption of grand narratives and argues instead for situated knowledge. Suspicious of what she sees as an essentially male-centred criminology, she argues that the truth claims of criminology have to be deconstructed and challenged from a feminist standpoint. Although rightly critiquing situated views of the world that claim to be universal, Smart wants to replace these one-sided, partial views with another set of partial views. As John Lea (1998) has argued, replacing the views of the dominant group with those of marginalised, victimised and excluded women is to replace one form of fundamentalism with another. In the end Smart muddies the waters rather than constructing a basis for the development of a feminist criminology. By advocating a form of standpoint feminism together with anti-modernism and anti-realism, Smart gravitates towards relativism and foundationalism. From this perspective it is difficult to see, as Pat Carlen (1992) has argued, how she might develop a policy response that would reduce rape, domestic violence and other crimes that victimise women.

Maureen Cain (1990), like Carol Smart (1990), advocates standpoint epistemology, but in contrast to Smart she wants to combine it with what she claims to be a realist approach. However, while realists recognise the situatedness of knowledge, most would take issue with Cain's claims that the standpoint of women is epistemologically privileged or that it is a position from which 'it is easier to understand more and better'. From this position Cain argues that 'feminists' are defined as those 'who work to advance the situation of women' in order to reduce suffering and oppression. Thus, not all feminists are women and therefore it is not clear who is eligible to claim this privileged standpoint. Moreover, it cannot be assumed that there is a unified women's standpoint while this form of essentialism overlooks that knowledge is often borderless and located in wider networks of communication.

There has also been a growing antipathy amongst some feminists towards the label 'victim', as it is argued that it removes agency while essentialising the woman and should in some cases be replaced by the term 'survivors' (Lamb 1999; Pease 2007). However, the term 'survivors' suggests that the impact of victimisation has been overcome, which is not necessarily the case, and is in danger of losing sight of the gendered significance and impact of victimisation. All forms of categorisation are essentialising to some degree and, although the term 'victim' can have pejorative connotations, defining oneself as a victim can be a first step to removing vulnerability and may trigger a process of action and defence which may prevent future victimisation. It is the refusal to acknowledge victimisation that gives perpetrators impunity.

Over the last decade or so, however, feminist criminology, like feminism in general, has lost much of its radical impact and has gravitated towards liberal feminism, focusing increasingly on specific issues rather than engaging in wider debates about patriarchy and gender inequalities. Feminism has moved from a focus on gender oppression and the sharing of experiences to an autocritique in which the traditional object of feminism, woman, has itself become the object of critique.

Administrative, pragmatic and managerialist criminologies

Although there is a long history of governmental approaches to the prevention and reduction of crime, there was an unprecedented growth of what has now become known as 'administrative criminology' in the 1970s and 1980s (Tilley 2002). In the United Kingdom, the establishment of the Research and Planning Unit in the Home Office under the leadership of Ron Clarke in the late 1970s provided a pragmatic approach to crime prevention and community safety. The establishment of a Crime Prevention Unit in 1983 provided a major impetus to the development of administrative criminology and sought an immediate and tangible response to the claims by liberal pessimists that 'nothing works', while also providing an alternative to 'dispositional theories' (Clarke 1997). Closely linked to this well-funded crime reduction agenda was the development of the British Crime Survey, which presented itself as the authoritative representation of crime. It was held to provide a more comprehensive picture than official police statistics since it shed some light on the so-called dark figure of crime. As an ostensibly reliable source of data it became not only an essential point of reference for the public debates about the changing nature of crime but also the major academic resource for explaining crime trends and the distribution of victimisation.

An indication of the conceptual weakness of administrative criminology, however, is evident in the very title of the 'British Crime Survey'. The survey is in fact not about Britain but is limited to England and Wales and is not about crime but victimisation. Crime and victimisation, of course, are not the same thing. It also excludes young people under sixteen. Therefore, it should more accurately be called the 'Adult Victimisation Survey of Households in England and Wales'. The name has recently changed to the 'Crime Survey for England and Wales', but it has taken twenty years and a number of prompts to introduce this limited corrective. Moreover, as left realists have argued, one of the implicit objectives of this survey when it was introduced was to 'define deviance down' by generalising from national rather than local samples and by placing an arbitrary limit on the number of victimisations each respondent was allowed to report. In this way the survey was designed to downplay the risk of victimisation and thereby provide some reassurance to the general public in a period of rapidly rising crime rates (Jones et al. 1986).

There is a discernible overlap between administrative or managerialist criminology and neo-conservatism. However, unlike conservative criminology, administrative criminology claims to be non-ideological, pragmatic and technocratic. Administrative criminology aims to respond to the immediate concerns of government by bringing together summaries of what is known about specific issues in order to develop crime-control policies and practices. It sees itself as providing value-free knowledge and operates on a presumption that the facts speak for themselves. Managerialism expresses no interest in the origin or validity of criminal sanctions, nor does it have much interest in traditional causal questions or in understanding the wider social context that shapes and 'produces' crime.

Administrative criminology draws freely on situational crime prevention, rational choice and routine activities theory, focusing mainly on opportunity reduction strategies. Apart from its affinity with these perspectives, it adopts a largely atheoretical, pragmatic approach that takes for granted the given categories of crime, which are notoriously wide ranging and imprecise. Thus, while it claims a degree of methodological and statistical rigour, the vagueness of the categories and concepts that underpin its analysis often serves to undermine the quality and value of the findings. Consequently, conclusions are often weak or equivocal and, although there is a commitment to finding out 'what works', the frequent adoption of a multi-factorial approach, which seeks out correlations rather than causes, often leads to an inability to produce firm conclusions. As a result there is little consistency in the development of research findings and not much in the way of cumulative knowledge or theory building.

Despite these limitations there has been a significant growth in the scale and influence of administrative criminology over the last three decades. The steady increase in government funding of crime control has resulted in a growing number of agencies and organisations that engage in different forms of criminological investigation, as well as a number of academic researchers and departments that rely on official sources of funding for their existence. In this way, official bodies have acquired the ability to direct the focus of research, influence the methodologies used and shape outcomes. Researchers who are critical of the selection of issues or the choice of research instruments are likely to fall quickly into disfavour. On the other hand, those who do receive funding are likely to be micromanaged, and the capacity for independent or critical investigation is often severely limited (Hope 2004).

The rise of administrative criminology has no doubt been encouraged by the general administrativisation of society. The rise of the 'new public management', with its emphasis on cost effectiveness, the setting of targets, the construction of performance indicators and the like, has gradually permeated large sections of society, including the criminal justice system (McLaughlin and Murji 2001). This new style of managerialism has also made its way into academic life, with a growing preoccupation with setting targets, measuring performance and increasing outputs. These developments, it has been argued, have led to the increasing commodification of knowledge with the consequence that critical scholarship has been sidelined (Walters 2003). As Pat O'Malley (1996) has noted, in the era of 'post-social' criminologies there has been a loss of independence amongst academic researchers and a blurring of the distinction between academic and administrative criminologies. The establishment of the European Society of Criminology in 2000, involving closer collaboration between government departments across Europe and academic criminologists, signalled the growing ascendancy and acceptability of administrative criminology in academia.

Administrative criminology is tied to the 'what works' agenda and is committed to 'best value' reviews. The problem that arises with this approach is that the data collected are always selective, and there is a tendency to focus on that which is easily measurable. Evidence does not speak for itself but needs to be interpreted, and this involves judgements of value. This is not to say that policies and practices should not be informed by evidence, but there are clear limits to the extent to which policies can simply be derived from evidence. A particularly weak component of the 'what works' approach is cost-benefit analysis, which assumes that the economic costs of interventions and outcomes can be calculated with some degree of accuracy and consistency. Unfortunately, different inputs produce different outcomes in different contexts. Moreover, not all costs and benefits are financial or have a cash equivalent value (Tilley 2001).

The contours of right realism and conservative criminology

Right realism, or what might be better characterised as 'naive realism', takes the category of crime and the functioning and purpose of the criminal justice system as given. By focusing on that which is immediately given, this form of neo-conservative criminology adopts a largely commonsensical approach to crime control, which has the considerable advantage of avoiding the difficulties of having to deconstruct categories and concepts. Right realists also tend to avoid explanations that include considerations of 'root causes' and 'deep structures', such as poverty and inequality, and instead focus on the more visible but arguably more superficial aspects of crime and its control. This, in part, is the basis of its widespread appeal. By avoiding challenging conceptual issues and engaging in 'straight talking', the policies presented often resonate not only with academics but also with politicians and the general public. Thus, right or naive realism is realist inasmuch as it takes crime seriously and aims to reduce crime and victimisation, but is naive inasmuch as it takes social reality as self-evident.

Probably the most powerful neo-conservative thinkers are James Q. Wilson and George Kelling, who published the highly influential article

'Broken Windows' in 1982, and Charles Murray (1996, 1997), with his depiction of the 'underclass' and his claim that 'prison works'. Indeed, it has to be acknowledged that during the 1980s and early 1990s conservative criminology was enormously influential and had a major impact on policy in many countries. Richard Herrnstein and Charles Murray's *The Bell Curve* (1994) was among the best-selling criminology books in the English-speaking world in the early 1990s, as was Wilson's *Thinking about Crime* in the 1980s. In both of these books crime is depicted as a function of human nature and is seen as residing in the individual personality or genetic structure (Cullen et al. 1997). These approaches draw largely on notions of individual pathology. However, they do not go very far in explaining why crime tends to be more concentrated in some localities rather than others, or why the rich steal.

These conservative thinkers, however, are different from those fiscal conservatives who see the motivation to engage in crime in terms of cost-benefit analysis. Rational choice theorists, for example, claim that offenders are not different from other persons; only their opportunities, benefits and costs differ. Both approaches, however, call for tough punishment. Despite the fact that America in the 1980s and 1990s had more people under the control of the criminal justice system than any other advanced industrial nation, conservatives repeatedly call for the intensification of punishment as a way to reduce crime.

Charles Murray's (1997) claim that prison works caused a considerable stir in the liberal academy, but it deeply influenced penal policy in the United Kingdom in the 1990s, with the British home secretary of the time, Michael Howard, publicly echoing this sentiment. Murray claimed that the United Kingdom was imprisoning far too few rather than too many convicted offenders. His arguments in favour of prison expansion were indirectly linked to his claims about the growing underclass. It was Murray's contention that we were witnessing the growth of a social group that was become increasingly disconnected from the mainstream society, not only economically but also in terms of their social and moral values. For Murray (1996) the signs of a growing underclass were to be found in the growth of crime and illegitimacy in conjunction with increased economic inactivity amongst men of working age. His response, however, did not involve overhauling the system of unemployment benefits or restructuring the labour market. Rather, it aimed at restoring the two-parent (heterosexual) family as the norm throughout society, despite the fact that all indications were that the modern family was undergoing a protracted crisis and that the traditional 'cornflake' family was in terminal decline, despite repeated attempts to prop it up.

At this point, Murray begins to merge with the third strand of conservative thinking, which sees crime not only as a consequence of dysfunctional families but also an outcome of moral decline, liberal tolerance and growing permissiveness.

However, probably the most influential contribution from the conservative right realists has been the widely quoted 'broken windows' thesis, in which Wilson and Kelling (1982) presented what at first sight appears very plausible. The thesis has two main components. The first focuses on the relation between low-level incivilities and crime, while the second concerns the perceived benefits of public order policing. Underlying both theses is a conservative conception of small-town America. The article provides a thinly veiled rationalisation for cracking down on incivilities and forms of anti-social behaviour on one hand and justifying greater use of public-order policing, using extralegal methods to manage 'the usual suspects', on the other (Harcourt 1998; Sampson and Raudenbush 1999). What is remarkable about these theses is how widely they have been accepted and quoted by academics, politicians and practitioners not only in America and the United Kingdom but also in other parts of the world. The broken windows thesis has had a major impact in relation to policing strategies, shifting the focus towards disorder and anti-social behaviour as well as contributing to the 'cleansing' of the post-industrial city (Beckett and Herbert 2008). Wilson and Kelling's thesis was also seen to provide a rationale for changes in policing and crime control in the Giuliani era in New York City in the late 1990s and was credited with the reduction of crime in that period.

Surprisingly, there was very little critical response from either American or British criminologists following the publication of the broken windows article and the majority of criminologists were keen to quote or at least to cite it. The initial critique of the broken windows thesis came from left realists, who argued that it was not so much the growth of incivilities that led to neighbourhood decline but rather economic instability and community fragmentation, which foster a breakdown of informal control and in turn lead to a rise in both crime and disorder (Kinsey, Lea and Young 1986; Matthews 1992; Kelling 2001). Some critical American commentaries began to appear in the late 1990s, but by that time Wilson and Kelling's theses had deeply influenced policy on both sides of the Atlantic.

Despite the enormous impact of these conservative right realists during the 1980s and early 1990s, all the major figures have now ceased writing for one reason or another and have not been followed by like-minded authors with the same level of influence. Consequently, the influence of conservative criminology has declined in recent years in both academic and policy circles.

The dimensions of liberal criminology

As the influence of conservative criminology began to wane during the 1990s, the other main political force in academic criminology – liberal criminology – gained ascendancy. For much of the 1980s and 1990s, liberal criminologists were, in policy terms, overshadowed by their conservative adversaries and liberals, with some justification, spent a considerable amount of time opposing what they saw as the undesirable effects of 'get-tough' policies and the expansion of state-sponsored forms of crime control. To some extent, however, liberal critics became an inversion of their conservative counterparts. Thus, while conservatives argued for tougher punishment and greater use of custody, liberals argued for decarceration and greater use of community-based sanctions. While conservatives focused on the criminal act, liberals concentrated on social reaction. Whereas conservatives argued for the regeneration of the family and community in order to reduce crime, liberals talked about the need for diversity, a rise in punitiveness and an increase in restrictions on personal freedom.

However, with the declining influence of the conservative 'heavyweights' at the end of the 1990s, liberals found the policy arena more open and accessible. Their achievements in policy terms, however, have been very modest despite their growing dominance in academic criminology. The reasons why liberals have failed to deliver are complex, but a number of features of liberal criminology have contributed to their declining influence on policy, particularly their conception of power, the state and freedom.

Within the classic liberal notion of 'freedom' as the individual being outside state control there is little recognition of the way that freedom is created through a whole series of governmental strategies and policies. As Lawrence Mead has pointed out:

> American political culture gives pride of place to the value of freedom. But a 'free' society is only possible when the conditions for order have substantially been realised. People are not interested in freedom from government if they are victimised by crime, cannot support themselves, or are in any fundamental way insecure. They will want more government rather than less. Nor are they likely to vote or otherwise participate politically unless they are employed or have their

personal lives in order. A 'free' political culture is the characteristic not of a society still close to the state of nature, as some American philosophers have imagined, but one far removed from it by dense, reliable networks of mutual expectations. (Mead 1986: 6)

From the liberal perspective, as Foucault (1991, 2007) suggests, 'one always governs too much', and he emphasises that 'freedom' is not achieved by a lack of state control but that it is one of the objectives of state intervention.

The appeal of liberalism derives in part from its emphasis on toleration and respect of others and defence of individual liberty. This is normally expressed in terms of the protection of rights. As Axel Honneth (1995) has suggested, the establishment of legal rights is an important aspect of recognising human dignity, autonomy and the capacity of persons to act as morally responsible subjects. Liberalism, however, has come under attack from a number of quarters, particularly from communitarians, who argue that the liberal notion of the rational free individual radically misrepresents real life and deprives us of the experience of communal embeddedness (Hancock and Matthews 2001). It is also suggested that the liberal notion of tolerance can be counterproductive in allowing young people, for example, to freely engage in various forms of anti-social behaviour without receiving appropriate sanctions. This can lead, it is argued, to an escalation and intensification of these problems (Braithwaite 1989). Communitarians argue that the notion of free choice is a myth and that our identities are partly defined by our communal attachments (Gutmann 1985). Moreover, the liberal conception of individual freedom as freedom from state 'interference' overlooks the extent to which state practices can secure freedom of movement and expression while protecting the vulnerable. However, in opposition to liberal claims that we are experiencing an expansion and intensification of state control, some sociologists have argued that the present is characterised less by increased restriction, subordination or colonisation than by deregulation, flexibilisation and increased fluidity (Bauman 2000; Weeks 2007).

Liberals claim that crime is a function of poverty and deprivation, and that the most appropriate way to deal with offenders is to provide better opportunities linked to rehabilitation and a more humane and less intrusive criminal justice system. This has been challenged, and to some extent discredited, by conservative critics who point to the fact that the crime rate continued to go up in the 1970s and 1980s, even as society became more affluent and more committed to action against poverty

(Wilson 1983). Although these critiques involved a considerable amount of exaggeration, liberals did not explain why so many of the poor are apparently law abiding or, for that matter, so many of the rich are not.

There has also been a tendency among liberals to suggest that crime is not really a problem and that the media and certain politicians talk up the issue of crime and exaggerate its extent. In this way, liberals have played down crime's seriousness and drawn attention away from its impact on the most vulnerable sections of the population. At the same time, liberals have been overly critical of state policies and institutions; some have argued that the aim should be to do less harm, rather than to do more good (Cohen 1985). The major failure of liberal criminology in the 1980s and 1990s was that it lacked concrete ideas for reducing the level of criminal victimisation and limiting its impact on individuals and groups. Although liberal criminologists were prepared to discuss the limitations of social reaction, they were noticeably less interested in crime itself. Where crime was referred to, it was either invoked as a signifier of institutional failure or presented as an amorphous and restrictive entity that was difficult to grasp or define. As Lucia Zedner (2011) has argued, insofar as (liberal) criminology engages with crime it either does so negatively or it dispenses with the category of crime altogether. Consequently, for the most part criminology has failed to address those issues of moral agency and individual responsibility that lie at the heart of criminal law. As a result there has been limited engagement with law reform and, in particular, a reticence to advocate new legislation. Underpinning this conspicuous omission has been a reluctance to engage in normative theorising and the widespread adoption of a detached and impersonal stance, which loses sight of the fact that crime is a moral issue and that policies and practices that respond to it involve judgements of value.

It is, however, the case that the majority of the most influential and widely read academic criminologists over the last decade or so have come from the liberal camp. They have also attracted a number of disillusioned critical criminologists, left idealists and libertarians, particularly those with serious misgivings about what they see as an increase in state power and control. This growing body of liberal criminology can be divided into three separate but overlapping strands: radical, humanist and pessimist.

Radical liberals. Probably the most influential strand of liberal criminology in recent years has been radical liberalism, which has focused on inequality and disadvantage in a context of what is seen as a growth of state intervention and the exercise of more authoritarian forms of political power. Radical liberals in general are deeply critical of current crime-control policies, which they claim are often ineffective and poorly implemented or result in unanticipated outcomes. At the same time they are uncomfortable with the growing focus on the victim and claim that politicians and policymakers are increasingly 'governing through crime' (Simon 2007; Garland 2001; Tonry 1995). In its more extreme form it embraces a libertarianism that adamantly defends the sanctity of the private sphere, while more egalitarian liberals tend to defend what they see as the dismantling of the changing welfare state (Sandel 1982; Wacquant 2009). As self-styled defenders of the economically marginalised, radical liberals aim to unmask the adverse effects of power and privilege.

In terms of theoretical orientation, radical liberals tend to incorporate a mix of conflict theory and strain theory. Thus, crime is seen to arise from disadvantage, limited legitimate opportunities and structural inequalities. What distinguishes radical liberalism from other strands of liberal criminology is a desire to move beyond single issues and engage in an examination of the complexities of the changing nature of social control. This is an ambitious project and unfortunately one which most radical liberals are ill-equipped to undertake (Matthews 2002; Garland 2001; Pitts 2013; Zedner 2002).

The inability to grasp the complexities of the changing nature of social control stem, in part, from the liberal assumptions underpinning the analysis, as well as being the consequence of the nature of the conceptual tools that are adopted. Thus, the drivers of changing forms of crime control are held to be such broad variables as neoliberalism, ontological insecurity, the demise of the welfare state and postmodern angst. However, the connections between these determinants and the presumed effects are rarely specified. The inability to identify the mediations and causal relations involved, or any suggestion of how neoliberalism or postmodernism are to be overcome, leaves these radicals in a position where they have little to say about how the apparent failings of the current situation might be addressed. Indeed, there tends to be a lack of concrete prescriptions about how to change or improve the situation; as a result we are left with a range of unresolved, and in some cases apparently unresolvable, dilemmas.

Radical liberals express a deep scepticism, both in relation to politicians, who are seen as opportunistic and pragmatic, and the general public, who are seen as gullible and ill-informed (Pratt 2007; Pratt et al. 2005). As they are also suspicious of state agencies and the managers of the criminal justice system, their audience is limited mainly to like-minded academics. Given their reluctance to engage these agencies and groups they are left with little incentive to develop viable reforms, let alone finding ways of implementing them. Thus, despite the high sounding rhetoric there is little end product in the form of intervention. Consequently, theories and propositions have little chance of being tested in a systematic way and any policy proposals are likely to remain at best speculative and at worst strategically irrelevant. For these reasons radical criminologists have little to say about developing more effective ways to reduce crime. They are mainly concerned with the possibility that interventions will restrict privacy and civil liberties. Interestingly, however, even radical liberals have been relatively quiescent in relation to the widespread introduction of CCTV and other surveillance measures in recent years.

Radical liberals for the most part operate with an essentially negative conception of power. For them power takes the form of repression and subjugation exercised by one group over another, resulting in a domination–resistance binary. There is little appreciation of how power can be constructive. As Foucault (1978) argued, power is to be understood as a relation which is always in play. Power relations may be asymmetrical, but they can be positive, productively shaping subjectivities and identities. Rather than see power in these terms, radical liberals tend to operate with a top-down conception of power, at times presenting conspiratorial and functionalist accounts of how policies are implemented and the public manipulated (Wacquant 2001, 2005). In this way, there appears a certain inevitability about the direction and development of criminal justice policy, and little consideration is paid to the contradictions, tensions and struggles associated with policy development.

Liberal humanism. This is often associated with a conception of a universal 'human nature' and of the individual as free creative subjects. Humanism expresses an endorsement of human self-determination and places man squarely at the centre of any analysis. Consequently, its emphasis is on engaging directly with human experience in order to understand the role of individuals in pursuing moral and political objectives, including justice and equality. According to Ken Plummer (2001) humanism aims to develop an understanding of human needs, desires and frailties. It proclaims what it sees as the natural dignity and inherent equality of all human beings in all places and all circumstances. It suggests that the focus should be on the person and situating the human being at the centre of our thinking, while being humane and operating with a certain sympathy and benevolence towards others. In this way, Plummer suggests, we seek to avoid inflicting pain on others and aim to be kind.

There are often religious undertones associated with humanism, coupled with a desire to 'make good' or 'do good'. This finds expression through a certain evangelical fervour which has been linked, for example, to restorative justice (Pratt 2006). Thus, the aim is not so much to sanction 'deviants' as to heal broken lives (Pepinsky and Quinney 1991). Opposed to notions of 'science' and value-free sociology, the role of values and meanings is stressed, and power is seen as 'the actualising of the life force' (Du Bois and Wright 2002). Humanists tend to favour positive reinforcement and reward rather than negative reinforcement and punishment.

There are also loose associations with counterculture and a perceived lack of self-fulfilment in an increasingly commercialised and materialist world. In psychology the work of Abraham Maslow (1970) and Carl Rogers (2012), who focus on 'self-actualisation' and 'self-realisation', has attempted to provide a positive vision of individuals in pursuit of a healthy personality, in opposition to studies that focus on the pathological and the abnormal.

Liberal humanism has been widely criticised by structuralists, postmodernist feminists and realists, particularly in relation to the implicit or explicit claim that there is a transhistorical human essence. For realists and others, sensibilities, identities and interests are seen as social products shaped by social conditions and constraints. The limited conception of power and a lack of appreciation of the role of economic, political and social structures in shaping identities makes it difficult from the perspective of liberal humanism to explain large-scale social change and how human values might be realised. The preoccupation with 'life histories' may be fascinating, but there remain issues about generalisability and validity. Social science has to go further than understanding the needs and aspirations of individuals if it is to engage with policy and effect meaningful change.

Liberal pessimism. A recurring feature of liberal criminology is pessimism and impossibilism. In its more extreme forms it claims that 'nothing works', while in more moderate versions it claims that there are serious obstacles to the implementation of interventions, which often suffer from problems of design, with the result that they either fall short of expectations or produce unanticipated or undesired outcomes. In its more moderate forms, liberal pessimism claims that the criminal justice system is inefficient, bureaucratic and discriminatory. There are in fact a number of overlapping themes repeatedly presented by liberal pessimists:

1. *Nothing succeeds like failure.* It is paradoxically through the continued failure of the criminal justice system that rationalisations for the expansion and intensification of interventions are formulated.
2. *The future is unpredictable and at odds with the intentions of reformers.* The claim is that social change has an uncanny capacity to take a different direction from that which was planned or anticipated. The corollary of this proposition is that social scientists in general are poor at prediction.
3. *There is a ghost in the machine.* The argument is that history is driven by an unforeseen and uncontrollable force, which operates with non-human or superhuman logic.
4. *The claims concerning human progress based on scientific evidence are unreliable.* Postmodernists and others claim that all knowledge is relative to the beholder or a specific group, and they are sceptical of the use of evidence-based approaches to addressing social problems.
5. *We are living in an 'iron cage' of bureaucratic rationalisation.* Drawing on the writings of Max Weber, it is argued that we are living in an increasingly impersonal society that is becoming more restrictive and intrusive.

The combination of these claims provides a convenient set of rationales for not engaging in social reform. In general, liberal pessimists like to claim that not only is social reform an uncertain and unpredictable activity but also we are becoming a more punitive and exclusionary society. The clear message is that things are getting worse and there is not much that we can do about it. In its more moderate forms liberal pessimism claims that we should be wary of those with good intentions. Drawing on experience of the destructuring ambitions of the 1970s and 1980s, it argues that the well-meaning intention of deprofessionalising and decentralising the criminal justice system merely extended the reach of social control (Cohen 1985).

The full implication of this disarming logic becomes apparent when approaches to penal policy are examined. Liberal pessimists have provided endless critiques of imprisonment, claiming that not only does it not reduce crime but it also produces a steady stream of recidivists at enormous social and financial cost. However, these liberal critiques, particularly those presented by abolitionists, are very sceptical of the possibility or desirability of prison reform. In fact, critiques of penal reform presented by liberal pessimists tend to involve a predictable set of self-defeating arguments, including claims such as these:

- However much you improve conditions a 'prison is a prison', which deprives people of their liberty.
- There is always a mismatch between intentions and outcomes.
- You may change or improve certain aspects of incarceration, but you leave the overarching structure intact.
- There maybe some improvements, but you could have done something else that would have been better.
- Rather than try to improve prisons, our efforts would be better spent diverting offenders from custody.

The classic response from liberal pessimists is that, on one hand, if you improve conditions you just legitimise the prison and reinforce and even extend the use of custody; on the other hand, if you do not improve conditions you increase the pains of imprisonment such that offenders are more damaged and marginalised and therefore more prone to reoffending. Women's prisons, which were once accused of infantilising prisoners, are now accused of responsibilising them (Hannah-Moffat 2001; Carlen 2002). While abolitionists are sceptical about the possibility and desirability of prison reform, other liberal penologists – the reductionists – see the problem of imprisonment mainly in terms of the number of people in prison. But, since there is no agreement about what the appropriate number should be, and because for reductionists there are always too many people in prison, the implicit logic of this position is a thinly veiled abolitionism. Instead of being drawn towards the utopianism of abolitionism or the pragmatism of reductionism, we need to recognise that prisons will be around for the foreseeable future and enter into a more meaningful debate about who should go to prison, for how long and for what purpose (see Braithwaite and Pettit 1990).

Some liberal critics argue that what needs to be done is replace imprisonment as far as possible with alternatives to custody, including community-based sanctions. However, other liberals argue that these alternatives involve 'net widening' and the expansion of the welfare–punishment continuum (Cohen 1985). There are, of course, others who advocate the expansion of welfare intervention as a more acceptable form of regulation, since it is held to be less punitive while providing support rather than punishment. However, some liberals claim that not only is the 'welfare sanction' a more invidious form of control but that in fact the poor end up making a disproportionate financial contribution to their own regulation (Garland 2001). Thus, within these unresolved debates dedicated pessimists can find good grounds for doing nothing except bemoaning the unfairness and unreasonableness of 'the system' as they sink deeper and deeper into the impasse of non-intervention.

In sum, liberal criminologists have little to say about controlling crime, protecting victims, reforming prisons or developing more constructive and effective forms of regulation. Thus, it is evident that it is the ascendancy of liberal criminology that lies to a considerable extent behind the recent debate on 'public criminology' and the apparent inability of the expanding criminological industry to make a significant contribution to crime control.

The failure of criminology and the need for critical realism

In this brief and somewhat caricatured history of criminology, it has been suggested that the subject area has become dominated on one hand by administrative criminology, which is pragmatic and managerialist and tends to provide at best short-term responses to pressing political issues but whose conclusions are often equivocal. On the other hand, liberal criminology in various forms is becoming more dominant in academic circles. The contemporary paradox, however, is that while administrative criminology is interested in policy formation, its theoretical and methodological limitations render it unable to perform this task effectively, while liberal criminology attempts to theorise criminological issues in an apparently radical manner but is conspicuously light on policy formation. Thus the immediate challenge for what we might call a post-adolescent criminology is to overcome this divide and develop a criminology which is critical, theoretically coherent and policy relevant. This is not to adopt a form of evangelical criminology, which Pat Carlen (2011) identifies in her anti-sermonising sermon on the current state of critical criminology. Rather, it is to develop a coherent and useful intellectual and epistemological approach, one involving a re-examination of the relationship between theory and method, and between values and policy, in order to develop a basis on which a viable public criminology might be constructed (Burawoy 2005).

The international impact of conservative criminologists during the 1980s and 1990s reminds us that criminological work, even if misguided, can be extremely influential in affecting public policy. Their influence also gives the lie to the claims that policymakers and the public have no interest in criminological work. The problem with a great deal of contemporary criminology is that it is either not presented in a way that makes it accessible to politicians and the general public, or that the policies presented are less than convincing. Moreover, as has been suggested above, there is a considerable body of criminological literature which has no identifiable policy relevance.

This is not to ignore the large body of informative, imaginative and interesting work published in the growing number of criminology journals and books. However, much of this work involves low-level or mid-range theorising and tends to focus on specific *topics*. It therefore becomes difficult to bring these theoretical and empirical threads together and build up a composite picture in order to address the wider questions of crime and justice. As a consequence, many of these middle-range theorists draw heavily on the writings of those radical liberals who do attempt to analyse broader social and political movements. This means, in effect, that their contributions have a high probability of becoming incorporated within an essentially liberal framework.

There is, of course, a significant body of criminologists around the world who have an affinity towards critical realism, although they may not define themselves in these terms. These are criminologists who have a left social democratic orientation and whose objective is to develop an evidence-based approach to crime and punishment in a conceptually coherent and practically effective way. Many criminologists share these aims, and are involved in forms of investigation designed to inform policy, while others act as advisors to different groups and organisations or are actively involved in campaigns and social movements working towards progressive reforms. In order to support and help develop these contributions, it is suggested that we need to build on the foundations that were laid by left realists in the 1980s and 1990s and extend and deepen this approach by drawing on the growing body of critical realist literature, which has added important epistemological and methodological dimensions to social scientific investigation.

2
A Framework of Analysis

From left realism to critical realism

The aim of this chapter is to provide an analytic framework that can be used to develop realist criminology. This is not a rigid or fixed guide but rather a set of reference points designed to provide the basis for developing a coherent and useful criminology. That is, it is an attempt to avoid some of the pitfalls that have beset positivist criminology, on one hand, and idealist forms of criminology on the other. It also represents an attempt to incorporate the theoretical and methodological insights that are associated with the growing body of critical realist literature (Bhaskar 1978, 1999; Sayer 2000; Archer et al. 1998).

Some twenty years ago left realists argued for the need to take crime seriously and suggested that much conventional criminology had failed to identify the causes and impact of crime, particularly amongst the most vulnerable sectors of the population. Left realists also stressed the need to link theory to practice and incorporate an analysis of both micro and macro processes, as well as focus on the lived realities of those groups that we wish to study (Young 1992). Left realism was essentially a political project aimed at providing a left social democratic response to the dominant liberal-conservative consensus within criminology. It provided a much-needed and important critical alternative to mainstream criminology and developed a range of useful concepts; most importantly it addressed the question 'What is to be done about law and order?' (Lea and Young 1984). The recent contribution by critical realists, however, offers the opportunity to develop left realist analysis further and to place it upon a firmer epistemological and methodological foundation. In this way critical realism provides a basis for developing an integrated and coherent approach, one that can more effectively link theory, method and policy.

The primacy of theory

In responding to what has been seen as the deepening crisis in criminology, realism aims to develop an approach that is theory-driven while being evidence-based. It is practically and politically engaged and takes the concerns of the members of the general public seriously, seeing them neither as dupes nor as irrational. Most importantly, it aims to develop a critical approach that stands in opposition to forms of naive realism that see 'crime' as unproblematic.

Indeed, one of the most remarkable aspects of criminological literature is how the notion of 'crime' is dealt with. On one side there are a large number of criminologists who adopt a predominantly common-sense, taken-for-granted approach; they present crime as an unproblematic given or simply equate crime with a particular act. On the other side there are those who overly problematise crime, arguing that it is a concept that has no 'ontological reality' and tend to gravitate either towards relativism or rampant idealism, claiming that the concept of crime is simply a matter of subjective interpretation or political manipulation (Hulsman 1986; Muncie 1996). In many respects, the inability to theorise 'crime' in a meaningful way is indicative of a lack of understanding of the role of theory and the process of abstraction. Understanding the significance of social categories and the processes of classification is fundamental to all forms of social scientific investigation. As Andrew Sayer has pointed out, a key part of social scientific investigation involves the process of abstraction:

Social systems are always complex and messy. Unlike some natural sciences, we cannot isolate out these components and examine them under controlled conditions. We therefore have to rely on abstraction and careful conceptualization, in attempting to abstract the various components or influences in our heads, and only when we have done this and considered how they combine and interact can we expect to return to the concrete, many-sided object and make sense of it. Much rests on the nature of our abstractions, that is, our conceptions of particular one-sided components of the concrete object; if they divide what is in practice indivisible, or if they conflate what are different and separable components, then problems are likely to result. So much depends on the modes of abstraction we use, the way of carving up and defining our objects of study. *Unfortunately the bulk of the methodological literature on social science completely ignores this fundamental issue, as if it were simply a matter of intuition.* (Sayer 2000: 19; emphasis added)

Theory construction is important for identifying the purported relation between events and the causal mechanism that promotes change. It is more than just a case of developing a few orientating concepts or general categories; it involves the development of an overarching framework composed of an interrelated set of assumptions, causal mechanisms and testable propositions. Central to this is the process of abstraction, whereby we isolate particular aspects of some object or situation. These abstractions in turn form the building blocks of theories by conceptualising their essential unifying qualities – their structure, powers and susceptibilities, together with their necessary conditions of existence. The aim is to identify the particular mechanisms and meanings which link their parts and explain their behaviour (Sayer 1992). Because for realists there is a social world existing outside the minds and sense perceptions of its participants, and because the causal mechanisms in play are often not observable, we rely on concepts and theories to help us explain these processes. We can then check these postulates against empirical observations of the world. Theory is judged not only by its logical coherence but also by how much it explains about relevant empirical observations (Kiser and Hechter 1998). Thus, critical realists give priority to conceptualisation and the process of abstraction, since how we conceive our objects of study tends to set the fate of subsequent research. In selecting a theory we need to consider the extent to which it can explain things and shed new light on particular problems. In the final analysis, theory is to be judged on the basis of its explanatory power. Social theory has to be useful and usable. Theory should never be an end in itself but a tool for analysing substantive social problems through supplying the terms or framework for their investigation (Archer 1995).

While critical realists see the appropriation of social reality as problematic, and emphasise the significance of concepts and categories in providing the conceptual grids through which we construct and appropriate reality, naive realists treat both social reality in general and crime in particular as pre-given and directly accessible. Whereas critical realism sees crime as a complex social construction, naive realism - in its various forms, including administrative criminology, purely descriptive criminologies and 'crime science' - tends to take the category of crime for granted and believes that the main aim of criminological investigation is simply to report, count, describe or map crime and victimisation. Although naive realists may express some concerns about the accuracy and reliability of the available data and acknowledge the gaps between recorded, reported and unreported crime, their work exhibits little reflexivity or detailed investigation into the meaning of the general category of crime or indeed subcategories, such as violence, robbery and theft.

Violence, robbery and similar terms denote generic categories that cover a wide variety of actions involving different offender–victim relations in different contexts. Thus, an initial task of investigation is to disaggregate these terms. In relation to robbery, for example, there is a need to distinguish between commercial and street robbery; the notion of street robbery itself needs to be broken down into its constituent parts: mugging, theft from the person and snatch thefts (Matthews 2001; Young 1988). This is critical to understanding the causal processes involved, which in turn will have more or less direct implications for analysis and the formulation of policy. Paradoxically, we find criminologists conflating commercial robbery and street robbery, with the result that in cases where the rate of one is decreasing and of the other increasing, researchers mistakenly conclude that the level of robbery is stable (Felson and Poulsen 2003; Wright and Decker 1997). In cases where loose and sloppy abstractions are used, they are unable to bear the explanatory weight placed upon them. They remain what Marx called 'chaotic conceptions'. No amount of methodological manipulation can compensate for such conceptual deficiencies. To paraphrase Margaret Archer (1995), the road to criminological hell is paved with poor conceptualisations.

We see similar conceptual issues arising in relation to the study of 'race' by criminologists. In America, one of the most ethnically diverse countries in the world, the bulk of criminological investigation divides the population into 'blacks' and 'whites' with little mention of 'Hispanics' (see, e.g., Tonry 1995; Wacquant 2009). This form of 'monochromatic' criminology is often reduced to a 'black' and 'white' opposition, which reinforces rather than elucidates racial divisions and ideologies. In the United Kingdom, which is also ethnically diverse, most criminological studies tend to break the population down into 'black', 'white' and 'Asian'. These categories, besides being too vague and too broad to conduct any meaningful analysis of race and crime control, are not even consistent, since 'black' and 'white' refer to skin colour, while 'Asian' refers to a geographical location.

As a substitute for theorising the process of crime control, criminologists have a strong disposition towards employing either/or dichotomies, resulting in what has been referred to as 'schizoid criminology' (Zedner 2002). Thus, we are presented with 'criminologies of the self' and 'criminologies of the other' (Garland 2001), the transition from 'old' to 'new' penology (Feeley and Simon 1992), and general claims that we are moving from 'inclusive' (welfare) to 'exclusive' (penal) forms of regulation (Wacquant 2009). Unfortunately, the empirical reality to which these dualisms refer is often more complex and nuanced than these suggested oppositions allow. Indeed, while these stark oppositions may appear at first sight a potentially useful way of making distinctions, all too often they serve to detract from the pursuit of a detailed examination of the processes involved and reduce complex social reality to simple dichotomies. Thus, instead of increasing the value of the explanation, they mostly act as a constraint, limiting the scope and depth of the analytic field and in some cases actively distorting the scope of inquiry. Moreover, one of the key features of 'liquid modernity' is that the firm divisions that characterised the Fordist era are increasingly giving way to more fluid social and cultural forms, including forms of transgression, that are making the language of strict binaries less and less appropriate (Young 2003).

Although theory development and good conceptualisation is important for realist criminology, there is little interest in theoreticism. All too often theorists become increasingly distant from the problematics and issues that they are attempting to theorise, and as they studiously refine their concepts, there is a danger that they will become lost in their own conceptual worlds.

The significance of social class

The whole of the criminal justice system – its personnel, its institutions and its practices – are deeply embedded in and reflect prevailing class relations. Most significantly, imprisonment, the central mode of punishment in most Western societies, is a punishment reserved almost exclusively for the lower classes. The uniformed police, on the other hand, are drawn mainly from the respectable working class, while lawyers and judges are overwhelmingly selected from the ranks of the middle and upper classes. These class divisions have an international significance and have remained the basis of the criminal justice system for the last two centuries, with a few minor exceptions.

Strangely, however, there has been a tendency in recent years for criminologists to ignore or play down the significance of class and instead to focus on variables such as race and gender. However, while the subjective experience of class is always mediated by gender and ethnicity, social class remains the best predictor of those sentenced to imprisonment as well as of the composition of the main criminal justice agencies and institutions. The proportion of women and ethnic minorities in prison who are middle or upper class, for example, is no more or less than that drawn from 'white' middle class groups in Western societies. Thus, the whole criminal justice system is highly structured along class lines, and one's class location will condition one's experience of crime and victimisation. However, in cases in which criminologists do acknowledge the significance of social class they tend to do so in terms of income differentiation or education status or, alternatively, prefer to talk about the 'poor', or the so-called underclass, rather than see social class, on one hand, as a function of the relations of production and, on the other, as a source of identity.

There have been a number of attempts to demonstrate the 'myth of social class', which aim to show that middle and upper class groups are equally involved in various forms of deviant or anti-social behaviour. This type of research, however, misses the point. It is not that the middle and upper classes engage in anti-social behaviour but that their actions have a different social significance to those of the lower classes and involve a different victim–offender relation, while the impact of these transgressions will have a different significance in different communities (Braithwaite 1981; Dunaway et al. 2000). The problem of crime is not reducible to acts but is a process of action and reaction involving specific social groups and the interaction between them, their relative social and geographical proximity and the type of threat that they generate. Thus the same actions engaged in by different social groups and classes can be interpreted very differently by others. Concepts of 'dangerousness', 'degeneracy' and above all 'criminality', for example, are widely reserved to describe certain activities of the lower classes (Pratt 1998). These discourses and associated images and perceptions have become deeply embedded in the social psyche.

Jeffrey Reiman, in his classic publication *The Rich Get Rich and The Poor Get Prison* (2004), argues that the criminal justice system conspicuously fails to eliminate crime and instead creates an identifiable group of 'criminals' whose incarceration serves both an ideological and a repressive function. The ideological function, he maintains, is to reassure 'respectable' society that it is being protected while reinforcing the notion that anti-social behaviour is mainly an activity engaged in by the poor, thereby diverting attention away from the activities of the rich and the powerful. At every stage of the process, Reiman argues, the criminal justice system targets the poor while weeding out the rich. From framing laws, to the use of police discretion, to the quality of legal representation and the decision making of the judiciary, the activities of the poor and powerless are more systematically and intensely regulated. The repressive function of prison, Reiman maintains, is achieved through the segregation of a selected group of offenders, which serves as a constant reminder to the working class of the potential consequences of non-conformity.

As Michel Foucault (1977, 2007) has explained, 'crime' has historically been constructed as a conflict between the lower or 'criminal classes', as they were once called, and the respectable working class. The respectable working class, particularly its most vulnerable sections, sought protection from the economically marginalised group, and it is no accident that the respectable working class has a vested interest in supporting property and theft laws (Thompson 1975; Ignatieff 1981), or that the modern uniformed police are primarily located in working districts in order to perform the dual roles of protection and surveillance (Silver 1967). At the same time the threat of prosecution and imprisonment has served to remind the working class, particularly in periods of economic crisis, that the real cost of crime is the possibility of exclusion from the legitimate labour force and the likelihood of propelling both themselves and their family into long-term destitution (Rusche and Kirchheimer 2003).

Left realists have also drawn attention to the class dynamics of crime and punishment, suggesting that crime is mainly intraclass rather than interclass. Crime, it has been argued, is socially and geographically concentrated and tends to compound other social problems. It is also socially and politically divisive and falls most heavily on the vulnerable and accessible (Lea and Young 1993). However, left realists have also been criticised for not taking white collar and corporate crime seriously (Pearce and Tombs 1992), particularly since, it is often argued, white collar and corporate crime cause greater social harm than street crime and therefore should be treated more harshly and be given more attention.

The response to white collar and corporate crime, it would seem, can take two non-exclusive directions. The first is that advocated by John Braithwaite (1982, 1989) and others; it places the emphasis on shaming and extralegal sanctions, since it is the case that the existing criminal justice system was never set up to deal with this type of transgression. While this approach has the merit of looking for alternative ways to sanction offenders, the effectiveness of shaming sanctions is limited. In many cases white collar and corporate criminals are 'amoral calculators' who are indifferent to a social sanction such as shaming. If they do wrong and are exposed, even in the mass media, many such offenders simply set up similar enterprises elsewhere.

The second alternative is to engage in an expansion, reclassification and reconstruction of the existing criminal justice system so that the various 'bourgeois' transgressions that have been carefully excluded from the remit of the modern criminal justice system can be included. Moves in this direction have included the introduction of changing forms of corporate liability, but a more systematic response would be necessary to make white collar and corporate transgressions more routinely punishable under the criminal law, while more rigorously enforcing legislation that does exist to prevent for example, tax evasion.

There is considerable public interest in prosecuting 'suite' crime. It is also the case that white collar and corporate offenders are easier to deter than 'common criminals' because their crimes are more calculating and they have more to lose through criminal sanctioning (Levi 2002). There are, however, at present problems of mobilising evidence and attracting witnesses, and the ability of both white collar and corporate offenders to obtain well-paid, effective legal representation can create prohibitive costs in pursuing prosecutions. Therefore, changes would need to be made to increase the chances of prosecution and to attach significant penalties to many of the transgressions committed by white collar and corporate offenders.

Although class consciousness and collective action on the basis of strong subjective class identities have declined in recent years, class remains a leading moral signifier in everyday life and, in particular, in the criminal justice process (Sayer 2000). Class position continues to shape people's sense of identity, interests and life opportunities, as well as their views on crime and justice (Haylett 2001). Class remains a relation of domination and subordination, although, as Bourdieu (1977, 1987) points out, the location of different classes in social space is determined not only by access to economic capital but also by the appropriation of cultural and social capital.

Crime as a social construction

The critical and radical criminologists of the 1970s were deeply influenced by Berger and Luckmann's seminal text *The Social Construction*

of Reality (1967). In this book Berger and Luckmann set out to challenge the views of positivists, empiricists and naive realists, who believe
that the world presents itself to us in a pre-given, unproblematic form.
In contrast, they underline the interpretative and interactive nature of
social life, as well as the importance of socially constructed categories,
which provide the conceptual grids through which we appropriate and
make sense of reality. These concepts, they remind us, are historically
and culturally specific. For example, the concepts of 'childhood' and
'youth' have different meanings in different parts of the world and have
changed considerably over time (Burr 2003).

Berger and Luckmann's work has had a profound influence on
criminology in general but particularly on critical criminologists,
who have widely adopted the mantra 'crime is a socially constructed
phenomenon'. In conjunction with this claim social constructionists
point to the importance of the role of social actors in defining their
experience (Houston 2001). The appeal of social constructionism is that,
in opposition to naive realists, it emphasises social and historical variability, the role of agency and the importance of discourse, meaning,
power and communication in making sense of the world.

Consequently, many constructionists have suggested that 'crime' is
an arbitrary construct with no ontological reality and that we should
talk instead about 'problematic situations' (Hulsman 1986). However,
there is an important distinction between 'crimes' and 'problematic situations'. For an act to become a crime several conditions must apply.
First, it has to be blameworthy and potentially interpreted as illegal.
This presupposes the existence of the criminal law. Second, it needs
legitimate and recognised actors (usually victims) to define the act as a
possible crime and report it to the authorities. Third, there needs to be
a normative structure in place to support the definition of the type of
act committed by relevant actors as being blameworthy and potentially
a crime. Fourth, there needs to be some recognition within the criminal
justice system that the claims of the victim and the perceived blameworthiness of the offender are appropriate. In cases in which stages three
and four are missing, a 'problematic situation' will not become 'crime',
although some form of transgression or victimisation has taken place
(Pires and Acosta 1994).

Left realists have argued that crime is not an act or a reaction but a
process involving what they refer to as the 'square of crime' (Lea 1992).
This model is designed to draw attention to the role of the four central
components involved – the offender, the victim, the state and public
opinion. This approach draws on the interactionist emphasis in human

interpretation while recognising the significant role of both formal (state) and informal (public) reaction. Thus the difference between crime and 'problematic situations', 'harms' or forms of 'deviance' is that:

> The concept of deviance does not require reference to a group of constitutive rules. This concept could then simply *describe* non-conforming behaviours. The concept of crime, on the contrary, recalls a constitutive set of rules. If this concept also describes an event, it has a distinctive characteristic in that its application to a concrete problematic situation *accomplishes* the very situation it describes. The existence of the criminal justice system, and the power of criminal law ideology, add a strong extra linguistic value to the language. (Pires and Acosta 1994: 27)

Thus, up to a point we can go along with social constructionism and recognise the need to understand and problematise a key concept like 'crime'. However, in the more extreme versions constructionists seem to suggest that social control is exercised to a degree that is independent of the individual act or the harm caused. In short, it is suggested that the majority of those targeted do not deserve targeting and that social control is largely random, unnecessary and, in some cases, counterproductive (Goode 1994). At a certain point there is a tendency to descend into relativism and suggest that social categories like 'crime' are arbitrary or fictional, discursively revisable, and that social processes and institutions can be dissolved by collective wishful thinking. This relativism can be disabling, since it often suggests that all viewpoints are equally valid, and can lead to a strategic impotence, since it precludes the formation of a normative base from which constructive reforms could be developed. In its more extreme forms this approach has potentially serious personal and political consequences:

> For we simply cannot construct the world any old way we choose and if we persistently attempt to do so we are ultimately more likely to come to the attention of psychiatric services than to gain academic approval. However, realising that our world is socially constructed need not force us to adopt a promiscuous and unbridled relativism. Social constructions are all around us and include such diverse features as racism, marriages and marriage guidance, government policies, governments themselves, child abuse, crime, disease, psychology including social constructionist psychology, buildings, people and cities (to name but a few). None of these things are any

the less real for being socially constructed, although the dominance of the processes of construction, as compared to other influences, may vary from one to the other. (Cromby and Nightingale 1999: 9)

The failure to adequately conceptualise the nature of crime and to identify an appropriate definition has led some social constructionists to conclude that there is little point in engaging with practical or political matters such as law reform and crime reduction. From a critical realist perspective, therefore, there are some serious limitations to the social constructionist approach, mainly in the form of an astructuralism – an inability to offer an explanation how structural forces constrain human development and ultimately how these structures might be transformed. Thus, realists can accept a weak form of social constructionism, which emphasises the socially constructed nature of knowledge and institutions, but reject the strong form, which suggests we cannot successfully identify real objects that exist independently of the researcher (Sayer 2000). For critical realists the social world is relatively inaccessible precisely because it is not reducible to our construction of it. Concepts like 'class' and 'crime' have materiality and objectivity and are not readily revisable by changing definitions and subjective conceptions.

In sum, although hard-line constructionism appears to provide a radical approach that problematises the notion of crime, it easily dissolves into relativism and inaction. As a central component of much self-styled critical criminology, it acts as a double-edged sword, inspiring critique on one hand and undermining it on the other. It results too often in 'fantasy radicalism', which largely involves a gestural politics, and makes little contribution to developing a public criminology.

The structure and agency debate

The relation between structure and agency remains a central, but as yet largely unresolved, issue in social science. It is, however, an issue to which critical realists have paid significant attention (Archer 1995; Sayer 2000). The sociological debate over structure and agency has been dominated on one hand by individualists and relativists, who have argued for the primacy or determinism of individual actions, while on the other hand the collectivists have focused on how social structures and constraints 'shape' individual actions. An alternative position is a form of dualism, which either collapses one into the other or alternatively presents them as 'both sides of the same coin'. The latter position is presented by Anthony Giddens (1979) in his widely referenced account of 'structuration theory', which attempts to address the vexed question of the relation of structure and agency. Giddens sees structure and agency as inseparable and mutually constituted. In doing so, Giddens aims to present the agent as someone knowledgeable, enjoying some autonomy from the social and structural constraints that confront them. That is, he wants to avoid social reductionism. In attempting to do so, he rejects the concept of 'role' in favour of the notion of 'positioning', which is produced through 'social practices' and consequently contains the potential for transformation at any moment. At the same time 'institutions' are held to be nothing more than regularised practices involving fluid processes of 'becoming'; they are consequently never something concrete. Thus, according to Giddens the 'integration of the social system is something that is constantly reproduced through the actions of agents' (1979: 79). That is, through their social practices. In this account, agency and structure must always co-vary because they are inseparable.

In contrast to Giddens's 'integrationalist' account, critical realists have argued that structure and agency should not be conflated and that structure can be pre-existent and causally influential. The idealist claim that structures exist only in the heads of social actors is firmly rejected by realists. We see this, for example, in the case of law and the panoply of institutions it generates and operates through. Without legal prohibition and its associated institutions being in place prior to its enactment, an act could notbe called a 'crime' as such. Thus rules, norms and laws not only regulate and respond but are also constitutive. In football, for example, if there were no rules there would be no 'football', only people kicking a ball around (Pires and Acosta 1994). Thus, it is correct to claim that the law 'creates' crime but is not constitutive of the blameworthiness of the act itself.

For the realist the task is to separate structure and agency while simultaneously showing their connections and their interplay. The essence of the realist approach is an examination of the temporal relationship between structure and agency, emphasising that structure necessarily pre-dates action, which leads to its reproduction and transformation and that the structure also post-dates action sequences that have given rise to it. Structures, it is argued, have 'emergent' and 'causal' properties, which implies a stratified world that is not reducible to the intentions of individuals (Sayer 2000).

The important point that realists make is that structure and agency are analytically separable and, because of the time element involved, are also factually distinguishable. Thus, according to Margaret Archer

(1995), to explain what happens in society it is necessary to differentiate the properties of structure from those of different actors.

> In brief, it is necessary to separate structure and agency (a) to identify the emergent structure(s), (b) to differentiate between their causal powers and the intervening influence of people due to their quite different causal powers as human beings, and, (c) to explain any outcome at all, which in an open system always entails an interplay between the two. In short, separability is indispensable to realism. (Archer 1995: 70)

Roy Bhaskar (1979) questions the interplay of social structures and human agents and calls for the employment of mediating concepts to explain how structures actually impinge upon agency and how agents react, in turn, to reproduce or transform structures. At the same time, it is noted that social structuring as a process is not always predictable. This is not to suggest that all things social are a matter of contingency. Rather, that society is ordered and the task is to understand how it is ordered and how structures change shape (Porpora 1998). Moreover, it is recognised that people are capable of resisting or circumventing structural tendencies and that all structural influences are mediated by people shaping the situations in which they find themselves.

Some of the aspects of the structure–agency debate have recently surfaced in criminology in relation to the issue of desistance. In their pioneering work on desistance Robert Sampson and John Laub (1993) claim to address the structure–agency debate but, in effect, present an account that focuses mainly on changes in structures, particularly the role of employment and marriage, and the ways in which people adapt to these roles and constraints. Offenders engage in desistance, they suggest, because once involved in these structures they find criminality less alluring, usually without even realising it. But, as Barry Vaughan (2007) as argued in drawing on critical realist literature, Sampson and Laub do not explain the moral and emotional elements of this process or how agents originally submitted to these 'turning points'. Neither do they explain why these individuals sustain these commitments or why they believe that these commitments are incompatible with their ongoing criminality.

A considerable amount of research indicates that structural changes such as getting married and taking up employment have a limited impact on offending behaviour (Farrall and Bowling 1999). There is therefore a need, as Archer (1995) has argued, to examine the internal process and narrative of change and the willingness of agents to consider different options. It is also important to consider the significance for the desister of wider social networks of people who provide emotional and material support.

Shadd Maruna (2000) in his account of desistance recognises the role of social bonds and attachments. However, he presents a 'phenomeno-logical' approach which focuses on individual decision making and the subjective experience of 'making good'. While providing some useful insights into the process of 'going straight', Maruna's account focuses almost exclusively on agency and so fails to squarely address the rela-tion between structure and agency. He also fails to identify how personal decision making is routinely structured and constrained. Maruna and his colleagues are, however, aware of the difficulties of addressing the structure–agency issue, as are Laub and Sampson (LeBel et al. 2008; Laub and Sampson 2001). While Laub and Sampson claim that there is currently 'no way to disentangle the role of subjective vs. objective change as the cause of desistance', Maruna and his colleagues ask the question 'which came first?' and conclude that subjective changes may precede life-changing structural events and that individuals 'can act as agents of their own change'. They do, however, call for more research to try to disentangle the sequencing of subjective and situational factors.

Thus, it is evident that amongst some of the leading commentators on the issue of desistance the relationship between agency and structure remains unresolved, with different parties emphasising either subjective or structural factors while largely ignoring the role of the other. Other researchers advocate an integrationalist approach, based on the work of Giddens, that collapses both sides of the process (Farrall and Bowling 1999). A realist approach calls for: a deeper understanding of the inter-play between agency and structure; an appreciation of the mediations in play, particularly the role of agencies and significant others; how struc-tural constraints are resisted and circumvented; and the identification of the causal powers of structures in order to overcome the one-sided approaches prevalent in much of the criminological literature.

Working in and against the state

One of the main features that distinguishes realist criminology from much mainstream criminology is its relation to the state. While liberals tend to be either anti or minimal statist, the more conservative strands in criminology tend to accept state actions uncritically and assume that the state works in the common interest. Thus liberals, being mainly opposed to different forms of state intervention, feel that one of criminology's main tasks is to point to the apparent failures and limitations of state policies and practices, while conservatives remain largely silent on the legitimacy and impact of state actions (Held 1989). Consequently, within mainstream criminological literature, the principal criminal justice agencies and institutions, such as the police and prisons, are either seen as perennial failures or accepted as a necessary, if expensive, element of social control. Where change is suggested, liberals tend to argue for a curtailment of police powers and a reduction in the scale of imprisonment, while conservatives argue for the extension of police powers and the development of more cost-effective forms of punishment.

A critical distinction between liberal and realist approaches to crime control is that, while both are critical of the operation of certain agencies and policies, realists are also interested in engaging with state agencies and contributing to policy and practice in order to increase, in some respects, the effectiveness of the criminal justice system, reduce forms of victimisation and work towards social justice. This may involve extending the range of state agencies or intensifying state intervention. Feminist criminologists have shown the way in working in and against the state to change policies on such issues as rape, domestic violence and sex trafficking (Horvath and Brown 2009; Raymond and Hughes 2001). In addition, feminists have drawn attention to the gendered and patriarchal nature of state institutions, practices and policies (Kantola 2006).

For realists the challenge is to move beyond merely criticising aspects of state policies in contemporary society and to engage constructively in the development of progressive and positive interventions. In short, there is a need to engage both analytically and politically with state policies and practices and to work both *in* and *against* the state. This may involve a whole range of activities: framing and processing legislation; participating in official committees; working with specific state agencies to develop new policies and practices; and criticising and changing existing policy approaches.

There is, however, a growing consensus amongst criminologists that the nature and direction of the state is changing, although there is little agreement about the exact nature of this change. Two opinions currently circulate in criminology concerning these changes. On the one hand, radical liberals like Loic Wacquant (2009) and Jonathan Simon (2007) claim that the state is becoming increasingly punitive, while others argue that more subtle and less punitive forms of state regulation are emerging that aim to 'shape' and 'responsibilise' subjects through a number of diverse strategies (Rose 1999; Deleuze 1995; Pykett 2012). On the other hand, there is a related debate in which one camp claims that the powers of the national state are being reduced as a result of globalisation, while others claim that state powers are being extended through the development of new forms of 'networked governance', which involve decentralised management, contracting-out of services and devolved budgets (Crawford 2006a; Garland 1996). Realists, like other criminologists, need to make sense of these changes since they clearly have implications for the regulation of crime control and will affect policy formation and interventionist strategies. While there is a danger of exaggerating the extent of these changes and taking attention away from the continued anchoring role of the state, the reality would seem to be, as Adam Crawford (2006a) has suggested, that in some areas state intervention is being withdrawn, in other areas it is being redrawn and in still others it is being extended.

Power

Any critical criminology must operate with a conception and an appreciation of power. Every facet of 'law and order' is infused with power relations ranging from those who engage in violence, to parents abusing children, to the judges who pass sentence on offenders. In the vast majority of offender–victim confrontations, whether they concern normal crime, corporate crime or state crime, there is a power differential in play. From the interpersonal to the structural, power operates at every level (see Box 1983).

The problem in analysing power is that it manifests itself in multiple forms, from the brutal and repressive to the more subtle, manipulative and ideological. Power appears to be everywhere and nowhere. At one moment tangible and overt, at another subtle and invisible. Thus, social theorists have found it necessary to distinguish between potential power and actual power.

In his review of power Steven Lukes (2005) dismisses behaviouristic conceptions that attempt to identify power in relation to immediate individual decision making or to pluralistic conceptions which claim that competing interests tend to balance each other out. Instead, Lukes offers a radical account of power that involves consideration of certain parties who are able to exercise control over the political agenda and are identifiable by the range of issues they can control or the different contexts in which they can achieve desired outcomes. Lukes suggests that notions of power commonly employed by social scientists are unsatisfactory in a number of respects.

First, there is what Lukes refers to as the 'exercise fallacy', in which the examination of power is limited to situations that involve power's actual exercise. Second, he is critical of forms of analysis that equate the exercise of power with domination rather than seeing power as productive. He rejects approaches that depict the exercise of power as essentially negative, repressive or constraining. Third, he sees accounts which focus on 'power over others' as inadequate, arguing in line with Michel Foucault (2002) that power is *relational*.

Foucault's conception of power, although it has been through a number of mutations over the years, challenges some traditional accounts. Foucault's main argument is that power is not simply repressive but productive and positive. Thus, Foucault suggests in *Discipline and Punish* (1977) that the study of punitive mechanisms does not concentrate 'on their "repressive" effects alone, on their "punishment" aspects alone, but situates them in a whole series of their possible positive effects, even if these seem marginal at first sight' (Foucault 1977: 23). More specifically, he argues, power produces 'subjects' forging their character and 'normalising' them.

> This form of power that applies itself to everyday life categorises the individual, marks him by his own individuality, attaches him to his own identity, imposes a law of truth on him that he must recognise and others have to recognise in him. It is a form of power that makes individuals subjects. There are two meanings of the word 'subject': subject to someone else by control and dependence, and tied to his own identity by conscience and self-knowledge. Both meanings suggest a form of power that subjugates and makes subject to. (Foucault 2002: 331)

Through the exercise of an array of disciplinary mechanisms involving the organisation of time and space, Foucault argues that power can be exercised through architectural design as well as direct interpersonal relations. Thus, power itself can be manifested in prison design, such as the panopticon, or in practices, such as the treadmill, which operate independently of any individual will. Foucault is interested in the different ways that power manifests itself; how it becomes objectified and internalised, and ultimately how it affects attitudes, actions, shapes bodies and structures discourses. In *Discipline and Punish*, Foucault conceptualises power very broadly in terms of changing productive relations and examines how the shift from sovereign power to disciplinary power not only determines the nature of punishment but becomes embodied in the creation and operation of the modern prison and associated disciplinary practices.

In the *History of Sexuality* (1979) and later writings Foucault modified his 'analytics' of power, as he calls it, in response to the various criticisms of the conception of power presented in *Discipline and Punish*, which argue that it is presented as being too unidirectional. The whole project of the *History of Sexuality* involves the elaboration of a modified theory of power, in particular the processes of subjectification.

Rather than seeing power primarily in terms of law or an expression of state control, Foucault sees it as incorporating a multiplicity of forces involving ceaseless struggles and confrontations. Thus, the exercise of power is always unstable and power is, in a sense, always 'in play'. In this way, Foucault also tried to develop a conception of power that moved beyond the coercion/consent dichotomy, wherein power is seen either as an expression of violence or force or as an effect of ideology. Nor did he want to present power predominantly in terms of capitalism or patriarchy, but rather as emanating from below and involving different lines of force and new knowledges whose outcomes can never be certain and whose effects may be different from those expected.

One theme that Foucault took up in the *History of Sexuality* is the operation of the family, in which the sexuality of children and adolescents was first problematised. This was also the theme of Jacques Donzelot's (1979) incisive analysis of the development of the modern family. Donzelot described how the family became responsible for the sexual and physical health of the children. Following Foucault, Donzelot does not see the modern family primarily as a site of repression, coercion or ideological manipulation, but rather as the product of a number of developments – the promotion of hygiene, the changing of gender roles, the deployment of medicine – all of which allow for the development of new modes of socialisation. Thus, Donzelot saw the modern family not functioning as a manifestation of state repression or an expression of patriarchal authority, but as offering women and children the possibility of increased autonomy. Once constructed, the modern family came increasingly under state control. At the end of the nineteenth century, the process involved the creation of a new, professional body of social workers who were able to provide a strategic link joining the child, the family, the school and the community. In addition, a number of newly formed regulatory bodies – the juvenile court, boarding schools and the like – emerged in this period. They created a network of social guardians, adjudicators and experts who gradually came to colonise the family.

Foucault's conception of power, however, is not without its critics. J. G. Merquior (1985), for example, argues that the conception of power presented in *Discipline and Punish* presents power as too comprehensive and monolithic, 'a machine in which everyone is caught', and that this has led to a reading of Foucault that conceives of power as omnipresent and all-embracing. This conception is reinforced by Foucault's avoidance of human agency and, ultimately, what seems to be a denial of the possibility of any political potential for the human subject. Andrew Sayer (2011) has argued that Foucault does not distinguish between malign and benign forms of power. Thus it is difficult to distinguish the operation of democracy from that of dictatorship. It is also suggested that Foucault presents a dystopian view of the world without offering any specific critique of social arrangements and consequently provides no basis for critique.

Feminists too have taken issue with Foucault's conception of power, arguing that Foucault never specifically examines the subordination of women or the sources of their subjectification. Nancy Fraser (1981) argues that Foucault lacks a normative framework and has thereby removed the possibility of providing a basis for developing an emancipatory politics. Other feminists have argued that Foucault presents a gender-neutral, and ultimately gender-blind, theory of subjection. He does not provide an account, for example, of how prison regimes differ in their treatment of male and female prisoners and how this relates to dominant conceptions of masculinity and femininity (O'Brien 1982). Lois McNay (1992) argues that despite Foucault's assertion that power is diffuse, heterogeneous and productive, his historical analysis tends to depict power as centralised and monolithic. These criticisms notwithstanding, Foucault has seriously challenged, if not dislodged, some of the conventional conceptions of power and engendered a rethinking of the nature of power amongst a broad range of social scientists, including criminologists.

Defending human rights

Recurring themes in criminology over the past fifty years or so have been what is the proper form of inquiry and what are the appropriate parameters of this sub-discipline? A major contribution to this debate was made by Herman and Julia Schwendinger (1975) in asking whether we are or should be defenders of order or guardians of human rights? In a similar vein a number of contemporary critical and radical criminologists argue that the traditional focus of criminology is too narrow and that we should concern ourselves with a wider range of social harms (Hillyard et al. 2004). Critical realists are not overly concerned about disciplinary boundaries and recognise the validity of those social scientists who want to reduce suffering, abuse, exploitation and oppression in its various forms. Moreover, as Amartya Sen (2004) has suggested, there is something deeply attractive in the idea that every person, anywhere in the world, irrespective of citizenship or territorial legislation, has some basic rights that others should respect. However, a number of issues arise in moving from this idealised vision to reality issues about competing rights, including the threshold of rights (with implications of which rights should be taken seriously), the enforcement of rights, the relation between rights and duties, as well as cultural variations in the identification of rights. Thus, while there may be broad agreement about certain 'basic' rights or so-called natural rights, such as the freedom of movement and expression, some critics are sceptical of 'second-generation rights' involving economic and social rights or welfare rights, which have mostly been added relatively recently to earlier enunciations of human rights. Rights to medical care, for example, should not be included, it is argued, since they are dependent on the availability of specific social institutions that may not exist. Thus there is a feasibility issue and it may not be possible to realise certain rights for all.

However, Zygmunt Bauman (2011) has argued that in a more globalised, individualised and 'liquid' world characterised by greater fluidity and uncertainty, the notion of basic human rights lays the foundation, at the very least, for mutual tolerance. The recognition of human rights provides an important normative point of reference that goes beyond the interests of national states and local conflicts. Moreover, it is the case that the pursuit of freedom of religion, expression and association not only serves to protect specific individuals but can provide protection, directly and indirectly, for all groups in society. At the same time it is recognised that the pursuit of individual rights has social implications:

> Although the notion of 'human rights' was created for the benefit of individuals (concerning the right of every individual to be seen as separate and distinct from others, without the threat of punishment or banishment from society, or human company in general), it is obvious that the fight for 'human rights' can only be undertaken with others, since only a joint effort can secure its benefits. ... To become

a 'right', a difference must be common to a sizable group or category of individuals, rich in bargaining power, it must also be sufficiently glaring not to be ignored, to be taken seriously; the right to difference must become a stake in the joint manipulation of demands. (Bauman 2011: 90)

To whatever extent contemporary international political life can be seen to have a sense of justice, its language is the language of human rights. Human rights provide a standard of evaluation for the policies and practices of a range of economic and political institutions (Beitz 2001; Blau et al. 2007). Human rights discourse identifies the conditions that societies and institutions should meet if we are to consider them legitimate. In this way there is no contradiction between defending human rights and simultaneously addressing crime and victimisation.

Intervention: beyond 'what works'

Realism is oriented towards a modernist problematic. That is, it stands in opposition to those forms of relativism and impossibilism which claim that effecting social change through the application of knowledge and understanding makes no real difference or that 'nothing works'. It is also opposed to forms of idealism which claim that piecemeal social change is irrelevant and only a major transformation of the social structure is worthwhile. For realists even small gains are gains, and it is recognised that piecemeal reforms often lead to further reforms.

Criminology, it should be noted, has a long history of pessimism and impossibilism and of dystopian images of the future. In issuing repeated warnings of the dangers of 'social control' and particularly in dwelling on the insecurities of late modernity, criminologists tend to present a negative interpretation of social change. In emphasising the growing concerns with insecurity, there is a tendency to downplay the ways in which social reforms have improved the quality of life for certain groups, reduced victimisation and increased personal freedoms (Ericson 2007; Simon 2007). A disproportionate focus of attention on a perceived increase in the range and intensity of controls and restrictions may explain why so little has been written on the most remarkable development within criminology in living memory – the crime drop (Blumstein and Wallman 2000; Karmen 2000).

There is, however, a more general problem of liberal pessimism that runs though criminology and goes beyond the claim that nothing works. Some versions of this pessimism claim that not only does nothing work but interventions often make things worse. In contrast, the realist project, closely tied to conceptions of emancipation, believes that there is no point in social science if it does not at least offer the possibility of some kind of social improvement. This may involve challenging and changing various (mis)conceptions or material conditions or both (Bhaskar 2002). As crime and punishment are enormously contentious issues, critique and debate should be central to the subject. The act of engaging in debate and critique presupposes change and the possibility of social improvement.

As a result of their interest in practical issues and fostering social change, realists are often accused of pragmatism. This is a serious mischaracterisation. It demonstrates a fundamental misunderstanding of the realist project (Pavlich 1999). Although realists are interested in *what* works, they are more concerned with *why* and *how* things work. Understanding why and how things work, critical realists argue, involves identifying the causal mechanisms that foster change. Thus a claim of critical realism is that it is not something inherent in particular programmes that makes them work. Rather, it is through the propensities and capacities of the agents or objects that such programmes are directed towards that allows them to work. Thus, whether rehabilitation programmes, for example, work as intended depends on whether the subjects go along with them and choose to use the resources as intended (Pawson and Tilley 1997). Realists aim to look beneath the surface of what works with the objective of identifying the generative mechanisms that produce change. It is this unique conception of causal processes and how they work that distinguishes critical realism from pragmatism, empiricism and positivism.

Critical realists also have a distinctive view of the nature and meaning of interventions (Pawson 2006). Interventions are not just practices but are theories or explanations that postulate the possibility of bringing about improved outcomes. Consequently, interventions are potentially fallible, particularly since they deal with complex social realities as well as with different groups of subjects, and may be implemented differently in different contexts. Therefore, all of these elements must be considered when addressing what works in order to find out what works for whom, under what circumstances. Thus, there are a number of different ways in which programmes may be said to work.

Although realists are committed to developing evidence-based policy, it is recognised that it is not possible to provide definitive 'solutions' to policy issues in open and complex social systems. Social interventions are complex and are rarely implemented in the same way twice.

Evidential truths are therefore always partial, provisional and conditional. It is not so much a question of presenting facts but of developing *explanations*, for justifying taking one course of action rather than another. As opposed to the notion that policies can be simply 'read off' from the data or that certain 'facts' are likely in themselves to change the direction of policymaking, what realists argue is that the objective of gathering and synthesising data is to make sense of the processes involved (Pawson 2006).

Engaging in intervention is always subject to political pressures, and so a realist approach is itinerary and processional. Engaging in effective intervention requires considerable skill and imagination, an ability to converse with policymakers and practitioners, the majority of whom are not 'agents of social control' but are often problem-solvers looking for direction and guidance. The failure of criminology has been that it has failed to provide this service in recent years, particularly on the most pressing problems of crime control.

Conclusion

The aim of this chapter has been to outline a framework of analysis for guiding realist investigation. It has emphasised the primacy of theory and the central role of conceptions of class and the state in examining the criminal justice process. This involves affording a limited role to social constructionism and a simultaneous recognition that social forms exist independently of human consciousness. There is also a growing interest in human rights in a period of 'liquid modernity', in which state power is becoming important in securing and legitimising an increasingly fragmented social world. The aim is to work 'in and against' the state in order to implement positive changes. Achieving this objective involves more than presenting 'solutions'. It often involves an attempt to develop explanations that evaluate the relative strengths and weaknesses of different options.

It is in the context of a rapidly changing post-Fordist world that realist criminology offers an effective alternative to both mainstream criminology and the available versions of critical and radical criminology. Fully developed, it offers the possibility of a paradigm shift within criminology. It has firm roots in social philosophy and adopts an open-door policy on evidence. It is theory-driven and critical. It maintains that social science has an emancipatory potential. It is flexible in terms of disciplinary boundaries and aims to draw on whatever sources of help are available to address the issues at hand. Finally, it has a clear commitment to policy development while recognising that this involves engaging with politicians, policymakers and practitioners at a number of different levels, often over a considerable period of time.

3
The Problem of Method

Engaging with social reality

Most books on criminological research methods have a great deal to say about designing questionnaires, developing interview techniques, conducting surveys and formulating sampling strategies but have much less to say about the process of conceptualisation and theorisation. Although mastering such techniques is no doubt an important part of producing quality research, there is a danger that the connection between theory and method is downplayed, and in some cases these two processes are treated as if they are separable and autonomous. The disconnect between theory and method is reflected in academic life when courses in criminological theory are taught without much reference to research methods and vice versa.

As has already been suggested, however, if we are to develop a viable 'public criminology' and avoid the deficiencies of 'so what?' criminology, we need to develop a 'joined up' approach that connects theory, method and policy in a coherent manner. For this reason the choice of methods is central to the objective of developing a consistent, realistic and useful criminology.

Selecting an appropriate method is not just a question of dipping into a methodological toolbox. Rather, the focus on method, like the focus on theory, raises the issue of how to appropriate, understand and investigate a complex and messy social reality. This is a challenging task since, unlike the closed world of natural sciences, social sciences deal with open systems and with a social reality that is often opaque, presenting itself in mystifying, illusionary and distorted forms. The primary concern, therefore, is how to conceptualise and investigate the complexities of the social world, with its layers of meanings, motivations and actions.

Beyond cookbook criminology

It is a characteristic of certain schools of criminology that they have a preferred methodology, which they claim is in some way superior, more rigorous or more reliable than any other. Consequently, they produce basic methodological textbooks containing a list of instructions which readers are expected to follow religiously. These can take the form of standard positivistic approaches based on observation, data gathering and statistical analysis, ethnographic research and participant observation, grounded theory or forms of discourse analysis (Layder 1993; Jupp 1995).

One example of such cookbook criminology, which has been very influential in academic circles, is that associated with the Maryland Group. It presents itself as a scientific, evidence-based approach to crime reduction. Although this approach has the commendable objective of developing a rigorous approach to crime control, it is conservative, or 'right realist', in orientation inasmuch as it adopts a common-sense view of crime and the criminal justice process, and formulates a methodology based on the natural sciences. It also rejects accounts of crime based on 'root causes' and aims to identify the independent effects of specific interventions within different institutional settings (Sherman et al. 2002; Maxwell 2012). The main purpose of research, it argues, is to find out 'what works, what does not work and what is promising'.

The main aim in employing the Maryland Scientific Methods Scale (SMS) is to disentangle the effects of specific interventions by testing causal hypotheses. The SMS involves a five-point scale in which: research based on cross-sectional design would score 1; while a simple before-and-after quasi-experimental design would score 2; cases that involve a control group would score 3; and using multiple sites and controlling for other variables would score 4. However, the 'gold standard' of evaluation design, according to its advocates, is randomised controlled trials (RCTs), where subjects are allocated blindly and randomly to experimental or control groups. In an RCT there is normally an experimental group that is subject to intervention and a control group that is not. Both are measured before and after the intervention; any differences in outcome between the groups is attributed to the intervention.

The main point of reference for the use of RCTs is medical research and the development of various scales of reliability (Farrington et al. 2002). Studies are assessed on several bases: statistical sophistication, the size of the samples used, response rates and perceived impact. Not only is this approach directed to conventional notions of crime reduction, but is seen to be equally applicable to the evaluation of the police and courts. In reviewing 675 programmes on the Maryland Scientific Scale, Lawrence Sherman and his colleagues (2002) reported that 29 were seen to work, 25 did not work, and 25 were identified as 'promising' in terms of preventing crime. However, 68 programmes were of unknown effectiveness. Significantly, only 13 programmes were reviewed in more than one setting, and 12 more reviewed in only two settings.

The most immediate problem with this approach is that most crime prevention interventions are multifaceted, involving interagency cooperation. Therefore, it is always difficult to identify the effectiveness of single interventions with any degree of certainty. In addition, it is acknowledged that the context in which different interventions are carried out is critical to their success or failure, but it is not always clear what it is about different settings that facilitates or limits the effectiveness of specific interventions.

Evidence, however, does not speak for itself. It has to be interpreted and this invariably involves value judgements. Moreover, the rapidly changing nature of the social world means that interventions which are seen to work in one place at one time may not work elsewhere or in the future. The enduring concern, however, is that evaluations will be taken at face value and qualifications about their effectiveness that are noted in research reports and summaries will be disregarded later. Further, there are serious concerns about the rigour and reliability of this approach:

> One of the questionable attributes of this project, however, concerns the decision to set the criteria for determining that a programme area 'works' at two level 3 studies indicating statistically significant findings of its effectiveness. On its face this does not seem to be a remarkably high threshold. We might expect much more from the multi-million dollar global criminological research enterprise than two methodologically sound studies showing positive results before we unequivocally conclude that an entire field of intervention works. As the editors put the matter, they chose not to use more demanding criteria of success because this 'would leave very little to say about crime prevention, based on existing science'. Actually, it would leave them with a tremendous amount to say, but it would almost all be bad news, as they would have to conclude on the basis of the existing evidence almost nothing works. (Haggerty 2008: 166)

As Nick Tilley (2001) has suggested, having a recipe is probably better than having nothing, and some recipe books are better than others.

However, an accomplished cook makes little use of cookbooks. The use of such rigid guides tends to result in standardised and unimaginative research practices, which are unlikely to produce satisfying outcomes.

The lure of empiricism

In the philosophy of science empiricism is, broadly speaking, the view that scientific investigation can be confined to observable phenomena and their formal relations. Realism embodies the view that there is a reality independent of our knowledge and that this reality is stratified, containing emergent properties whose effects should not be conflated with our experience of them (Bhaskar 1979; Dilworth 1990). Whereas empiricism is inductive and empiricists believe that 'facts speak for themselves' and that theories can be constructed by collecting and sifting data, realists believe that social scientific research should be theory-led and that we use theories and concepts to carve up the world and make sense of the multitude of 'facts' that compose reality (Manicas 2006).

For the most part, empiricists emulate the methods of the natural sciences and frequently claim that their endeavours are 'scientific', whereas realists maintain that social scientific investigation necessarily involves the interpretation of human meaning, intentions and actions and therefore requires a range of methods, the choice of which will be dependent on the nature of the object under study and what one wants to learn about it. Realists argue that, because social systems are always open and usually quite complex, it is very difficult, if not impossible, to isolate the components we want to examine under controlled conditions, contrary to what may occur in the natural sciences (Sayer 2000, 2010).

As C. Wright Mills argues in *The Sociological Imagination* (1959), abstracted empiricism tends to be atheoretical, with little conception of the historical and social forces that shape both natural and social scientific investigation. Indeed, where structural and historical factors are used in empiricist studies, they are often 'above' the level of the data made available in the research or alternatively refer to psychological factors that operate 'below' the level of data presented. Typically, when literature reviews are conducted, Mills suggests, it is not to develop a theory, or to test assumptions, or to give the study meaning. In many cases the literature review is presented independently of the research report and is often written up *after* the data are collected.

Despite warnings from C. Wright Mills and other major sociologists, empiricism and positivism remain prevalent in social science in general and in criminology in particular. The growing body of government-sponsored administrative criminology operates with a predominantly empiricist methodology. Typically light in theory and heavy on statistical manipulation, these studies collect data on different aspects of crime, victimisation and the operation of the criminal justice system such that the work is often small scale, localised and descriptive, producing equivocal conclusions. A major limitation of these studies is that they make little contribution to the development of cumulative knowledge and theory building.

Empiricism, however, can take a number of forms, some of which are more subtle than the usual abstracted empiricism. For example, a popular strategy in criminology is to take two phenomena that appear to be changing simultaneously in related ways and to claim that one must be causing the changes in the other. Identifying these forms of correspondence has become a major preoccupation for criminologists, even amongst those who have radical pretensions. One of the most influential representatives of this form of 'functional empiricism' is Loic Wacquant (2000, 2005), who has presented a number of explanations of the changing nature of crime control on the basis of observing two phenomena changing simultaneously. Thus he observes the decline of the ghetto in the United States and the expansion of the prison and concludes that the prison must be replacing the ghetto. In a similar vein he sees the demise of the Keynesian welfare state and the simultaneous growth of the prison and concludes that they must be functionally related. In addition, he claims that the rise of the prison population in the United States is a function of the rise of neoliberalism and postmodern insecurity, despite the fact that the number of people sent to prison has decreased in periods of neoliberalism (as occurred in the Thatcher era), and he seems impervious to the fact that neoliberals are generally interested in minimal statism rather than expanding state provision, particularly in the very expensive form of incarceration.

In the same way there is little support for Wacquant's thesis that declining welfare budgets in most advanced Western countries are primarily responsible for the expanding prison populations. In the United States, for example, the state of California significantly increased welfare expenditure in the 1990s as prison populations were expanding (Greenberg 2001). To the extent that changing forms of welfare provision are likely to have an impact on prison populations, it would seem that it is not so much a question of a reduction in welfare expenditure per se, as of the reorganisation and redistribution of welfare. However, the attractiveness of the form of functionalist empiricism presented by Wacquant is not difficult to understand for those who want simplistic answers to complex issues. These types of accounts are superficially attractive, but the complex ways in which these phenomena may be connected are not explored, and it is the regularity of their appearance that provides the (questionable) basis of explanation.

Another prevalent example of empiricism involves what we might call 'inverted empiricism'. This approach assumes that because we cannot observe simultaneous changes in two phenomena, they cannot be causally related. This type of empiricism is evident in the majority of studies in criminology on the relationship between crime rates and the prison population. Since imprisonment rates in the United Kingdom and America have increased significantly over the last decade or so while recorded crime rates have fallen, it is frequently concluded that there is no discernable causal link between crime and imprisonment rates. Michael Tonry, for example, in *Penal Reform in Overcrowded Times* (2001), asserts in a section ironically entitled 'crude empiricism' that the 'explanation for why so many Americans are in prison, that our crime rates are higher or faster rising than in other countries, has virtually no validity' (Tonry 2001: 54). In an impressive piece of logic, Tonry concludes his discussion of crude empiricism with the startling and unverified claim that American imprisonment rates rose because American politicians 'wanted them to rise' (2001: 57). Thus the complex dynamics of prison expansion are reduced to a form of voluntarism.

However, it makes little sense to compare changes in the overall recorded crime rate and the imprisonment rate since a large percentage of recorded crimes are unlikely to warrant a prison sentence. To better understand the connection, we need to examine the process of attrition, particularly for those offences that are highly likely to end in a prison sentence if the offender is found guilty, and to examine the forms of decision making at various points in the criminal justice system, particularly by the police and sentencers. The causal connections between different types of crime may be indirect, heavily mediated and subject to an array of different forces and forms of decision making, but it does not mean that causal connections cannot be identified (see Matthews 2009a).

The problem, as always, is that there are a number of causal processes in play with different, and at times contrasting, impacts. Our aim however, should not be to engage in a fruitless and meaningless form of inverted empiricism. Instead, it should be to identify the causal mechanisms which shape and produce the outcomes that we are examining.

Moreover, the denial of any meaningful relation between recorded crime rates and imprisonment is one of the major conceptual fault lines running through criminology, almost creating two distinct sub-disciplines – 'crime' and 'punishment' – that are studied independently of each other, with the consequence that punishment tends to appear arbitrary. This in turn makes informed and normative discussions of punishment and imprisonment extremely difficult and tends to disconnect academic criminologists from the concerns of the public and policymakers.

Thus, in order to avoid the excess of voluntarism and reductionism, realists place considerable emphasis on *causal* explanations. The main objective is to distinguish the causal from the contingent. Rather than engage in empiricism, with its interest in statistical correlations and recurring events, or present pure descriptions, realists focus on why and how change occurs and on identifying the causal dynamics that produce non-random outcomes.

On causality

In everyday life we repeatedly ask what makes something happen. That is, we want to know what produces or creates change. In positivistic social science, causal explanations are translated into the language of cause and effect or, more ambitiously, 'laws'. For many positivists the aim of identifying causes centres on the search for regularities, but observing regularities may not necessarily identify the causal relations involved. As Andrew Sayer (2010) has pointed out, what causes an event has nothing to do with the number of times a particular association has been observed to occur. This is not to say that the existence of empirical regularities may, in some cases, draw attention to causal processes, but confirmation of this causal relation will require qualitative information about the nature of the objects and relations involved.

We may find, for example, that prison riots or disturbances tend to occur in overcrowded institutions with poor conditions, but this does not identify the mechanisms that are responsible for generating the riot. Thus statistically we may find a high correlation between overcrowding and riots, but this does not provide a convincing causal account and indeed may obscure the actual causes. Often what we need is qualitative investigation to narrow the list of possible causal factors. Rather than simply seek associations between 'factors' or 'variables', qualitative research with those involved in prison riots may reveal that they were caused, for example, by a sense of injustice or as a result of rigid rules following the actions of prison officials (Player and Jenkins 1994).

In contrast to the consequentialist account of causation, the major difference for realists is that the causal powers of objects and relations are seen more generally as their ways of acting. Thus, people have causal powers, including being able to work, speak, reason, whether they choose to exercise those powers or not. Causal powers also reside in objects or institutions, such as bureaucracies and prisons. Bureaucracies have the power to process large volumes of standard decisions over time, while their hierarchical and rigid structure limits their flexibility and adaptability to novel situations. That is, causal powers are not so much about the regularity between separable things or events, but the properties and liabilities of particular objects. Thus, we need to understand what it is about certain objects or relations that is likely to produce change. Importantly, causal powers exist independent of their effects. Therefore, the fact that certain effects are not observed does not mean that causal powers do not exist. The aim is to identify the *mechanisms* that are able to activate certain powers.

Three additional considerations make the identification of causal processes difficult. The first is that processes of change often involve several causal mechanisms, not all of which are pushing or pulling in the same direction. Second, we need to distinguish between necessary and contingent causes. That is, between causal mechanisms that are necessary or generative and those that have minimal effect. Third, it is important to be aware that the same causal mechanisms can produce quite different results in different contexts.

Thus, particular drugs possess certain causal powers, but their effects will not only depend on the context in which they are consumed but also vary according to the individuals or groups that consume them. For instance, injecting heroin to reduce pain and suffering in hospitals is interpreted differently from the use of heroin and related drugs by marginalised populations living in urban ghettos. Identifying what a given mechanism can and cannot do requires considerable effort and ingenuity. It is not reducible to the search for regularities.

The identification of causal mechanisms stands in contrast to the attempt in criminological research to introduce intervening variables into the account. The aim is instead to identify the mechanism responsible for producing, shaping or transforming the process under investigation. Thus, a mechanism is not a variable but an account of the make-up or behaviour of the processes responsible for the observed regularities.

In these situations it is necessary to develop a research design geared to identifying such possibilities, coupled with a more rigorous attempt to theorise possible relations and processes. This will often involve studying examples that provide contrasts in aetiology, such as the absence of an otherwise common condition, or asking what it is about a phenomenon that enables it to do certain things. Alternatively, the question can be posed whether this outcome would happen in the absence of certain mechanisms. In realist terms these mechanisms will be 'fired' only in certain conditions. Therefore, explanations must include reference to the prevailing conditions. For example, reasons may be given for joining a gang, but these actions presuppose social structures, rules and systems of meaning in terms of which reasons are formulated (Pitts 2008). Social scientific explanations often begin with an account of actions, then proceed to the reasons given in actors' accounts. This, in turn, will invite some consideration of the rules, both formal and informal, in terms of which the actions and accounts make sense (Sayer 2010). This leads to broader questions such as: How do such rules come to exist? How is compliance (or otherwise) with these rules achieved?

Voodoo criminology?

Jock Young (2004) has described the prevalent fetishism with numbers and statistical analysis as 'voodoo criminology', for it attributes certain magical powers to the representation of crime and punishment by presenting them in terms of mathematical formulations. Thus,

> We are confronted at this moment with an orthodox criminology which is denatured and desiccated. Its actors inhabit an arid planet where they are either driven into crime by social and psychological deficits or make opportunistic choices in the criminal marketplace. They are either miserable or mundane. They are, furthermore, digital creatures of quantity, they obey probabilistic laws of deviancy – they can be represented by the statistical symbolism of lambda, chi and sigma, their behaviour can be captured in the intricacies of regression analysis and equation. (Young 2004: 13)

In a post-Fordist world characterised by fluidity, mobility, contested values, increased emphasis on personal identity, expressivity, excitement and reflexivity, it is ironic, Young argues, that criminology fails to capture this changing sense of movement and purpose and, instead, becomes increasingly preoccupied with translating social action and social relations into the dry language of mathematics.

It is not that mathematical or statistical analysis cannot be useful in some situations, but that there is a danger of attributing too much credibility to studies where the results are stated in purely mathematical forms, since there is a tendency both inside and outside criminology to believe that such studies provide precise and rigorous conclusions. In many cases the analysis has limitations, not only of conceptual weakness but also of the sample's representativeness, variations in response rates, as well as systematic uncertainties about how responses are interpreted. These limitations are, however, often overlooked when the findings are presented in what appears to be the definitive language of mathematics.

The problem with quantifying social process is that many of the main processes involved – motivation, values, attitudes, other context-dependent activities – are unsuitable for quantification and cannot be cardinally measured in a meaningful way. Interval scales can only be effectively developed for objects and processes that are qualitatively invariant (Sayer 2010). Thus, we cannot measure the processes of socialisation or rehabilitation, for example, along scales of linearity.

From a realist perspective the main limitation of the language of mathematics is that it is acausal and astructural. To say that the, so-called, independent variable varies in relation to the dependent variable may impute a notion of cause, but it fails to reveal what it is about the independent variable that actually changes the dependent variable. Thus, any imputation of causality associated with the decision to define one variable as independent and the other as dependent must be based on non-mathematical causal criteria. Additionally, this type of analysis is unable to clearly distinguish causal from accidental relations.

Similar problems arise in relation to statistical methods, whether descriptive or inferential. Statistical methods have a limited descriptive capacity. At best they indicate patterns within a set of observations that may be a starting point for investigation. Inferential statistics treats processes as random or chance elements and thus, by implication, uncaused. Regression equations, for example, say nothing in themselves about causal or conditional relations, yet there is a widespread assumption that causal analysis and regression analysis are virtually synonymous. Identification of regularities is not a sufficient condition for identification of causes. To say that crime rates vary by area does not 'explain' what it is about different areas and the populations inhabiting them that causes the variations. In fact, the more we understand the causal relations involved, the less relevant statistical representations become. Those who are committed to mathematics and statistics forget that the analysis they conduct is often based on unexamined assumptions and that decisions about whether a sample is distributively reliable, for example, require qualitative analysis and conceptual preparation.

A further difficulty arises from an explanatory point of view, in terms of the presumed independence of variables or in seeing their combined effects as purely additive. In reality, these variables interact and are interdependent and combine and conflict in ways that standard forms of variable analysis are unlikely to capture. Thus, the verdict on statistical methods must be that, despite their logical rigour, they are primitive tools as far as explanation is concerned (Sayer 2010). Indeed, 'sophisticated' statistical analysis is often used to compensate for conceptual weaknesses. Experience suggests that there is a close correlation between the level of statistical 'sophistication' and the degree of conceptual ineptitude.

The difficulties associated with multivariate analyses are considerable. First, the variables selected are often assumed to occur at the same level of aggregation, but the social world is a complex interweaving of structures operating at many different levels. Second, any perceived association between selected variables may be causal or merely coincidental, or it may be a function of a mutual relation with an underlying variable. Third, many variables will be excluded from the analyses because the data are not available, because certain factors are not measurable or because investigators are unaware of them. Fourth, there is often an implicit assumption that the individuals studied are inherently rational. Finally, there is the enduring problem of spurious correlations (Mingers 2004). Assessing the viability of the effect of different variables or correlations requires a degree of intuition, often based on personal and practical experience, in order to interpret and justify outcomes accurately.

This is not to suggest that quantitative and qualitative methods cannot be usefully combined. Great care needs to be taken, however, not to engage in contentless abstractions, losing sight of theory and becoming enmeshed in a numbers game. The complexity of social life and criminality cannot be reduced to a combination of simple behaviours seen as responses to set stimuli, as if such stimuli have a single meaning regardless of context. Thus, rather than examine the differences between variables or factors, it is more productive to identify the causal processes involved, an approach which potentially produces a more powerful and useful form of analysis.

We also see the limitations of statistical modelling in relation to prediction and forecasting. While there are good reasons to try to anticipate future possibilities, statistical methods in criminology have been notoriously poor at predicting future crime levels. The crime drop – probably the most significant development in criminology in living memory – was not predicted. Indeed, it took criminologists some years to even begin to appreciate its significance. To some extent, the failure to predict and recognise this development was a function of the dominant methodological stance in criminology combined with widely held assumptions about the 'law' of the inexorable rise of crime (Young 2010).

Ethnography

Ethnographic research has become increasingly fashionable in criminology. It is seen as providing a more relevant and meaningful alternative to the perceived rigidity of quantitative research. The growing interest in the cultural dimensions of crime and punishment has called for a methodological approach that is interpretative and sensitive to the cultural dimensions of social life. Ethnographic research is seen to have the capacity to demonstrate the richness and diversity of social life and to go beyond the examination of behaviours towards an understanding of the meanings and motivations of the populations studied.

It is the case that ethnographers often choose to study esoteric and marginalised groups with the aim of showing how they make sense of reality and construct their social worlds, in order to identify the rationalities they employ. In this form of naturalism, the aim is to provide an authentic account of the groups' lives and provide some insight into the social relations involved, while implicitly or explicitly challenging some of the conventional depictions mainstream society holds of such groups. Thus, ethnographic research aims to understand from the inside, not judge from the outside. Ethnographers claim that in this way, in contrast to quantitative approaches, they:

- can take into account a diversity of perspectives
- can identify beliefs and attitudes that are normally obscured
- are able to draw on multiple sources of evidence
- are able to discover the unanticipated consequences of action or inaction
- are more flexible and more able to adjust to the situation on the ground
- can examine processes as well as outcomes.

Most of these claims, however, are not unique to ethnographic research. They can also be attributed to a number of different methodologies, including some forms of quantitative research. However, in the long and distinguished tradition of ethnographic research, which goes back to the Chicago School and includes David Matza's naturalism through to more recent work on youth cultures and gangs (see Hobbs 2001), a number of questions have arisen about the validity, policy relevance and generalisability of this approach. Thus, although there is a critical component in ethnography – its ability to challenge conventional conceptions of social relations – there is also a conservative tendency associated with those forms of ethnographic research which are purely descriptive and which present uncritically the views of those studied. The danger is that ethnographers inadvertently create rather than represent the social worlds they describe. This form of naive realism mirrors the naive realism of much positivistic criminology. In many cases the relation between data and theory is unclear, and much ethnographic research involves a process of analytic induction, in which the theory and concepts are seen to arise from the data. From a realist perspective this is untenable. Researchers always carry theories and concepts into the field, and these invariably shape how they conduct their research.

Thus the question arises, as Martyn Hammersley (1992) suggests, of what distinguishes a good from a bad ethnography. He suggests that a good ethnography must involve more than systematic or detailed data collection. In addition, ethnography cannot be judged purely on its ability to maintain the integrity of the phenomena under study, since all phenomena are empirically inexhaustible. It is therefore possible to construct multiple 'true' descriptions of any social phenomena. Hammersley's version of 'subtle realism' claims that ethnographic research is determined by assumptions about what is socially and politically relevant. Much will depend upon the plausibility and credibility of accounts. The aim, he suggests, as do other realists, is not to make claims of certainty but to identify patterns and processes that have a degree of generalisability. This may involve engaging in comparative research or, at least, in research in different but related sites and contexts. In this way, Hammersley argues, there can be an affinity between realism and ethnographic research, inasmuch as it can get closer to social reality and capture the richness and diversity of social life in a critical and reflexive way (Hammersley and Atkinson 2007).

One study frequently cited as an example of a good ethnography is Paul Willis's *Learning to Labour* (1977). In this book Willis explains how working-class kids in the act of defiance create oppositional cultural forms which, in the process of challenging authority, reinforce and maintain the structures of domination that confront them. That is, what at one moment appears a rational and creative action can serve to reinforce existing class relations. Willis makes a strong case for the advantages of ethnographic research over survey methods and all forms of investigation that just report or summarise verbal or written responses. He argues that such approaches are unable to uncover the complex social relations and processes by which working-class 'lads' become complicit in their own subordination and exploitation. It is necessary, he suggests, to penetrate the surface, the immediate representations and the appearances, in order to understand the nature of working-class culture. Importantly, he adds, the form of consciousness adopted by 'the lads' is not imposed on them, nor is it accidental. Rather, it is an adaptation acted out, not only in the particular school that he studied, but also in schools up and down the country. This study therefore has a level of generalisability. It captures some of the essential elements of this complex, but what seems an ultimately self-defeating, process of resistance. Moreover, as Beverley Skeggs (2001) reminds us, even in those studies that claim to 'give voice' to respondents, it is ultimately the researcher who guides the project, sets the terms of reference and interprets the responses.

The power of Willis's analysis derives in part from his ability to identify the subtleties of class and cultural relations and to do so within a form of analysis that explores the links between agency and structure while exploring the relevant mediations. The processes are influenced by dominant ideologies of masculinity and power, which are in turn represented through the attitudes and practices of working-class 'lads'. It is the role of the researchers, as Willis ably demonstrates, not to dismiss these ideologies as illusions or simple conspiracies but to interrogate and unpack them in order to reveal their structure and functioning. In this way Willis provides, according to Manicas (2006), an account that includes some of the essential features of a realist approach, particularly in relation to Willis's account of how social structures are able to reproduce themselves (Willis 2000). Although Willis himself considers the policy and political implications of his analysis, an overly functionalist and pessimistic reading of his text might suggest that it is not worth putting resources into working-class schools or encouraging working-class students because the notion of upward mobility is a myth and all working-class kids are destined to 'fail'. However, in the years since *Learning to Labour* was published, we have seen notions of masculinity change considerably. Significant changes have taken place within both the educational system and the labour market in the United Kingdom, as well as in working-class culture.

Thus, a good ethnography will have a number of key attributes. First, it is necessary to formulate a generic conceptual framework that elucidates key concepts and theorises the patterns and processes that may be in play. Second, it needs to be reflexive and to consider power relations, not only relations affecting the actions and interactions of those being studied but also those between researcher and the researched. Third, it must try to identify the main causal relations that affect the social processes under investigation. In this way the aim is to move beyond description and towards an explanation. Fourth, it should link the analysis of people's accounts to the structures in which they operate and, at the same time, identify the mediations that connect the two processes. Ultimately, the aim is to move beyond individual accounts, recognising how structures and contexts shape processes and outcomes. Fifth, it should move from the specific to the general in developing investigations, either through use of comparisons or repetition to maximise the research's generalisability. Finally, it must develop research which is policy relevant and based on causal analysis, while linking action to structure in a way that is ultimately able to construct credible and convincing explanations.

However, even in good ethnographies and, so-called, deep ethnographies there is an unfortunate tendency to focus on one particular group in one location. Consequently, the group concerned is treated in isolation as if its members' lives were hermetically sealed off from the wider social world. Indeed the layers of social interaction and social relations that are frequently found in good novels rarely appear in ethnographic research. Few groups are isolated in reality, and in modern society there is considerable overlap of different social groups, all of whom derive some of their relevant characteristics, views, identities and aspirations through social interaction with others.

In contrast, we see some of the limitations of ethnographic research in relation to 'grounded theory', which is sometimes seen as having an affiliation to realism in being 'grounded' and having some relation to theory. Its approach, however, is essentially inductive, involving the gathering of information that is deemed to provide the researcher with the data necessary to build up a theory (Glazer and Strauss 1967). This approach tends to encourage researchers to focus on the 'close up' features of social interaction and to neglect wider and less visible structural phenomena and power relations (Layder 1993). Moreover, Glazer and Strauss (1967) define 'formal' theory in a way that excludes types of theorisation that are not grounded on data, with the consequence that there is a lack of dialogue between theories that arise from the data and those which guide data collection. This results in a narrow focus that plays down the relevance of grand theories, such as feminism and Marxism, which are often dismissed as being 'speculative'.

Instead, grounded theorists insist that concepts should emerge out of the observed data and should directly represent the perspectives and attitudes of the people being studied. Besides raising the age-old problem of induction, there is a tendency to focus only on those causal relations that are directly observable and to ignore or play down the wider structural mechanisms. Such an approach fails to acknowledge that observation is conceptually mediated and that all researchers enter the field with a set of assumptions, theories and concepts which guide research. However, if objects lack structure and are unconnected to one another, the structure of knowledge is built on sand. The identification of causal powers involves not induction but retroduction. That is, where it is possible through subsequent investigation to identify the causal processes involved, there is no need for induction.

Doing realist research

Ray Pawson and Nick Tilley (1997) summarise the logic of realist explanation in the following terms:

> The basic task of social inquiry is to explain interesting, puzzling, socially significant regularities (R). Explanation takes the form of positing some underlying mechanism (M) [a hypothesis] which generates the regularity and thus consists of propositions about how the interplay between structure and agency has constituted the regularity. Within realistic investigation there is also investigation of how the workings of such mechanisms are contingent and conditional, and thus only fired in particular local, historical or institutional contexts (C). (Pawson and Tilley 1997: 71)

There is no set formula for doing realist research. Much depends on what you want to know and what you are investigating. The main objective is to work towards a causal explanation. The general procedure is, in essence, much the same as in standard forms of research – developing theory, formulating research questions, examining empirical details and engaging in analysis.

The difference from standard forms of investigation is in the research process itself. Thus, while the forms of research are fairly familiar, the content is different. Some of the main obstacles to developing useful and coherent forms of research have been identified, and the types of research strategies that are likely to be of value have been outlined. However, at this point we need to put a little more flesh on the bone and spell out in a little more detail how to do realist research and evaluation.

Drawing on the work of Andrew Sayer (2010), Ray Pawson and Nick Tilley (1997) it is possible to identify a number of stages in understanding realist research and evaluation. This involves adapting the familiar research cycle, which moves from theory to method and policy, but changing the emphasis and the nature of the research strategy. Thus, engaging in realist research involves not so much a change of form as a change of content.

Stage 1: theorisation, conceptualisation and abstraction

What distinguishes realist research from other popular approaches is that it aims to move beyond description, or limit its focus to what is observable or directly measurable. In doing so it places great emphasis on the processes of theorisation and abstraction. By starting with a particular problematic the aim is to theorise the nature and capacities of the object under study (Pawson 2013). This involves moving beyond 'chaotic' and one-sided conceptions and developing concepts and categories that are consistent and coherent. In practical terms this will involve examining the relevant literature in order to develop an awareness of current debates and issues related to the problematic. It is important to ensure that the investigation is socially relevant and allows some critical purchase on existing knowledge while allowing the possibility of clarifying ideas (Ackroyd 2004). How we 'carve up' and define our objects of study will seal the fate of subsequent research. Theories are also concerned with developing propositions which might explain change or certain outcomes. Having critically engaged with the available literature, an important element of theorising is to identify issues that require further investigation or else remain unsolved. These questions are formulated as research questions and hypotheses, which can then be subjected to empirical investigation.

Stage 2: formulating research questions or hypotheses

Developing well-fashioned and well-focused research questions or hypotheses is critical to the research process. Poorly conceptualised questions will lead almost certainly to unfocused and unrewarding forms of inquiry since the research questions will specify what it is that we want to know and, at the same time, determine the direction of research. The research questions or hypotheses will determine the data to be collected, which will in turn be checked against theoretical expectations.

Stage 3: deciding on a research strategy

This stage involves a combination of experience and imagination. Realists are methodological pluralists. Although critical of certain methodological approaches, such as purely descriptive studies or forms of statistical analysis which have little explanatory value, realists argue that the choice of method is a function of the nature of the research questions on one hand and the nature of the object under study on the other. Thus realists advocate the use of quantitative or qualitative methods or a combination of both, depending on whether the aim is to engage in intensive or extensive forms of research. Intensive research is concerned with identifying the causal processes in operation; extensive research is normally concerned with describing some of the common properties and general patterns of the population as a whole (see Sayer 2010: 42–43). Thus realists are open to a range of methods, including certain forms of ethnography, participant methods, survey methods, structured and unstructured interview techniques, historical investigation, case studies and action research.

Stage 4: analysing the data

Data analysis has a number of objectives, including the identification of patterns and processes and the attempt to understand the causal mechanisms involved. There is a need to identify as far as possible the structures that support and activate particular mechanisms. At the same time the aim is to identify the mediations between agency and structure as well as the rules and norms that shape and constrain action. Research analysis often involves moving from the level of action, to identification of the rules that govern actions, to identification of structures and their powers and effects.

The analysis must also be sensitive to context and the conditions in which causal powers are activated. Also, since there is often a plurality of causes, the challenge is to identify the operation of specific causal processes and control for others. At the same time it is important to distinguish between necessary and contingent causes. Identification of causes may involve reasons and motivations, as well as acts, either individual or collective.

Stage 5: developing explanations and policy implications

Although realists believe that all knowledge is limited and fallible, the ultimate aim is to develop *explanations* of social phenomena and processes in order to contribute to policy development. The more powerful and plausible the explanation, the more likely it is to be policy relevant. Developing such explanations often involves formulating critiques of previous research and existing knowledge. It also necessarily involves modifying and extending existing theory. The ultimate aim is to contribute to the accumulation of knowledge.

In terms of realist evaluation, the question is to identify not only what works but also how and why it works, for whom, and under what conditions. In developing such explanations it is important to note, as Pawson and Tilley (1997) point out, that interventions will work only to the extent that they connect with the propensities and capacities of the populations to whom they are directed.

Ultimately, the objective of realist research and evaluation is to contribute to the development of constructive evidence-based forms of intervention. Intervention in itself is not so much the presentation of a 'quick fix solution' as an attempt to lend weight to certain policy options. Research should never be naive, disinterested or trivial.

Conclusion

Engaging in criminological research may appear at first sight a relatively straightforward process, but producing meaningful and worthwhile results is a difficult and challenging activity. Things are often not as they seem. People say things they do not mean and mean what they do not say. Frequently, they do not have fully thought-out responses to questions and in other cases remain unaware of how the contexts in which they operate structure and condition their responses. At other times they are ambivalent and contradictory. Methods that are designed only to measure unequivocal responses are unable to capture these complexities and are ultimately in danger of misrepresenting individual and social attitudes.

The open nature of social systems, their continuous transformation and variability, creates problems of prediction and replicability. At the same time there is the recurring issue of generalisability, particularly in relation to 'intensive' qualitative analysis. Most importantly, it can be difficult to understand the process of change and, by implication, identify the various causal mechanisms in play and distinguish contingent from generative causes. Ultimately, the aim is to develop an explanation of social change rather than presume that facts speak for themselves. Thus the aim is to link methodology to theory and conceptualisation, and move towards producing a more plausible, consistent and coherent account, one that has some policy relevance and is able to clarify the original problematic.

4
Rational Choice, Routine Activities and Situational Crime Prevention

The new criminologies of everyday life

Notions of rational decision making play a central but often implicit role in criminological explanations. Most commonly associated with opportunity theories, situational crime prevention and routine activities theory, rational choice is widely used by administrative and conservative criminologists interested in developing practical, if not pragmatic, ways of reducing or preventing crime. The notion of the rational actor has its roots in classical criminology, which aimed to develop a system of punishment in which the gain from crime would be outweighed by the severity of the sanction, and as such it would deter any rational person. Classicism was characterised by a focus on the act rather than the actor and was less concerned with the social and economic causes of crime than with controlling human 'passions' (Beccaria 1963).

For much of the nineteenth and twentieth centuries, however, the ideas of classicism were moderated by a growing emphasis on the personal and social conditions that were seen to cause crime. A range of so-called dispositional theories began to explore the psychological make-up of offenders on one hand and the social and economic conditions that were likely to propel them into crime on the other. In this way they went about constructing the 'criminal' as a distinct type of person with identifiable characteristics (see Taylor, Walton and Young 2013; Roshier 1989).

The 1970s saw a growing disillusionment with these dispositional theories and, relatedly, with attempts to rehabilitate offenders. Instead, many ideas and sentiments resurfaced, particularly those relating to the rationality of offenders, and became central components of emerging forms of administrative criminology, often with a strong conservative bias. This involved a shift in the discipline's focus away from theories of social deprivation towards explanations couched in terms of self-control and what has been termed 'the new criminologies of everyday life' (Garland 1999; Felson 1994). These involve mainly rational choice theory, routine activities theory and situational crime prevention. From these perspectives the focus is on the daily activities that produce criminal opportunities and finding ways of removing, or at least reducing, them. It is argued that it is availability of opportunities coupled with access to attractive targets that creates the conditions for crime to take place. All rational actors, it is suggested, are likely to take advantage of these opportunities in situations where the rewards clearly outweigh the risks. Thus, there is no real or intrinsic distinction between offenders and the rest of the population. Criminals are only rational individuals who take advantage of available opportunities.

In the seminal publication *The Reasoning Criminal* (1986), Derek Cornish and Ron Clarke set out to provide a pragmatic approach to the problem of crime and to counter claims made by pessimistic liberals that nothing works. In contrast to approaches which seek to identify 'deep causes' or to 'psychologise' offenders, Cornish and Clarke outline the basis of a rational choice perspective on criminal behaviour, which, they state, rests on 'the assumption that offenders seek to benefit themselves by their criminal behaviour; that this involves the making of decisions and choices, however rudimentary on occasion these processes might be and that these processes exhibit a measure of rationality' (1986: 1–2).

In addition, Cornish and Clarke (1987) argue that focusing on the choice-structuring nature of different types of crime is a useful way of understanding the involvement in crime by different actors. These actors themselves might not be fully aware of these properties, but different crimes have different attributes involving different challenges, costs and benefits that give each a unique character. Thus it follows that a person prevented from committing one type of crime is not necessarily going to switch to another type. Someone prevented from engaging in burglary is unlikely to turn to violent crime or fraud. This observation has direct implications for thinking about displacement, since the choice of crime, it is argued, is not so much structured by the predisposition of the offender as by the characteristics of different offence types. Clarke (1997) gives the example of gas suicide to support his argument about the choice-structuring properties of different types of suicide. He points out that the elimination of gas suicides following the introduction of non-lethal natural gas in Britain in the 1970s was not followed by a substantial displacement to other forms of suicide.

In contrast to the forms of rational choice theory developed by those economists who explain actions in purely monetary terms and in relation to reward maximisation, Cornish and Clarke adopt a 'thin' or 'bounded' notion of rationality. They argue that offenders are motivated not only by financial gain but also by a search for status or kudos, and a desire for emotional release or the pursuit of power. By adopting the notion of 'bounded rationality' they acknowledge that offenders are not always in possession of all the relevant information to make precise calculations of the risks and rewards associated with their actions, but often operate on a 'good enough' knowledge base.

The attractiveness of rational choice theory lies in its attempt to provide a seemingly straightforward conception of human action, drawing on common sense and everyday understandings. Rational choice theory, particularly as applied to crime, offers the possibility of a direct no-nonsense approach to crime prevention and is presented in terms that are likely to resonate both socially and politically. It avoids awkward questions about the role of poverty, disadvantage and other 'deep causes' and provides an explanation that can be applied to a wide range of situations, particularly those where the actions of individuals are expressed in relation to identifiable goals.

In *The Reasoning Criminal* (1986) the authors aim to lay out the basis of their approach in a clear and concise manner. However, even in their short introductory chapter there are some inconsistencies, which stem from claims concerning the forms and range of rational choice theory, the role of 'dispositional' or 'background' factors, the theoretical status of rational choice models of the decision-making process in the context of crime and, finally, whether rational choice theory is adequate to cover all forms of crime or only certain crime types.

Cornish and Clarke (1986) are very critical of those versions of criminological theory that look at disadvantage, socialisation, psychological issues and the like to explain criminal involvement. However, after expressing serious reservations about such approaches and claiming that criminals are normal rather than pathological, they present models of criminal involvement which include reference to 'background factors', such as upbringing, psychological temperament, social class and education, parenting and the like, which they suggest *predispose* certain people towards criminal involvement. These background factors, we are told, dictate a person's 'readiness' to commit crime. Although they claim they are not interested as much in the offender as in analysing the criminal act, they do implicitly identify certain people as having criminal traits or predispositions. They are careful, however, to refer to 'offenders' rather than 'criminals'. Nevertheless, other authors in the same publication refer, explicitly or implicitly, to people as 'criminals' and, by implication, as a particular type of person.

There is also some confusion over the perceived range and focus of rational choice theory. At one point Cornish and Clarke suggest that the rational choice perspective fits some forms of offending better than others. At other points they claim that rational choice provides a framework for understanding all forms of crime. On the other hand, the authors seem to suggest that rational choice provides an *additional* approach to existing criminological approaches, such as learning theory and control theory, focusing not so much on the predispositions of offenders but the subsequent decisions relating to the commission of the criminal act.

However, their discussion of the actual decision-making process involved is conspicuously limited. Instead of critically engaging with the different psychological accounts of decision making, the authors tirelessly reiterate that such processes are essentially rational, although they make little effort to deconstruct this fundamental concept. Alternatively, when decision-making processes are addressed, traditional psychological perspectives are drawn upon, or common-sense assumptions are mobilised.

These ambiguities, which reoccur throughout the rational choice literature, are taken up and discussed in the course of this chapter. From the outset, however, this apparently no-nonsense, hard-hitting approach is full of unresolved issues and uncertainties, which, it is suggested, seriously detract from its claim to provide a rigorous and coherent theoretical approach to crime.

Routine activities theory

Routine activities theory and rational choice theory are seen by Ron Clarke and Marcus Felson (1993) as 'mutually supportive'. Neither theory is particularly interested in offender motivation, psychological or dispositional accounts. Instead, they place considerable emphasis on the situational nature of crime. Both approaches focus on temptation and opportunity and assume that offenders are goal directed. Offenders are not seen as pathological but as rational actors responding to incentives and opportunities. Neither approach believes that the way to reduce crime is to change the minds of offenders or rehabilitate them. Rather, the situation in which crime occurs should be changed. Felson (1994) argues that whereas rational choice theory deals mainly with the content of decisions, the routine activities approach, in contrast, deals with the ecological or situational contexts that supply the range of options from which choices are made.

Cohen and Felson (1979) claim that for a crime to happen a likely offender, a suitable target and the absence of capable guardians must all come together. In this way this approach aims to bring together the basic ingredients for a crime event and incorporate them in dynamic relation. Routine activities operate on both micro and macro levels. At the macro level, it is argued that changes in the community, working practices, and the volume and nature of goods available all affect the level of crime in various ways. Thus, the increase in the number of women involved in the labour force will both reduce the guardianship of the home and affect the socialisation of children. Also, the proliferation and increased attractiveness of goods such as mobile phones, cars, and fashionable clothes is seen to be strongly associated with the increase in property crime.

At the micro level, potential offenders are held to respond to available opportunities in situations where there is a lack of suitable guardians. These guardians can be formal agencies, such as the police, or informal agents, such as members of the public. Like rational choice theory, routine activities theory draws readily on ecological concepts of spatial distribution and the ways in which different settings constrain behaviour.

Although this approach claims that it is not particularly interested in the issue of motivation, it is clearly the case that the motivation of the offender – the degree of intensity and the level of commitment – is central to this process. The assumption that the offender is merely rational and will necessarily take advantage of opportunities or the lack of guardianship is unconvincing, since perceiving opportunities and being sensitive to the level of guardianship is not part of most people's agenda. The vast majority of people routinely pass open windows or unlocked cars without thinking of stealing.

This raises the issue of the decision-making process and the role of risks and rewards. In approaching a particular target, prospective offenders have to ask themselves whether they have the guts or the skill or the equipment to commit the offence. They are more than spontaneous decision-makers. Offenders have agency and will often need resources to commit an offence. This reduces the sense of 'opportunity' and suggests that in many cases the offender needs to be predisposed (Ekblom and

Tilley 2000). Moreover, when discussing routes to offending, Clarke and Felson (1993) talk not only about opportunity but also about temptation. Temptation is an interesting, though largely unexplored, concept in this literature, but reference to this and related concepts suggests that the decision-making process is much more complex than simply maximising utility.

At the same time an offender must perceive a certain target as 'attractive'. However, there is no inherent feature of any object that makes it intrinsically attractive. Attractiveness lies in the eye of the beholder (offender). Even more uncertain is what is meant by 'capable guardians'. There is often a certain circularity attached to this notion. An available level of guardianship that does not deter offenders is deemed retrospectively not to have been capable or sufficient. On the other hand, if a crime does not occur, are we to assume that the level of guardianship was adequate?

In short, routine activity theory is not so much a theory as a set of fairly vague propositions, which are formulated at such a level of generality that they have limited explanatory power and tend to involve ex post facto rationalisations. As such, routine activities theory by itself is able to explain very little about crime. No doubt part of its attraction, like rational choice theory, is its apparent simplicity and its claim to universal applicability. The three-part mantra of 'motivated offenders, attractive targets and suitable offenders' can be easily learnt and parcelled out as criminological wisdom. However, the world is a messy place and explanations of a complex activity like crime are unlikely to be reducible to a set of vague propositions. A number of criminologists, including Felson himself, have come to recognise these limitations and have tried to provide more plausible accounts of crime by combining rational choice and routine activities perspectives with control theory and social disorganisation theory, albeit with limited success (Chamard 2010).

In earlier formulations routine activities and rational choice tended to concentrate on everyday transgressions, mainly in the form of acquisitive crime. More recently there have been attempts to broaden the approach and apply these perspectives to more challenging issues. One such issue is terrorism, which is often depicted as an irrational or mindless act. Clearly, if rational choice and routine activities can provide insight into the nature of terrorist activities and help reduce or prevent terrorism, this would be seen as a major achievement and provide an example of the general applicability and utility of these perspectives.

Preventing terrorism?

In an intriguing and ambitious publication Ron Clarke and Graeme Newman (2006) aim to combine the analytic powers of rational choice theory with the strategic processes associated with situational crime prevention in order to address the issue of terrorism. On the basis that terrorists, like criminals, are not 'mindless' actors but are rational calculators responding to available opportunities, they apply the methods of situational crime prevention equally to both groups. They thus reject popular attempts to psychologise terrorists, arguing that a more effective response would be to block opportunities through weapons control and the protection of targets. They emphasise understanding the *how* of terrorism rather than the *why*.

As with crime prevention, Clarke and Newman (2006) argue that it is necessary to separate terrorists into a number of different types, such as hijackers and suicide bombers, and to tailor intervention specifically to each type of terrorist attack. This in turn requires a detailed analysis of the forms of preparation, target selection, types of weapons used and the actual commissioning of the act which involves a need to understand the decision-making process and to 'think terrorist'. Doing so, it is argued, reveals that terrorists' decision-making processes are little different from those of everyday life and that, despite the uniqueness of their objectives, they ought to be deemed entirely rational.

This 'rational' decision-making process may not be perfect. It may be based on limited or unreliable information, be falsely optimistic or be swayed by opinions or passing emotions. However, it is suggested that we need to confront these forms of 'bounded rationality' in order to understand what terrorists hope to gain from their actions. Although rational choice theorists are not particularly interested in changing the minds of terrorists or engaging in questions about the legitimacy of terrorists' goals, they are drawn repeatedly into the issue of motivation and the question of the relation of means to ends. This creates a tension in their analysis between explaining individual and collective behaviour and, in particular, altruistic motives and forms of self-sacrifice (Coleman 1986). On one level the authors argue that terrorism is the culmination of a series of individual acts motivated by the promise of martyrdom or rewards in the afterlife. However, as terrorists operate in groups, there may be a contradiction between collective and individual decision making in terms of both object and motivation. This makes the injunction to 'think terrorist' very difficult. Indeed, the requirement to 'think terrorist' begs the question of how terrorists think. The authors seem to assume that the logic adopted by terrorists, either individually or collectively, involves the same forms of 'bounded rationality' as they themselves have developed.

For some the emphasis on the group nature of decision making differentiates terrorists' activities from crime, with the possible exception of organised crime. Terrorism is also distinguishable from crime in that, whereas crime is mainly a social transgression, terrorism is a political act little concerned with criminal adjudication and the conviction of offenders in the criminal justice system via due process. Rather, regulation involves the abrogation of rights in pursuit of the wider objective of maintaining security (McCulloch and Pickering 2009; Zedner 2009).

The particular and diverse nature of terrorism raises issues concerning the relevance and usefulness of social and environmental forms of intervention developed by situational crime prevention theorists in order to prevent and reduce crime. There are limits to how far the vast array of potential targets can be 'target hardened'. Targets selected by terrorists are often public places. The IRA, for example, targeted pubs, parks and shopping districts. Other terrorist groups focus on kidnapping individuals, while others detonate explosive devices in such public spaces as markets and recreational centres. As with the proliferation of situational crime prevention strategies, there is a problem of creating a 'fortress society' and reducing freedom of movement, civil liberties and privacy. At the same time the preoccupation with 'target-hardening' and the like directs the focus towards defence, rather than addressing international political and cultural differences (Tilley 2002).

In many respects the combination of rational choice theory and situational crime prevention is not as powerful or radical a combination as Clarke and Newman (2006) claim. There is a lack of understanding of both the decision-making processes involved and the pursuit and formation of objectives. The authors see the infliction of violence as the primary objective but, as other commentators on terrorism have pointed out, there are a number of different objectives often being pursued involving intimidation, publicity and propaganda, political manoeuvring and 'spoiling' peace regulations, which create a complex interplay between means and ends (Kydd and Walter 2006). It is not that rational choice theory cannot be applied to some degree in making sense of this process, but it would need to take a more elaborate form than that presented by Clarke and Newman. Such an approach would have to attempt to explain collective actions and the role of solidarity, revenge, self-sacrifice, trust and loyalty (Elster 1993).

At one point Clarke and Newman (2006) present their thesis as a fundamental critique of dispositional theories and present it as a more effective alternative to traditional approaches. However, elsewhere in the same publication they conclude that 'people's disposition is part of the equation that makes up the event'. At the same time they acknowledge in their discussions of suicide bombers that 'they simply do not have enough direct information about how suicide bombers and their handlers conduct their acts'. Instead of offering policymakers an innovative way of developing existing preventive approaches for dealing with terrorism, they end up calling for more research into the motivation and target selection processes. Thus, while the authors have a great deal to say on reducing opportunities, they are much less instructive about the actual decision-making processes involved, or in specifying the values and beliefs that motivate terrorists, or identifying the range of goals and objectives they aim to pursue. Engaging in this form of inquiry would take the authors some way beyond the established boundaries of rational choice theory and situational crime prevention approaches and would involve incorporating dispositional and other theoretical approaches.

Is it a theory?

There has been an ongoing debate about the theoretical status of rational choice theory. Questions have been raised about the theory's explanatory power and predictive ability (Trasler 1986). The immediate question that arises is whether all actions can be explained by rational choice theory. Raymond Boudon (1998) argues that rational choice may be useful in explaining forms of individual action deemed instrumental and goal directed but is less relevant when non-instrumental action needs to be explained. If rational choice theory cannot explain non-instrumental action, Boudon argues, it cannot claim to be a general theory of action. He also makes the point that the Dutch adopted the use of methadone to cure drug addiction while the French did not. Rational choice theory, he suggests, is of little help in explaining these different choices.

In other cases we may impute rationality by claiming that, although a man did not behave as predicted, there was an alternative underlying rationality which the man himself may not have been aware of. This raises the issue of false consciousness. For the psychoanalyst explaining these hidden motivations may cause no problem in itself, but the theorist is on shaky ground where the rationale presented to explain an action is at odds with the person's own explanation of the action. Where actions are guided by certain principles, an obligation falls on rational choice theorists to explain why the actor endorses these principles. In addition as Max Weber (1968) suggested there are different forms of rationality and those versions of rational choice theory that stick to a narrow conception of instrumental rationality, in which the actor applies a strict cost-benefit analysis, are too rigid to provide a general theory of action.

The focus on background factors raises issues of the relation between rational choice theory and other theories. There is considerable ambiguity here. At one point Cornish and Clarke (1986) seem to suggest that rational choice approaches *complement* rather than supplant existing theory. However, further on in the same text, they state that they see the rational choice perspective as providing a framework that is able to *incorporate* existing theories. In addition, they suggest a need to *integrate* theory and claim that their perspective represents such an attempt. However, incorporating is a different theoretical activity from complementing, which in turn is very different from integrating different theories. Elsewhere, Clarke (1997), in his articulation of 'bounded rationality', claims that the rational choice perspective provides 'not an organising theory of crime but rather an organising perspective or "blueprint" for which theories of specific crimes could be developed' while simultaneously arguing that the rational choice perspective 'constitutes a theory of both crime and criminality'. Later in the same article Clarke suggests, in line with Cornish (1993), that rational choice is a *metatheory* within which existing theories can all find a place. Thus it would seem that within the space of one article rational choice is a perspective, a theory and a metatheory.

The central issue, as Green and Shapiro (1994) suggest, is the explanatory power of rational choice theory and what this approach has contributed to our understanding of crime. They argue that in the field of political science the models of rational man that have been developed by rational choice theorists have done little to advance our understanding of how politics works in the real world. The propositions developed can only be characterised as banal, as they do little more than restate existing knowledge in rational choice terminology. Green and Shapiro also raise issues about how the propositions of rational choice theorists are tested. They argue that:

When systematic empirical work is attempted by rational choice theorists, it is typically marred by a series of characteristic lapses that are traceable to the universalist ambitions that rational choice theorists mistakenly regard as the hallmark of good scientific practice. These pathologies manifest themselves at each stage of theory elaboration and empirical testing. Hypotheses are formulated in empirically intractable ways; evidence is selected and tested in a biased fashion; conclusions are drawn without serious attention to competing explanations; empirical anomalies and discordant facts are often either ignored or circumvented by way of post-hoc alterations to deductive arguments. (Green and Shapiro 1994: 6)

Similar critiques, of course, could be directed at a number of contemporary approaches to crime control, but the problem that confronts rational choice theory is that propositions are often formulated in ways resistant to genuine empirical testing and that there are serious misgivings about its predictive ability. These problems arise in part from the underlying assumption that the forms of rationality are identical for all agents and a reluctance to engage with interpersonal variations, since this would generate insuperable problems of tractability (Lilly et al. 2011).

In terms of prediction it is very difficult to demonstrate intentionality. Consequently, this is often assumed or applied retrospectively. The problem of applying intentional causal mechanisms also creates problems for empirical testing. As a result, the researcher often has difficulty pinning down the processes involved or knowing what would count as evidence to support or deny the theory. In practice, however, rational choice theorists are not particularly concerned with explaining the behaviour of specific individuals. Instead, they focus on the regularities that are held to govern the behaviour of all agents. The lack of specificity about what it means to be a rational actor means that it is far from obvious what sorts of behaviour, in principle, could not fail to be explained by some variant of rational choice theory. Rational choice theorists seldom make a clear statement about what data or observations would warrant a rejection of a proposed hypothesis, and it is always possible that different rational choice models may generate diametrically opposed predictions. Moreover, rational choice explanations involve an array of unobservable entities – tastes, beliefs and rules–which form an essential, although often unchallenged, part of most rational choice accounts.

Colin Hay (2004) has argued that rational choice theory is incapable of capturing the complexity of social interaction because it cannot deal with the indeterminacy of human agency.

It is moreover based upon a methodology which seeks (even when this may prove elusive) fully determinate predictions. Just as an object dropped from a tower cannot choose to ignore the theory of gravity, so too a political subject facing a strategic conundrum has no choice other than to select the rational course of action. As this suggests, if the choice is 'rational' it is no choice at all. (Hay 2004: 40)

Thus, despite the emphasis on choice, rational choice theory presents a conception of the human subject who is ultimately determined by the context. This in turn raises the vexed question of the relation of structure and agency since, in most formulations of rational choice theory, the actor is devoid of the capacity to exercise genuine choice in a given context. In effect rational choice turns out, Hay argues, to be an unacknowledged structuralism which sidesteps the problem of agency by appearing to be both voluntarist and structuralist. Rational choice theory's enduring problem, however, is that not all people act in the same way when placed in the same situation and exposed to the same temptations or incentives. To explain these variations would require an understanding of individual agency. Thus, the ultimate limitation of rational choice theory is that it is too one-dimensional and does not adequately capture the complexities of social life. People act out of habit, jealousy, friendship, loyalty and sympathy, as well as self-interest.

A further difficulty arises in relation to the identification of goals. If these are not specified, or are vague, it becomes difficult to explain causal relations or the process of decision making. Jon Elster (1993) raises three questions in this respect: (a) Is the action the best way to satisfy the desire? (b) Is the action consistent and free from internal contradictions? (c) Does the action achieve the desired effect? In general, Elster asks the basic question: Does rational choice theory actually tell us what people do? The difficulty in answering this question is that there are too many situations in which we know too little about the choices available to be able to make a clear decision. Relatedly, there is the problem of how much information people need to make rational choices.

There are also those who are deemed incapable of making rational choices, such as those suffering from mental illness. It is well documented that a significant proportion of those in prison suffer from at least one type of mental illness (Davies 2004; Human Rights Watch 2003). Although this group represents a relatively small percentage of those who commit crime, it should be remembered that 1 in 16 people in the United Kingdom and 1 in 20 in the United States will spend some time in prison during their lifetime. Does rational choice apply to all of this population? Are they capable of making fully rational decisions?

Cultural wars

Cultural criminologists have taken issue with rational choice theorists, arguing that, while rational choice theory may be useful in preventing and reducing property and acquisitive crime, it is less relevant in relation to 'expressive crime' (Ferrell et al. 2008). Drawing on the work of Jack Katz (1988), cultural criminologists emphasise the emotional and sensual nature of offending and claim that in 'late modernity' rational choice theory fails to grasp the meaning and significance of these forms of transgression.

Keith Hayward (2007), a leading cultural criminologist, argues that expressive crimes, such as joy riding, drug abuse, binge drinking and producing graffiti, require a cultural explanation and cannot be seen in purely instrumental terms. In general, Hayward argues that rational choice theory lacks reflexivity and provides a limited and blinkered perspective from which to examine the complexity and diversity of crime and criminal motivation.

Graham Farrall (2010), in reply, argues that situational crime prevention has been effective in reducing a wide array of criminal activity by 'designing out crime' and increasing the risk of criminal activity. Farrell, like Clarke, also defends the notion of bounded rationality while claiming that rational choice theory is applicable to emotive as well as to acquisitive crime. If the objective of the individual is to seek thrills or to experience excitement through the expression of apparently gratuitous violence, this is no less rational than stealing cars or engaging in burglary.

However, if we look at the activities of graffiti writers, for example, the aim is, as Sloan-Hewitt and Kelling (1997) point out, 'getting up' so that as many spectators as possible will see their work. The authors explain that in order to reduce graffiti on the New York subway, it was necessary to understand the motives and psychology of those involved in painting graffiti on the trains. Consequently, trains were kept in the depot and the graffiti removed before they were put back in use. In this way the transport authorities aimed to undermine the logic of the graffiti writers. Ironically, this article was published in a collection edited by Ron Clarke entitled *Situational Crime Prevention: Successful Case Studies* (1997), despite the fact that it involves an implicit critique of the type of target-hardening measures previously widely adopted in New York and London, such as applying anti-graffiti paint, which had proved to be very expensive and time-consuming and of limited effectiveness. Thus it was understanding and explaining the goals and objectives of the graffiti artists, rather than engaging in forms of target hardening, that proved effective.

In his response to Hayward, Farrell (2010) launches into a critique of cultural criminology. He questions the use of key concepts like culture and the adoption of limited methodologies as well as the failure to address the harms experienced by victims. While Farrell is no doubt correct to point to the limited policy relevance of cultural criminology and their rather romantic picture of offenders as 'urban adventurers', he seems unsure about the explanatory potential of rational choice theory. On one hand, he seems to acknowledge that rational choice theory provides a limited account of human action and little purchase in understanding the role and impact of cultural developments. At best it is only able to identify the effects that cultural shifts have in changing offending behaviour, induced by changes in (criminal) opportunities. On the other hand, he claims that the rational choice perspective can be used to inform situational crime prevention strategies 'in relation to all crime types involving criminal acts labelled as expressive or irrational'. Thus, for Farrell all criminal activity is 'rational', even when considered irrational by those who engage in it or those who observe it. The task of criminologists and policymakers is therefore to find the rational in the irrational on the assumption that all offenders are driven by a largely undifferentiated notion of 'rationality'.

In response, Hayward (2012) argues that leading economists, social psychologists and policymakers are becoming increasingly sceptical about applying rational choice theory to either economic processes or individual behaviour. This is an indirect reference to the increasingly influential work of Thaler and Sunstein (2008) who, with others, have come to question the claims of rational choice theorists in relation to decision making. Ironically, Farrell also claims that he has much in common with these writers despite the fact that they appear to be involved in developing a fundamental critique of rational choice theory.

Predictably irrational

Two influential books have recently appeared which challenge the notion that the decision-making process is entirely rational. The first, by Dan Ariely (2008), is entitled *Predictably Irrational*; the second is by Thaler and Sunstein (2008) and is called *Nudge: Improving Decisions about Health, Wealth and Happiness*. The first is a prize-winning book, the second has been highly influential in policy circles on both sides of the Atlantic.

These authors argue that people are anything but predictably rational goal-directed actors. Most decisions they make, it is suggested, are conditioned by situational and structural processes. In fact, they claim that most people do not know what they want until they see it in context, and even then their decisions are subject to a range of influences. Decisions to purchase certain goods or services, for example, are based not so much on rational calculations of the expected utility to be derived from these goods against the cost as on how manufacturers and retailers display these items and on the prices of related goods. The basic point is that in everyday life consumers do not have a clear idea of their own preferences or what they are willing to pay. Consequently, many people buy things that they did not know they wanted or needed before entering the shop, or buy things that they cannot afford.

Decision making, according to Thaler and Sunstein (2008), is an uncertain business. Most of the time it follows certain rules of thumb because we do not have the time or inclination in our daily lives to analyse everything. These rules of thumb involve processes that they call anchoring, availability and representativeness. Anchoring involves basing judgements on existing knowledge. For instance, if we are asked to estimate the population of New York, we might believe it is about the same size as London but a little more densely populated. In turn, we know London has a population of eight million people, and so we might estimate that New York has a population around ten million.

Availability refers to the likelihood of risks. How often people think about, or how seriously they take, an issue is linked to how likely or how often that issue is likely to arise in their lives. Representativeness is how people link and group different categories of events. Most of the time people necessarily operate with stereotypes, which may be more or less accurate. People also operate out of habit, and in many cases decision are heavily influenced by the actions and assessments of others. Whether we decide to leave work or college at the end of the day by the stairs or by lift has little to do with an assessment of the costs and rewards of each option. It is more likely to be influenced by the choices made by friends or colleagues. Much of this makes sense in relation to crime. We know from biographical accounts that many people become involved in crime because of peer pressure and informal associations rather than spontaneously making a decision in isolation to commit an offence.

Adopting a position they describe as libertarian paternalism, Thaler and Sunstein emphasise freedom of choice rather than attempt to restrict choice. Their aim is to 'help' people make choices by 'nudging' them in the desired direction. Applying the notion of 'nudge', it is argued, allows policymakers and politicians to formally maximise choice while effectively influencing and (re)directing behaviour. This can take a virtuous or sinister form. Not surprisingly, the work of Thaler and Sunstein has been taken up by policymakers on both sides of the Atlantic who are attracted to this more subtle, and potentially more effective, way of influencing behaviour. In a recent Cabinet Office paper, for example, indicatively entitled *MindSpace: Influencing Behaviour through Public Policy*, there is a clear indication of a move away from 'hard' instruments, such as legislation, to adopting what are seen as potentially more cost-effective techniques of shaping and influencing behaviour:

> Influencing behaviour is central to public policy. Recently, there have been major advances in understanding the influences on our behaviours, and government needs to take notice of them. This report aims to make that happen.
>
> For policymakers facing policy challenges such as crime, obesity or environmental sustainability, behavioural approaches offer a potentially powerful new set of tools. Applying these tools can lead to low cost, low pain ways of 'nudging' citizens – or ourselves – into new ways of acting by going with the grain of how we think and act. This is an important idea at any time, but is especially relevant in a period of fiscal constraint. (Dolan et al. 2010: 7)

Significantly, in this and related publications there is an explicit, or at least an implicit, critique of rational choice theory as a way of explaining the decision-making process. The report goes on to say that, in order to change behaviour, an alternative model has to be constructed in which the processes of decision making can be understood in relation to the context and environment in which decisions are made, taking account of the influence of significant others. Successful attempts to shape behaviour, the authors of the report maintain, require the integration of cultural, regulatory and individual change. Thus there are signs that the model of man as rational calculator is gradually being replaced by the irrational subject, who is to be governed through the cultivation of particular emotional and behavioural responses. The ideal subject is one who can govern temptation by developing models of reflexive responsibility.

Freakonomics and the crime drop

An interesting and provocative variant of the application of rational choice theory to criminology can be found in the best-selling books by Steven Levitt and Steven Dubner, *Freakonomics* and *Super Freakonomics* (2006, 2010). In these books the authors aim to present novel explanations of the nature of a range of criminological concerns, including drugs, prostitution, terrorism and crime. Although the authors are presented as 'rogue economists', their accounts of these phenomena adopt an essentially rational choice perspective in which they raise a number of unusual and intriguing questions: 'Why do drug dealers still live with their mother?', 'How is street prostitution like a department store Santa?' and 'Why should suicide bombers buy life insurance?' Their aim is to explore, they suggest, the 'hidden side of everything'. They claim that morality represents the way that people would like the world to work, whereas economics represents how it actually does work (Hindmoor 2010).

Levitt and Dubner (2006: 12) claim that incentives are the cornerstone of modern life; dramatic events often have subtle and distant causes, and it is important to use information carefully. They suggest that 'if you learn to look at data in the right way...you can explain riddles that otherwise might have seemed impossible'. Just as previous scholars have argued that if you want to gauge the health of a firm, do not look only at the accounts, but also take note of the number of days that employees are off sick or the rate of staff turnover.

For the most part Levitt and Dubner explain the use and organisation of drug dealing and prostitution in terms of 'demand and supply'. This, they inform us, fixes prices, the supply of labour and the scale of the trade. More difficult questions – changing patterns of drug use or the association between different types of drugs and different socioeconomic groups – are ignored. At the same time they argue that the price charged by those involved in prostitution for different services is mainly a function of supply and demand. However, as more detailed studies on prostitution suggest, demand and supply do not arise spontaneously from biological need, on one side, and poverty on the other. Rather, they are brought into being by an extremely complex mixture of social, political, cultural and economic processes (Anderson and Davidson 2002). In addition, there are critical questions about the social construction of desire. Thus although it is a truism that without either demand or supply, prostitution would disappear, its functioning and social acceptability depend on a much wider combination of processes (Matthews 2008).

It is, however, in relation to the dramatic decrease in crime, which has occurred in America and elsewhere over the past two decades, that Levitt and Dubner present their most influential thesis. Rather than attribute the unprecedented decrease in crime to mass imprisonment, new policing strategies or changing patterns of drug use, they claim it was the legalisation of abortion in the 1970s that has had the most significant impact on the crime rate. Interestingly, in this account they move beyond a purely economic explanation. The unanticipated consequence of bringing in legislation to allow abortion in America has been, they suggest, that the number of unwanted babies decreased; and they claim that most of those babies would have been born into the poor or the 'criminal' classes. In order to give some credence to this thesis, Levitt and Dubner produce correlations showing that crime went down faster in the 1990s in those states that had high levels of abortion. In this way they aim to show that the rational decisions of individual women resulted in unanticipated and unexpected outcomes.

There are a number of problems with this thesis. First, there is an issue of timing. If abortion is a major cause of the crime drop then, given that pro-abortion legislation was introduced in the 1970s in the United States, the crime drop should have started in the mid to late 1980s. Second, a large number of legal abortions that took place after the 1970s were probably illegal abortions before then. Third, abortions were by no means limited to the poor and single mothers. As Franklin Zimring (2007) points out, births to single mothers increased in the United States after the legalisation of abortion, and evidence from other countries where abortion was legalised in the 1970s fails to show a clear relation between liberalisation of abortion and the crime drop. However, Zimring himself produces equivocal conclusions after assessing the evidence.

Zimring's account, in fact, reflects the failure of much liberal criminology. He claims that there was no single cause, or even an evident cause, for the decline of crime at the national level. Thus, instead of identifying the causal relations involved, he claims the crime decline was a classic example of multiple causation, with none of the many contributing causes playing a dominant role. The same conclusion is to be found in Andrew Karmen's *The New York Murder Mystery* (2000), in which he argues that the decline of homicide in New York was a 'fortuitous confluence', where every one of the causal factors known to affect crime moved in the same direction. How convenient. In a similar way John Conklin (2003) seems to attribute the crime drop to a range of 'factors' but fails to provide a compelling explanation of this important development. This is mainly because he, like Zimring and Karmen, adopts an approach that tries to identify the key variables or factors by a process of elimination and by adopting a successionist conception of causality. However, the wider socio-economic and cultural dynamics are not investigated, and the crucial relations between these factors remains unexplained (Young 2011).

In contrast to these rational choice and multifactor approaches, the international nature of the crime drop suggests that neither legalised abortion nor other factors cited could explain the simultaneous decrease in different countries. Developing an explanation of this decrease in crime would arguably involve an analysis of the shift in productive relations from a manufacturing to a service economy, coupled with the development of the information society, as well as changes in the nature of masculinity and other cultural shifts.

Assessing the utility of rational choice theory

Rational choice offers, at best, a limited vision of human action while downplaying agency in favour of structure. However, the structure mobilised in most criminological investigations is not the social structure, or even criminal justice agencies or institutions, but the structuring processes of crimes themselves (Kiser and Hechter 1998; Somers 1998). As cultural criminologists have pointed out, the situations in which offenders consciously decide on goals and weigh the costs and benefits of committing a criminal act are the exception rather than the rule. To understand the relation between ends and means and the motivation of offenders requires some appreciation of emotions, capacities, predispositions and values. That is, without an appreciation of 'dispositions', it is difficult to provide a comprehensive explanation of crime. It is not enough to claim that there is an 'interaction' between the type of crime and the type of offender. The nature of the interaction needs to be spelled out and explained (Manicas 2006). Thus, as Thaler and Sunstein (2008) argue, much behaviour is 'anchored' in past experience and is deeply influenced by significant others instead of being determined by 'human nature', as some rational choice theorists suggest.

Let us take the example of commercial robbers, who are widely seen as amongst the most organised, committed and 'rational' offenders. Research suggests that in the majority of cases they do not know how much money different premises hold at any given time, the type of security in use or how they might escape if things turn ugly (Matthews 2001). In fact, for many commercial robbers the ability to calculate the relation of risk to reward is extremely limited; many admit they are motivated, at least in part, by the excitement and risks involved. In other cases, individuals become involved in robberies not because they have assessed the benefits and risks but because friends and acquaintances draw them in.

That is, they may be motivated more by a sense of loyalty and 'keeping face' than by the promise of riches.

The focus on ends raises the distinction between the rational and the reasonable. Rational action is normally assessed in terms of means, whereas reasonable action is assessed in terms of ends (Sayer 2011). Actions are deemed rational in as much as a person is seen to efficiently and successfully pursue a given goal, although the worth of the particular goal is a matter of indifference. By contrast, we describe people as reasonable and unreasonable in terms of how they respond to particular situations and balance particular priorities and goals. Thus, a person who robs a local corner store by brandishing a shotgun may be considered unreasonable, although the robber may feel he has used the most effective way to persuade the storekeeper to hand over the money and minimise resistance (Cook 1991). However, in most cases of robbery and burglary, how offences are executed is not reduced to instrumental rationality but is conditioned by values, norms and reason. Paradoxically, most crime is a surprisingly moral activity guided by considerations about what is reasonable and morally acceptable. As Matza and Sykes (1961) and others have pointed out, 'delinquent' actions are infused with subterranean values and operate in relation to an identifiable moral code.

What this means, in effect, is that rational choice theory operates with an impoverished and, at best, one-sided conception of human action. For a more rounded picture of human action, it is necessary to consider goals, desires and values. Why do some people want to take illicit drugs? It is not just their availability that structures demand. In terms of addressing crime and deviance, it is necessary to address some of these 'irrational desires' (Archer 2000). In short, we are drawn back into a more detailed consideration of 'dispositions' if we want to seriously address the issue of crime. This necessarily takes us away from the methodological individualism underpinning rational choice theory. No doubt the widespread appeal of both rational choice and routine activities perspectives is their apparent simplicity. However, the enduring problem of social scientific investigation is dealing with complexity (Pawson 2013).

Moreover, as Alan Norrie (1986) has argued, there are direct and indirect policy implications of rational choice and routine activity perspectives. Amongst the more direct policy implications are forms of target-hardening, the use of different types of surveillance and varieties of situational and spatial controls. More indirectly, measures follow from the image of the individual offender as a rational decision maker; hence, one fully responsible and punishable. This lends weight to both retributive and deterrent forms of punishment, while expressing deep scepticism about the role of rehabilitation. This in turn fuels conservative 'get-tough' policies and supports 'just deserts' approaches to punishment. Norrie's observations remind us of the relation between theory and policy and that even those approaches which appear to be largely pragmatic, technical and administrative are never politically or morally neutral.

Conclusion

Rational choice and routine activities perspectives have considerable currency in academic criminology. However, it has been argued that these theories involve a number of relatively vague propositions with limited explanatory power or predictive capacity. Nevertheless, these approaches have been widely adopted by administrative criminologists, in part because they allow a focus on the immediacy of the criminal act and serve to avoid awkward questions about disadvantage, poverty and inequality. Their simple formulae and common-sense approach also appeals to those policymakers and politicians looking for quick fixes and convenient sound bites. The major weakness of rational choice and routine activities, however, is that in themselves they cannot account for the selection of one outcome rather than another. Second, most studies that draw on these perspectives involve post-hoc accounts of known facts. Third, there is a lack of specificity about what it means to be rational.

At the same time notions of rationality underpin a great deal of analysis within criminology, even amongst those who are sceptical of the value of the rational choice perspective. Four possible responses have been suggested to the various critiques of rational choice theory (Hay 2004; Green and Shapiro 1994):

1. Rational choice should be seen not as a theory but as a useful heuristic device for providing explanations.
2. Rational choice theory should be complemented with other criminological theories; namely, learning theory, control theory, social disorganisation theory and psychological or cultural theories, which can include aspects of motivation and emotions.
3. Rational choice theory should be restricted to explanations of certain forms of instrumental action or situations in which choices are highly structured and straightforward and the goals and objectives are clear.

4. The rational choice perspective should be limited to understanding the more immediate processes involved in carrying out specific forms of crime.

Whichever one of these options is adopted, the debate about the value of rational choice theory will no doubt continue as new variants of the approach are refined and developed. However, a reasonable response would be to advocate a combination of all four options. That is, there is some justification for accepting that rational choice could be a useful heuristic strategy and would be most relevant in situations with limited choices and clearly identifiable goals. Ultimately, however, rational choice would need to be located within a broader theoretical framework that could more effectively accommodate an appreciation of the dynamics of structure and agency and simultaneously incorporate considerations of values and social norms.

5
From Cultural Criminology to Cultural Realism

The cultural turn

Over the past three decades we have witnessed what has been referred to as the 'cultural turn'. Culture, which was once seen as a secondary derivative of the 'economic base', has now come to assume a central place in sociological thinking, while the economic is either marginalised or subsumed under the cultural umbrella (Ray and Sayer 1999). The growing preoccupation with culture has been associated with the declining influence internationally of Marxism and the growth of postmodernism, as well as with an increased interest in debates about identity, recognition and diversity.

The term 'culture' is used to signify a range of different modalities, ranging from high culture to street culture and to what Zygmunt Bauman (2011) describes as modern forms of 'liquid culture', characterised by an increasingly seductive and rapidly changing consumer-orientated society. Within the various uses of the term culture there is a focus on meanings, symbols and representations within different groups. Cultural phenomena in some sense must be shared even if they are contested. Consequently, cultural forms are widely treated as positive achievements to be celebrated and understood.

The contribution of cultural criminology

As one strand of this 'cultural turn', cultural criminology has changed the balance within academic criminology by providing a greater emphasis on the cultural aspects of crime and punishment. Over the last two decades it has made a significant impact, particularly amongst critical criminologists. It has injected considerable energy into a subject which seems to have less and less interesting and informative things to say about the topical issues of the day and which is gradually becoming more distant from the everyday realities of crime and crime control. It has also challenged much of the thinking of mainstream academic criminology by emphasising the cultural dimensions of crime and punishment and by arguing for a critical re-examination of criminal motivation and values while drawing attention to a number of 'crimes of style', including creating graffiti, gang activities, base jumping, protest music and other popular subcultural forms which are seen to challenge dominant social norms (Ferrell 1996).

Engaging with these deviant and marginalised populations, cultural criminologists call for different and more imaginative methodologies to target hard-to-reach and outcast groups. An essential starting point of investigation for cultural criminologists is the exploration of the complex symbiotic relation between culture and crime. Drawing on the work of Jack Katz (1988), they claim that criminal involvement is neither a purely rational act involving a calculation of risk and reward nor an irrational act carried out by pathological subjects. Rather, criminal involvement is seen as a function of boredom and limited opportunities or, alternatively, as a creative response to the pressures and demands of contemporary capitalism. Crime and deviance, it is claimed, involves a search for excitement or entertainment, or represents a form of resistance or risk taking. Cultural criminologists have coined the term 'edgework' to conceptualise this range of activities (Lyng 1990). Edgework constitutes purposive action grounded in the emotional and the visceral and involves the search for excitement and gratification. From this vantage point crime is no longer a routine or mundane activity but is a meaningful behaviour involving issues of identity, emotion and resistance. Although crime may be seen as an individual act, it is simultaneously viewed as a deeply cultural and social endeavour, often located within different subcultural groups. The formation of gangs, for example, is seen as a subcultural response to the pressures and constraints of urban deprivation, particularly amongst ethnic minority groups (Brotherton 2008).

The relationship between culture and crime is seen, on one hand, to involve a conflict between the dominant cultural norms and particular subcultural groups, resulting in the 'criminalisation' of certain aspects of popular culture. On the other hand, crime and culture are held to be mutually reinforcing, principally through the ways in which the media preoccupies itself with reporting, shaping and in some cases manufacturing deviant or criminal images and stereotypes. Thus it is argued, there is a symbiotic relationship between crime and culture, and part of the excitement of engaging in crime stems from challenging or breaking cultural norms. Therefore, the mobilisation of the criminal law and related sanctions, it is suggested, often serves to heighten criminal motivation.

In rejecting positivism, rational choice theory and administrative criminology, cultural criminologists seek to re-engage with a range of theoretical perspectives: labelling theory, subcultural theory, critical theory, feminism, as well as theories of late modernity. It adopts a fundamentally social constructionist approach in opposition to those forms of administrative criminology and crime science that take the concept of 'crime' as a given. In this way the aim is to develop a critical stance while synthesising a range of divergent intellectual perspectives.

Understanding motivation, emotions and identities requires, it is argued, a distinctly different approach than that provided by traditional forms of quantitative or survey methods. Two of the main methodological approaches advocated are ethnographic studies and *verstehen*. Drawing on studies such as Paul Willis's *Learning to Labour* (1977), cultural criminologists argue that ethnographic accounts offer the possibility of engaging with the lived experience of subjects, thereby allowing an appreciation of meanings and motivations in different contexts. At the same time, Jeff Ferrell (1997) has revisited Max Weber's concept of *verstehen*, which involves empathising with those being studied in order to highlight the importance of the lived meanings that are associated with criminal events. In this way, the aim is to 'get inside' and immerse oneself in different forms of illegality. In addition, cultural criminologists engage in the standard practice of critical theory by undertaking forms of ideology critique and unmasking the perceived negative effects of consumerism, and by demonstrating how the media mobilises images and forms of representation that serve to frame and commodify crime (Hayward and Presdee 2010).

Cultural criminology has sought to challenge conventional criminology, which it claims has not only lost touch with those people it attempts to understand but also lacks an appreciation of the changing dynamics and imperatives of late modernity and the rapid transformations taking place as a result of globalisation and migration (Young 2007). It offers an ostensibly radical politics while advocating an active engagement in the lives of the marginalised and the outcast, aiming to participate actively in the defence and support of these groups. In this way cultural criminology has sought to reinvigorate criminology by opening up new areas of investigation and challenging some of the conventional thinking in the subject area.

A realist response

It has been pointed out by critics that the concept of culture used by cultural criminologists involves a limited focus on the dynamics of popular culture and a neglect of the nature of the dominant or control culture, which is portrayed as monolithic (O'Brien 2005). The dominant culture is seen to manipulate images and ideologies in order to promote unwanted consumerism and to reinforce its own power base. Thus, although cultural criminologists provide detailed and often colourful depictions of aspects of popular culture, they often fail to locate them within the wider cultural contexts from which they have emerged, or to identify the detailed workings of the institutions of social control. In this way, they have moved away from the priorities of left realism, and present an inverted response:

> Since there is no clear definition of 'culture' in cultural criminology, its practitioners are given licence to make any and all kinds of sweeping generalisations about the wider contexts in which crime occurs.... Here, the ethical interests of left realism – especially the concern with the particularity of crime victims – are turned upside down in a kind of political critique of oppression and subordination characteristic of left idealism but, importantly, without a concomitant commitment to theorising the role of specific institutions in the process of social control. (O'Brien 2005: 610)

In this selective interpretation and representation of 'culture' there is, as O'Brien (2005) points out, no normative assessment of the issues under consideration but rather a general moralising about the perceived failures and inequities of capitalism and the misdeeds of the powerful (Presdee 2000). Consequently, all of the subcultural adaptions in advanced capitalism are seen as positive achievements, while the control culture is seen in essentially negative terms. Inasmuch as cultural criminologists focus on crime, they are mostly preoccupied with relatively minor illegalities, while largely ignoring the more serious and harmful forms of criminality. At the same time, by focusing on selected forms of micro resistance, narratives of dissent and alternative lifestyles, cultural criminologists are in danger of engaging in the kind of romanticism associated with left idealism.

What is missing from cultural criminological texts is any real appreciation of the victims of crime on the one hand and the role of public opinion and social norms on the other. In fact, cultural criminologists tend to use terms like 'deviance', 'crime' and 'transgression' interchangeably, thereby blurring the distinction between the serious and the trivial, between the legal and illegal. Where they do talk about crime, it is often so-called non-victim crime. At the same time, crime is frequently depicted as essentially a conflict between the actor/offender and the control agencies that seem to inexplicably 'criminalise' what are described as 'expressive' forms of behaviour.

Thus, in terms of graffiti, for example, there is little recognition of the opposition which large sections of the public express in response to having neighbourhoods defaced with unsightly 'tags', which they see as a blight on the urban landscape, particularly in run-down inner-city neighbourhoods. The vast majority of graffiti 'artists' are not Banksys or King Rollos, nor are they engaged in producing colourful and decorative street art or murals. Rather, they operate in the mistaken belief that writing their initials in oversize letters is visually attractive and aesthetically appealing. In the same way, gang membership may be seen as a subcultural response to the vagaries and insecurities of urban life, but where gangs threaten and intimidate local communities, or engage in gratuitous violence, their role must be questioned (Pitts 2008).

Although these minor offenders may see their actions as some form of resistance or as an attack upon the control culture, the majority of those who engage in crime and deviance do not destabilise the social order. They are not protorevolutionaries and are not engaged in constructive or progressive political action. Thus, the claim that the forms of transgression most subjects of cultural criminology engage in provide an effective critique of the authorities' claims about crime and justice is clearly an exaggeration. At the same time the libertarian and anarchistic orientation of some cultural criminologists involves a form of anti-statism and a conception of power antithetical to critical realists. It provides a barrier to engaging constructively in policy formation while presenting power in essentially negative and authoritarian terms. This not only militates against a detailed analysis of power in its diverse forms but also reinforces a conception of power as all-encompassing, which, needless to say, is a conception of power that the powerful are only too willing to endorse.

While there can be little doubt about the growing interest and influence of cultural forms in recent decades, the tendency within cultural criminology to dissolve the economic into the cultural by claiming, for example, that 'capitalism is essentially cultural these days' and that 'its crimes and transgressions rest precisely on its cultural accomplishments' is a serious misconception (Ferrell 2007: 92–93). In a period of increased globalisation, deepening capitalist crises and growing inequality, downplaying political economy seems to be particularly inappropriate (Hall and Winlow 2007). Although in practice it is difficult to differentiate the cultural from the economic, the heuristic and empirical distinctions between the two spheres remain important and real. Within cultural criminology, capitalism is frequently translated into cultural terms and mythologised. At the same time, the cultural forms referred to are not fully elaborated and are presented as unified and undifferentiated wholes or, alternatively, certain aspects of culture are isolated and decontextualised. However, when aspects of culture are separated out into rituals, knowledge, beliefs and values, it is not too difficult to show that the parts are tied to specific administrative arrangements, economic pressures or political imperatives. Thus:

> The difficulties become most acute when (after all the protestations to the contrary have been made) culture shifts from something to be described, interpreted, even perhaps explained, and is treated instead as a source of explanation in itself. This is not to deny that some form of cultural explanation may be useful enough, in its place, but appeals to culture can only offer a partial explanation of why people think and behave as they do, and what causes them to alter their ways. Political and economic forces, social institutions, and biological processes cannot be wished away, or assimilated to systems of knowledge and belief. (Kuper 1999: xi)

Cultural criminologists, like other social scientists, tend to talk in terms of the shift from modernity to 'late' or 'post' modernity, thereby couching the historical movements over the past two centuries in predominantly cultural terms rather than depicting them as a shift from Fordism to post-Fordism (see Hayward 2004: 50–61 for an exception). As Nancy Fraser (2003) has argued, the transition from the forms of 'discipline', which Michel Foucault has identified as being prevalent in the nineteenth century, to contemporary forms of 'flexibilisation' is more appropriately explained in terms of a shift to post-Fordist globalisation with its attendant forms of inequality, mobility and economic and social instability. The implications of Fraser's argument is that we now live in a post-disciplinary society involving new modes of regulation and subjectification, which are more directly associated with changes in political economy than with purely cultural shifts (Lemke 2003).

Cultural criminologists tend to adopt a selective view of culture, one that sees high culture or the dominant culture in predominantly negative terms or as an expression of the oppressive power of the ruling class with its ability to silence, mystify or co-opt the majority of the population through the manipulation of the mass media and the promotion of consumerism. Street or popular culture, on the other hand, is seen mainly in positive terms. Thus, while the task is to subvert, unmask, contest or delegitimise dominant cultural forms, street and popular culture are to be celebrated.

The analysis of the media by cultural criminologists concentrates on the ways in which the media are seen to construct, distort or amplify crime and deviance through a series of 'spirals' and 'loops', as well as through the mobilisation of 'moral panics'. Surprisingly, there is relatively little discussion of the new social media and their profound impact upon culture, politics and identities (Castells 1996; Ferrell et al. 2008; Young 2007). For a criminology which aspires to be 'critical and activist', this is a strange omission since the new social media are widely held responsible for transforming and undermining, as well as challenging, established forms of mass media and facilitating so-called cyber-activism. Recent events in Italy and elsewhere have demonstrated the role of new social media in mobilising political campaigns amongst otherwise diverse and uncoordinated groups (Albertazzi et al. 2009; Van Aelst and Walgrave 2002). A focus on the development and impact of these new forms of social media in the context of the information society could inject a much-needed materiality into the cultural criminological repertoire and a more detailed appreciation of the changing nature of global politics and wider social movements (Ayres 1999).

In a similar vein, there is the suggestion that consumerism is undesirable and somehow responsible for creating 'crimogenic expectations of material convenience' (Ferrell et al. 2008: 14). While some forms of crime no doubt involve the theft of culturally valued goods, the suggestion that consumerism 'contaminates communities' smacks of a certain nostalgia, and a desire to return to pre-capitalist social relations. This claim is, in part, a reflection of the underlying thesis that capitalism/consumerism is bad, while culture in its popular forms is good. For most of us, however, consumerism is one of the positive achievements of capitalism, and it is inconceivable that any future post-capitalist society would do away with consumerism.

Ferrell, Hayward and Young (2008) claim with some justification that 'nothing kills good criminology like bad method'. The main contenders for the title of 'bad method' are statistics and survey methods, the latter of which is claimed to 'simply create that which they wish to capture'. Cultural criminologists express a deep-seated hostility to the use of quantitative methods and instead advocate the use of qualitative methods, particularly in the form of ethnographies. Such an approach, it is claimed, is not only increasingly appropriate in late modernity but is also able to capture more effectively the motivational dynamics and meanings of both subjects and objects of crime. While there is a rational core to this argument, there is a danger of losing sight of the value of some forms of quantitative analysis and, in particular, the use of descriptive statistics. We need to know something about crime trends if we are to analyse the 'crime drop', for example. Similarly, we need to know something about the changing levels of imprisonment, the composition of inmates and changing levels of suicide and violence in prison if we are to engage meaningfully in penal reform. These numbers are never perfect, but they do provide a useful starting point for investigation, while drawing our attention to different processes and issues related to crime control.

If these quantitative methods have their limitations, so does ethnographic research. Within ethnography, as has been argued, there is a tendency to replace causal analysis by description and simultaneously to devalue theory. At its worst, ethnography – even so-called deep ethnography – simply reports the understandings, or in some cases the misunderstandings, of subjects or does little more than represent their interpretation of the social world, which may be woefully misguided or one-sided (Hammersley 1992). Given the privileged position afforded to method, there is surprisingly little discussion in the cultural criminological literature of what distinguishes good ethnography from bad ethnography. Rather, we are told that one of the significant attractions of ethnographic research is that it can be conducted without funds and theory, while research questions or hypotheses are apparently optional (Ferrell et al. 2008). Engaging in 'instant' or 'liquid' ethnography requires, it is suggested, little or no training, while difficult questions concerning the validity and generalisability of these ethnographic studies are conspicuously avoided. This is unfortunate because the problem of generalising from particular case studies is an enduring one for ethnographic research. In addition, the claim made by some ethnographers that focusing on the 'lived experience' of subjects overcomes the structural agency problem is misguided.

There is an emphasis on agency in the majority of the studies conducted by cultural criminologists, with little appreciation of how prevailing power structures shape or constrain social action. Moreover, the integration of agency and structure is not fully realised by pointing to the uncertainties and pressures of 'late modernity' and claiming that they have created new forms of transgression and exacerbated existing pressures towards crime (Young 2003). Such an explanation does not square very well with the remarkable decrease in crime that has taken place since the 1990s on both sides of the Atlantic. Although there are frequent references to capitalist globalisation, the links between these structural developments and involvement in crime remain tenuous. In sum, the repeated claims that increased cultural globalisation results, for example, in new or increased forms of transgression is no more useful as a form of explanation than the positivists' claim that unemployment or family breakdown causes crime.

In general, there is a deep ambivalence amongst cultural criminologists, whether they are involved in a radical critique and rejection of mainstream and conventional criminology or whether their aim is to contribute to its renewal and expansion. At one point they claimed that 'a new criminology is needed' (Ferrell, Hayward and Young 2008: 63) on the basis that much existing criminology is 'sanitised dross' involving frequent 'outpourings of astoundingly obtuse intellectual gibberish' (171). However, despite these protestations it is claimed elsewhere that cultural criminology 'does not undermine contemporary criminology as much as it expands and enlivens it' (Ferrell and Sanders 1995). At one moment it sees itself as salvaging and rejuvenating criminology, and at another it claims to be a post- or anti-conventional criminology. Thus, while it presents a challenge to mainstream criminology on a number of fronts, as with old-style radical criminology and 'left idealism', its assault on conventional criminology is often largely rhetorical. The danger is that it will not transcend conventional criminology, but that it will become an inversion or a mirror image of that which it criticises (Cohen 1979). In many respects its gravitation towards libertarianism and anti-correctionalism, its views of the state and its inability to effectively address contemporary power relations leaves it in danger of being incapable of responding effectively to crime and its control. Encouraging 'subversive symbolic inversion' and 'creative recoding' as central political strategies is unlikely to produce 'dangerous or useful knowledge' or for that matter bring global capitalism to its knees.

However, the struggles that characterise contemporary capitalism are more than a 'battleground of meaning' and a struggle over 'the transposition of images' (Ferrell, Hayward and Young 2008: 199–204). If cultural criminologists want to move beyond Marxist materialism and engage in a critical criminology, then it is imperative to incorporate questions of political economy and address normative questions while considering the feasibility of alternatives (Sayer 1997). It is not enough to talk about resistance or empowerment or engage in ideology critiques. Rather, the need is to change the material conditions in which people live. There is no point in a critical criminology that does not offer at least the possibility of some kind of improvement. Although removing illusions and enlightening people may be useful, it is also necessary to remove or block the mechanisms that generate these constraints or illusions. If we have a critique of law or inequality but no feasible or discernible alternative, the force of the critique is weakened, to say the least.

Cultural criminologists' claim that they are 'more attuned to prevailing conditions' than mainstream criminologists and are consequently 'more capable of conceptualising and confronting contemporary crime and crime control' (Ferrell et al. 2008: 2) is unconvincing. Indeed, it could reasonably be argued that cultural criminology is as much a reflection as an analysis of prevailing conditions, given its particular preoccupation with style, fashion and popular culture. Moreover, its inability to address adequately the relationship between agency and structure seriously limits its capacity to critically analyse the changing nature of contemporary society, while its anti-correctionalism and anti-statism leave it ill-equipped to engage seriously in crime control or a reduction of victimisation. The adoption of a social constructionist approach, combined with an affinity for postmodernism, leads to anti-objectivism and anti-realism. However, its claim that the dominant forms of media representation are distorted and one-sided and in need of demystification and correction implies an objectivism – otherwise it would be difficult to know what reality it is that needs to be unmasked.

Defending and reconstructing cultural criminology

In a spirited defence of cultural criminology Jeff Ferrell (2007) argues with some justification that Marxist materialism and contemporary political struggles have to take cultural considerations on board. He also addresses the important issue of what constitutes a critical progressive criminology:

> There are at least a couple of ways to engage in a critical progressive criminology. One is to analyse the criminal violence and interpersonal degradation spawned by social arrangements of exploitative inequality, including those of global capitalism and the other is to analyse moments and movements that resist inequality and predation, exploring the ways in which resistance emerges out of legal

marginalisation and in turn comes to be criminalised as a threat to the existing order. Ideally we would do both, since both in fact point to the possibility of a better world if 'we' is taken to mean the collective critical criminologists, then I suppose we do. (Ferrell 2007: 99)

Although this is the right question to ask, the answer given is inadequate and reflects the limited nature of much cultural criminological analysis. There is no appreciation in this account of personal responsibility or social norms, nor are all forms of popular culture positive and progressive. Although there is nothing wrong in examining the relation between inequality and crime, the options available to critical criminologists go far beyond this restricted dichotomy, with its limited conception of power, crime and culture. Ferrell's notion of the 'good society' would be a world in which graffiti 'artists' and gang members would be free to follow their desires with impunity. There is little appreciation in this statement of the productive nature of power or the role of the state in increasing personal security or reducing victimisation. In contrast to this narrow vision, a number of recent contributions to criminology have considered some alternative conceptions of the role and meaning of culture that signal the development of a broader approach, one which might allow us to reconstruct – or at least redirect – cultural criminology in a way that would make it potentially more critical, more progressive and, ultimately, more realist.

The first contribution is a recognition of the cultural dimensions of punishment. The work of Dario Melossi (2001) has drawn attention to the 'cultural embeddedness' of conceptions of punishment in different countries, pointing to the role of religious, political and social norms in shaping attitudes. David Nelken (2005) has shown that the 'culture of control' involves both informal and formal processes of regulation, arguing that while one may be liberal and tolerant, the other may be punitive. In addition, there may be significant differences in tolerance towards different crimes among different populations, for example, in Italy attitudes towards organised crime are relatively tough, while attitudes towards the young are more tolerant and forgiving. The implications of the 'cultural embeddedness' of punishment and the differentiation of norms and attitudes in different countries is twofold. On one hand, the deployment of punishment in different countries is not simply a question of rates of offending or forms of resistance; it requires an understanding of social norms within the wider culture. On the other hand, it reminds us that responses to crime are rarely homogeneous but are differentiated in terms of notions of seriousness and in relation to the activities and concerns of different social groups.

Relatedly, David Garland (2006), in an attempt to integrate cultural analysis into the sociology of punishment, has endorsed the 'cultural embeddedness' thesis, adding that penal institutions have historically been grounded and shaped by cultural values and perceptions. Garland suggests that, although the concept of 'culture' remains notoriously multivalent, incorporating cultural considerations into the sociology of punishment offers the promise of a richer and deeper form of analysis. This can include an appreciation of changing sensibilities, the role of cultural myths and symbols, and changing emotional responses to the infliction of punishment (Piacentini 2005).

Orlando Patterson (2006) has argued for the need to engage the dynamics of youth culture, particularly with reference to African American youth, if we want to develop interventions that will resonate with these young people. In recognising both the attraction of young black males to 'hanging out' in subcultural groups and their engagement with fashion, drugs, hip hop music and culture, Patterson argues that while this may increase their sense of self-respect, it all too often traps them and disconnects them from the socio-economic mainstream. Significantly, Patterson argues that engaging with ethnic minority youth in this way will require a different methodological approach than that which has been used to date.

> In academia, we need a new, multidisciplinary approach toward understanding what makes young black men behave so self-destructively. Collecting transcripts of their views and rationalisations is a useful first step, but won't help nearly as much as the recent rash of scholars with tape-recorders seem to think. Getting the facts straight is important, but for decades we have been overwhelmed with statistics on black youths, and running more statistical regressions is beginning to approach the point of diminishing returns to knowledge. (Patterson 2006: 2)

Thus, Patterson suggests that if we want to meaningfully engage with these young people, simply recording or replicating their views or engaging in linear regression analysis is unlikely to develop the type of understanding needed to change the situation.

Another area of criminological investigation where a cultural criminology could be of value is in relation to the crime drop. Most of the available explanations – increased imprisonment, new styles of policing, the war on drugs and the like – are, at best, partial explanations (Blumstein and Wallman 2000). However, Andrew Karmen (2000), in his study of the decreasing murder rate in New York and after a review of the leading explanations, concluded that the changing values of youth could be a major factor, while Robert Sampson (2006) has argued that the evolving multicultural mix in New York and other cities may have had a significant impact upon the level of crime. Sampson's controversial thesis suggests that an influx of first-generation immigrants into urban centres may have served to counteract the values of street culture, thereby depressing the level of offending (Hagan et al. 2008).

Surprisingly, James Q. Wilson (2011), in reviewing explanations for the crime drop, explains the decrease not only in terms of changing patterns of drug use but also principally as a consequence of what he refers to as an improvement in culture. He adds, however, that studying culture poses serious methodological problems for social scientists, since it is difficult to produce 'hard numbers and testable theories'. However, he concludes that 'we can take some comfort, perhaps, in reflecting that identifying the likely causes of crime decline is even more important than precisely measuring it' (29).

Research on commercial robbery has shown that the substantial decrease in recorded incidents in the United Kingdom in the 1990s was difficult to explain in terms of crime prevention measures or changing policing strategies. The most plausible explanation points to the changing culture amongst armed robbers, with the gradual replacement of the old-style professional 'faces' carrying a sawn-off shotgun in raids against banks, building societies and post offices by a more amateur and less specialised group of offenders engaging more spontaneously against 'softer' targets such as convenience stores, petrol stations, off-licences and the like, typically carrying a handgun or a replica. In many ways the new breed of commercial robbers can be seen as embracing a post-Fordist ethos with its emphasis on flexibility, mobility and diversity (Matthews 2001).

The preceding examples show that the focus on culture can be usefully broadened and differentiated so as to allow us to consider both the positive and negative aspects of culture and the relationship of the cultural, political and economic aspects of contemporary capitalism. Cultural criminology thus moves from a focus on the esoteric and exceptional towards more mainstream political and social issues and, ultimately, towards an approach which is theoretically and methodologically closer to realism.

Indeed, the development of cultural criminology to date can be divided into two discernible phases or dimensions (O'Brien 2005; Webber 2007). The first, identified as mainly socio-psychological in orientation, has focused on motivation, risk taking and forms of edgework. Drawing heavily on labelling theory, postmodernism and subcultural theory combined with libertarian politics, crime and deviance are seen as either arising from the pressures and uncertainties of late modernity or as a form of resistance. The second phase or dimension of cultural criminology takes broader themes, examining the role of the media, consumerism, globalisation and migration. However, there are signs that a new phase of cultural criminology is emerging, one drawn to questions of policy and a reconsideration of the role and meaning of culture. This approach involves a reconsideration of the relation between different forms of critical criminology; in particular, the relation between cultural criminology and realist criminology. Thus it is argued that cultural criminology and realist criminology have the same theoretical roots, and that while realism concentrates on the *form* of social interaction, cultural criminology focuses on the *substance,* and that what is required is a criminology that does both:

> There is a certain serendipity to the synthesis between realism and cultural criminology because both fit together like pieces of the jigsaw puzzle: one depicts the form of social interaction which we call crime, whilst the second breathes human life into it. If realism stresses that crime is a relationship between offender and victim and between actors and reactors, cultural criminology reminds us that such relationships are imbued with energy and meaning. They are cultural products not simple technical targets constituted by opportunity or pragmatic calculations of harm. (Hayward and Young 2012: 120)

In addition, it is suggested that cultural criminology brings to the 'square of crime' meaning, energy and emotion, thereby turning this formal structure into a lived reality. However, although it is the case that cultural and realist criminology have similar roots, they are not always moving in the same direction or drawing on the same sources. Indeed, the starting point for the development of cultural realism is not the combination of form and content; rather, it lies elsewhere, since it is not the case that realist criminology lacks content or that developing cultural realism involves simply inserting detailed descriptions of motivations and emotions into the 'square of crime'. There are, in fact, major questions regarding the validity of the descriptions produced by cultural criminologists and their attempts to identify offenders' motives, as has already been suggested. It is also not just a case of juxtaposing the 'foreground' factors of motivations and emotions with the 'background' factors of poverty and inequality but also of linking agency and structure in a meaningful way (Webber 2007). The considerable epistemological, methodological and political differences would need to be addressed if a 'marriage' of these two approaches is to have any chance of success. As is suggested above, a realist approach needs to be 'joined up' in a way that links theory, method and policy. It is also the case that critical realists have engaged in cultural analysis and looked in some detail at the role of emotions and identity formation in contemporary capitalism (Archer 2000; Sayer 2011).

A more constructive way of developing some form of cultural realism would be to begin by identifying some points of agreement that could usefully be developed. There are a number of areas of common ground. First, both approaches would agree that a greater understanding of the cultural dimensions of attitudes and behaviour is critical to the formulation of effective policy. Second, both cultural and realist criminologists argue that interventions are likely to work only to the extent that they connect with the sensibilities and propensities of the subjects to whom they are directed. Third, both approaches express deep reservations about the use of inferential statistics and the positivistic tendency to turn complex social relations into dry mathematical formulas. Fourth, both approaches have a commitment to naturalism and engaging in the lived experiences of subjects, since there is a need to establish a congruity of meaning between researchers and their subjects, combined with a need to understand their experiences, emotions and aspirations. Fifth, there is a mutual distrust of the overly rationalised conception of man in rational choice theory and of the overly routinised conception of order in routine activities theory. Sixth, the approaches agree that the forms of regulation themselves can be constitutive of the offence in question. Thus, the nature of crime or deviance is not reducible to individual motivation or opportunity but is created, to some extent by the modes of regulation directed towards it. There is, finally, a common commitment to the development of a critical or radical criminology that problematises the notions of crime and deviance, although there remain some differences in exactly what is 'critical' about these two approaches to criminology (Sayer 1997; Matthews 2010).

However, while these points of agreement may provide some foundation for developing a cultural realism, combining the two approaches is not a straightforward exercise. One of the main obstacles is linking the detailed case studies frequently undertaken by cultural criminologists to valid generalisations. In formal terms we face the problem of connecting the ideographic to the nomothetic (Hayward and Young 2012). This involves moving beyond pure description and an exclusive focus on human motivations, emotions and intentions or on accounts given by actors themselves, to a form of analysis that can identify the key *relations* between individuals and the way that they are structured in different contexts. This may involve identifying outcomes that the individuals themselves do not fully understand or expect (Carr 1964).

We generalise in part because we aim to learn lessons from studying different situations, and generalisations are often accomplished through a process of comparison. The comparative method is an effective way to test hypotheses and further theoretical development. For example, an attempt to explain the cause of a riot would need to consider the motivations and aspirations not only of the rioters themselves but also of the control agencies. We could also try to identify the causal dynamics involved in riots in different contexts and in different countries.

Recent comparative research on riots in the United Kingdom and France has identified a number of similar causal mechanisms in play, including absolute and relative deprivation, growing inequalities, increased tension between the police and sections of the population and growing issues of legitimacy (Waddington and King 2009). Riots have repeatedly been found to be concentrated in deprived inner-city areas, involving predominantly young males from socially and economically marginalised groups. Such comparative analysis does not, of course, allow specific predictions of the type that claim that a riot will take place at a particular time and place, but it does allow the identification of propensities and the spelling out of conditions that make riots more probable. From a realist point of view, comparative ideographic research moves beyond establishing similarities and differences of units of analysis. Instead, the aim is to approach the issue in a theory-driven way: postulating the existence of a number of generative mechanisms potentially responsible for producing the events under study. These can then be empirically examined.

Thus, the significance of this type of generalisation is that it emphasises the central role of causal analysis in developing meaningful explanations. Indeed, it is impossible to understand everyday life unless one assumes that human behaviour is determined by causes that are, in principle, identifiable. For critical realists, of course, causality is not associated with recurrent regularities but with the identification of causal mechanisms and tendencies. As Max Weber (1949) argued, the search for causal explanations does not necessarily involve an attempt to identify *laws* as such but causal *relationships*. Weber talks about 'adequate causation' and suggests that the aim is to identify the change in the existing state of affairs that produced a particular outcome. In this process, *verstehen* is seen as critical, since individuals are themselves causal agents who act for reasons that we need to identify. Thus for Weber, as Ferrell recognised, it is important to understand how people perceive the world and what they do or do not want to do about what they see.

For realists it is also important to identify the causal capabilities of structures and to recognise that institutions, like bureaucracies and prisons, have particular generative powers – even if those subject to those powers are not fully aware of them. As Erving Goffman (1968) has pointed out in relation to 'total institutions', they routinely generate particular social divisions, relations of domination and subordination, while creating and shaping identities. Typically for the inmates, removal from familiar social settings and interaction with significant others involves the 'mortification of the self' and the construction of an institutionalised identity. There may be resistance and different forms of adaption to the pressures and constraints, but this often only serves to reinforce the structures. In this way Goffman's account identifies the key social mechanisms at work in these institutions and explains the range of possible outcomes. It may be that different types of total institution operate in different ways, which can be identified through empirical analysis, but the power of Goffman's analysis lies in its ability to identify the core processes at work in these different settings and how they influence identities. As Willis (1977) has shown, a good ethnography does not simply describe or report. Rather, it uncovers the rules and norms that are implicit in everyday activity (Manicas 2006).

In this process the aim is to identify the causal mechanisms in play and to distinguish generic causes from contingencies. Thus, in contrast to the positivistic claim that research based on case studies is epistemologically inferior, from a realist perspective explanatory ideographic studies are valid inasmuch as they are concerned with the clarification of structures and their associated generative mechanisms. At the same time we need to dispel the twin myths that these intensive qualitative studies suffer from a problem of representation and objectivity. Since we never know the complete characteristics of the populations we wish to study, the question arises – representative of what? Where such research lays structures and mechanisms bare, it is no less objective than extensive quantitative research (Sayer 2010). It is also the case that qualitative studies can be exploratory in the strong sense inasmuch as they identify causal relations and processes, while in certain cases in which the population under study is not too diverse it may be possible to combine both qualitative and quantitative approaches.

Tsoukas (1989) has suggested that the movement from ideographic to nomothetic explanations can be achieved in three stages. This involves moving from an examination of actions and motives to that of reasons and rules and finally to that of structures and causal powers. Thus the investigation begins by theoretically identifying the inner constitution of those under study, then moves on to identify the reasons and rules by which actions are adopted and finally examines the associated structures and causal powers behind them and how these are exercised in particular contexts.

In search of cultural realism

One example of what might be called cultural realism is the work of Philippe Bourgois – although he himself might not accept this characterisation of his work. However, he can be considered a cultural realist inasmuch as his work embraces theory, cultural issues, political economy, power relations, normative concerns and a strong policy focus. He has been engaged in long-term ethnographic research with homeless drug users in New York and San Francisco and has produced a number of detailed studies of the meanings, motivation, emotions and values of this often neglected group. His aim is neither to romanticise the people he studies nor reduce them to statistical artefacts.

In relation to theory he draws heavily on the writings of Foucault, Bourdieu and Marx, as well as a wide range of anthropological and sociological literature. He adapts Foucault's conception of power, particularly bio-power, which he uses to critically engage the medical model of addictions. He also sees the regulation of drug use as a way of 'disciplining the misuse of pleasure' and 'controlling economically unproductive bodies' (Bourgois 2000). From Bourdieu he takes and explores the notion of habitus and the concepts of economic and social capital. From Marx he draws an understanding of political economy. In adapting the work of these authors, Bourgois examines the relation between class and culture, political economy and power, while exploring the links between theory and practice. Combining the work of these and other authors provides a basis for developing a useful conceptual framework for understanding both cultural and economic issues in a way that allows him to incorporate considerations of both agency and structure.

Bourgois places the normative concerns of suffering, abuse and exploitation at the centre of his analysis. He is therefore careful not to romanticise the suffering and misery that the homeless, drug-addicted population experiences daily. While he is critical of those ethnographies that focus on the exotic and esoteric, he is also at pains to point out how these subjects become active agents in personal degradation and community disorder. In contrast to the romantic vision presented by some liberal and cultural criminologists, he demonstrates how the drug trade can come to dominate public space and how local law-abiding residents come to live in fear and contempt of their neighbours.

> Illegal enterprise, however, embroils most of its participants in lifestyles of violence, substance abuse and internalised rage. Contradictorily, therefore, the street culture of resistance is predicated on the destruction of its own participants and the community harbouring them. In other words, although street culture emerges out of a personal search for dignity and a rejection of racism and subjugation, it ultimately becomes the active agent in personal degradation and community ruin. (Bourgois 2003: 9)

Thus, he suggests that street culture may be not only an alternative space for resisting exploitation, but also a site of violence, drug abuse and gang activity. Like Orlando Patterson he suggests that, while street culture may provide moments of creative response to exclusion, it can serve to maintain exclusion through semi-illiteracy, expressive violence and involvement in problematic drug use. Bourgois (1996), like Goffman, emphasises that through the cultural practices of opposition and resistance, individuals often shape the oppression that larger forces impose on them.

In opposition to the conservative vilification of street life, Bourgois (1996, 2002) approaches his subjects with respect and humanity, pointing to the way in which different cultural adaptions can provide a degree of mutual support while maintaining a sense of dignity and an element of comradeship. Thus, there is a need, he argues, to bring theory and politics to bear to uncover the layers of meaning that operate in this cultural milieu and provide a critical alternative to the dominant liberal and conservative perspectives.

In focusing on cultural dimensions, Bourgois describes how African American youth who witnessed the ravages of drug use and drug wars in their communities in the late 1980s desisted from using crack cocaine in the 1990s. Although heroin had become cheaper and purer in that period, it remained unpopular in its intravenous forms. In this way drug use is subject to cultural change. He argues that patterns of drug use are not random, however, since cultural and economic forces create different forms of vulnerability and demand (Bourgois 2003). Thus, it is no accident that crack cocaine became the drug of choice among inner-city subgroups suffering the most intense forms of racial and spatial segregation in 1980s America. Importantly, he argues, drug use is not reducible to the pharmacological effects of particular substances. The significance of different drugs should be seen and understood in relation to the social and economic context in which they are used.

Although Bourgois (2002a) favours long-term ethnographic research with his subjects, his ultimate aim is to help generate a critical debate around social suffering. For him, the role of ethnography is to provide a bridge between decontextualised theory and the reality of urban street life. He is critical of postmodernism, which he feels has removed ethnographic research from political and social engagement. He also distances himself from those approaches that have sanitised urban culture and ignored the painful realities of street life. He takes issue with the cultural relativists who avoid making judgements about the role and value of different cultural adaptions. He is also critical of 'ivory tower' academics who shy away from engaging in hands-on ethnographic research with the unemployed, the drug-addicted or violent criminals because they are incapable of treating these people with humanity and respect or of conducting the type of ethnographic research required if a meaningful dialogue is to occur.

In his work on HIV and needle-exchange programmes, he argues for a combination of qualitative and quantitative methods. Quantitative epidemiological studies, he suggests, can provide useful information on large-scale patterns and trends, and detailed ethnographic studies can help explain anomalies while identifying causal relations (Bourgois 2002a). In addition, by accessing large-scale quantitative datasets, which are easily accessible, it allows qualitative researchers to situate their research subjects. In this way, ethnographic research, which he suggests is often too narrowly focused, is able to place its investigations in a wider context. In a later work, *Righteous Dopefiends* (with Jeff Schonberg 2009), he advocates using photo-ethnography, which he maintains can greatly improve ethnographic techniques and provide a more powerful form of analysis by allowing discussion and reflection, particularly when carried out collaboratively.

As a consequence of his extensive ethnographic research, Bourgois (2000, 2010) finds himself drawn to critically rethink drug policy and what he sees as the undesirable consequences of the so-called war on drugs. His experiences encourage him to address the suffering, which he sees at firsthand, and to evaluate existing forms of treatment and social support. He is particularly critical of the medical model of addiction and also expresses serious reservations about placing heroin addicts on long-term methadone programmes. Drawing on comparative research involving Switzerland and Australia, he calls for a heroin prescription programme, which he argues would immediately reduce the everyday torments of the homeless drug user. Although he admits that methadone may stabilise the lives of some users, for others its effects are more mixed. In some cases it can be counterproductive, resulting in long-term dependency affecting personal and intimate relations and often involving bouts of anger and depression. Bourgois also calls for a range of treatments to meet the needs of different individuals combined with employment initiatives, which he suggests would be more cost-effective than continually recycling this population through medical and criminal justice institutions.

Arguably, Bourgois aims to make a significant contribution to the way that drug use and drug cultures are conceived, at the same time he has made a valuable contribution to the policy debate. Bourgois offers a joined up approach that links theory, method and policy while engaging in a detailed and sensitive investigation into the troubled and, at times, desperate lives of the economically and socially marginalised. He is able to combine qualitative and quantitative approaches, to focus on both agency and structure and incorporate considerations of politics and power, while developing a reflexive methodology that allows him to link theory to practice.

From the information and insights that Bourgois has been able to glean from his long-term ethnographic research in specific locations, we can see that he is able to draw out general themes and identify causal relations associated with drug use by marginalised and homeless populations in deprived US inner-city areas. He identifies the complex processes and tensions involved as well as the individual and social effects of this kind of activity. He shows that different forms of drug taking are a function of identifiable social and economic determinants. However, he claims that general processes and structures do not come from outside localities and then impact them. Rather, the structures are to some extent constituted by the agents themselves. In this way the local and the idiographic provide insights into the workings of more general processes (Sayer 1991). By adopting an approach which focuses on process and specificity as well as culture and political economy, Bourgois provides a telling example of what might be identified as cultural realism.

Philippe Bourgois is, of course, not the only author who might be described as a cultural realist. John Braithwaite, amongst others, could also be described in these terms. Braithwaite's work (1989) on reintegrative shaming, which is based to some extent on an examination of Japanese culture and its system of informal control, and his analysis of the power of emotions in modifying behaviour, can be seen as particular forms of cultural criminology (Braithwaite and Braithwaite 2001). In an influential work on corporate crime (Braithwaite 2005), in which he engages in serious discussion of policy options and the limits of criminal sanctions, there is a strong realist component and a serious commitment to empirical investigation and intervention.

Conclusion

There is no doubt that cultural criminology has deepened and enriched criminological investigation on a number of levels. Drawing on the critical tradition in criminology, it has challenged contemporary criminology and called for a radical rethink of the criminological enterprise. Unfortunately, however, much of its work on crime and deviance, particularly in its earlier manifestation, reverts towards a 'left idealism' that romanticises the deviant while failing to provide a detailed examination of the operation of control agencies. Like much liberal criminology, it is governed by an anti-statism and anti-correctionalism that push it towards an oppositional and abolitionist stance, which in turn undermines its ability to engage in the reduction of crime and social suffering.

It has been suggested, however, by Hayward and Young (2012) that elements of cultural criminology could be combined with a realist criminology, resulting in what might be called cultural realism. This, however, is not just a question of meshing the two approaches, since there are some serious epistemological and methodological issues that need to be overcome if a marriage is to be realised. Works of Philippe Bourgois and John Braithwaite offer two examples of how cultural realism might be constructed. Although the authors draw on different aspects of culture and have a different theoretical orientation, both link theory, method and practice in a way that draws heavily on cultural considerations, with the aim of ultimately contributing to the policy process. For cultural criminology to move forward into a third stage, there is a need, it is argued, for researchers to incorporate their work within a realist framework in order to develop an approach that is more theoretically and methodologically consistent while being more socially and politically useful.

6
The Myth of Punitiveness Revisited

The problem of definition

Over the past few years there has been a steady stream of books and articles that have provided some commentary on what is referred to as either 'populist punitiveness' or 'penal populism' (Bottoms 1995; Pratt 2007; Pratt et al. 2005). Significantly, this growing body of literature involves little discussion about what exactly is meant by 'punitiveness'. Consequently, the concept remains what Marx would have called a 'chaotic conception'. That is, it remains a thin concept, lumping together the unrelated and inessential and unable to bear the explanatory weight that researchers put on it, ultimately leading to a form of analysis that descends into voluntarism. Thus, rather than identify the causal processes and mechanisms involved in the changing nature of crime control, these voluntaristic accounts see the main driver of crime-control policies as a product of the will of different individuals or groups.

The lack of definition means that potentially all forms of regulation can be included under the conceptual umbrella of 'punitiveness', thus encouraging the belief that a shift towards punitiveness has taken place. In some cases prisons and capital punishment are taken as examples of punitiveness, while in other cases community-based sanctions and alternatives to custody, such as probation, are given as examples (Martinovic 2002). When most commentators speak of punitiveness, they seem to have in mind the deliberate infliction of pain and suffering on individuals, but since it is often used as a blanket concept there is little differentiation or recognition of the different intensity, purpose and effects of different types of crime-control measures.

The considerable evidence of what might reasonably be construed as examples of non-punitive policies – including welfare interventions, the widespread deployment of rehabilitative efforts in prisons, the increased use of surveillance and monitoring strategies, the growing use of diversion programmes and use of drug courts and community-based sanctions – the growth of informal and restorative justice and the increasing emphasis on crime prevention (none of which is designed to be overtly punitive in the sense of inflicting more pain and suffering on offenders) tends to be ignored or downplayed by those whose selective vision sees examples of punitiveness everywhere. It would, of course, be surprising if one could not find some examples of get-tough policies in a system designed to punish and correct problematic behaviour. However, there is a worrying tendency in the crime-control literature to desperately seek out examples of punitiveness while simultaneously ignoring the diversity of current crime-control measures. It is important in this context to distinguish *intentions* and *outcomes*. The history of penal reform teaches us that even well-intentioned interventions can have unexpected outcomes (Cohen 1985).

Many commentators, including those critical of the notion of punitiveness, find themselves trapped in a punitive/non-punitive dichotomy. The failure to engage with the counterfactual results in the construction of a simple zero-sum form of explanation, which is no doubt part of its attraction (Zedner 2002). The complexities, contradictions and tensions in emerging criminal justice policy thereby remain largely unexplored. Alternatively, those that see strategies of crime control only in terms of punitiveness tend to locate these policies along a punitive continuum, resulting in a form of one-dimensional criminology.

The aim of this chapter is to suggest that trying to explain the complexities of the changing nature of crime control predominantly in terms of the undefined notion of punitiveness leads to a conceptual cul-de-sac. Following previous critiques that suggest the notion of punitiveness is deficient and unduly constraining, this chapter argues that the growing body of literature which has adopted the notion of punitiveness as an organising concept for explaining the changing nature of crime- control has failed to develop our understanding in a meaningful way and is ultimately built on a foundation of sand (Matthews 2005). This debate, however, extends far beyond the limitations of the notion of punitiveness and the growing number of publications that have focused on it. The widespread reliance on this chaotic conception is indicative of the theoretical malaise within criminology in general and liberal criminology in particular.

Missing the punitive turn?

In a recent publication entitled *The New Punitiveness* (Pratt et al. 2005), we find an interesting mix of articles. Although it appears that this collection was designed to map the increase in punitiveness in different countries, it contains a number of articles that point out that some countries, including Canada, Italy and Scandinavia, had 'missed the punitive turn'. Despite the fact that these countries had experienced all or some of the same social, economic and political changes identified as the basis for the apparent rise in punitiveness in both America and the United Kingdom, little evidence was found that would suggest that changes in criminal justice policy in these countries have been associated with what might be seen as punitiveness.

Indeed, the prison population in Canada has remained relatively stable since 1960. Although there has been some tough rhetoric from politicians over the past two decades, Canadians have maintained a balanced approach, combining a commitment to the values of opportunity and diversity with an emphasis on rehabilitation and therapeutic interventions (Doob and Webster 2006; Meyer and O'Malley 2005; Moore and Hannah-Moffat 2005). Over the same period Scandinavia has maintained a relative stability in its use of incarceration even in a context of increasing recorded crime rates. The continuing low level of incarceration is combined with strong support for welfare programmes and a culture of tolerance (Bondeson 2005).

Prison populations in Scandinavian countries have been relatively low for many years. However, rather than seeing these countries as being more tolerant and less punitive, John Pratt (2008) has argued that they are examples of 'exceptionalism'. He maintains that they are increasingly coming under pressure from a number of forces, including high levels of immigration combined with neoliberal influences, to become more punitive. Weakening solidarity combined with a decreasing tolerance of the use of illicit drugs has served to increase punitiveness in recent years, which in turn has increased the prison population. Yet, while there has been a slight increase in the rate of imprisonment in Norway since 1990, it remains relatively low by international standards. In Finland the prison population decreased during the 1990s, though there has been a marginal increase since 2000 (Lappi-Seppälä 2007) and even Pratt describes Finland as 'the new standard bearer in penal tolerance and leniency' by advocating decarceration and promoting prisoners' rights.

Italy, where there appears to be an increase in recent years of 'benevolent tolerance' towards young Italians, provides an interesting example of non-punitiveness. The number of young Italians sent to prison has been going down since the 1970s, despite an increase in youth crime (Nelken 2005). The general presumption is that the use of custody should be avoided wherever possible for young people. While there is evidence of a relatively tolerant attitude towards youth crime, corporate and financial crime are often pursued with more rigour than in most neighbouring European countries. As Dario Melossi (2001) has argued after examining the differential use of imprisonment in Italy and the United States, levels of incarceration are a function of how 'cultural embeddedness' shapes specific policy orientations (Green 2009).

Thus, it is clear that a number of countries have not experienced what has been described as a 'punitive turn' in recent years. Although these examples are instructive in demonstrating the differing trends in criminal justice policy and practice, it is misleading to describe these countries as missing the punitive turn. Firstly, because the rise in punitiveness may be seen erroneously as a norm from which some countries deviate, and secondly because it assumes that punitiveness is a useful organising concept for thinking about recent changes in criminal justice policy.

Engaging with the counterfactual

Rather than spell out exactly what is meant by the concept of punitiveness or even provide a working definition, most who are drawn to the notion seem preoccupied with attempting to list various examples of punitiveness or, alternatively, devising more or less imaginative ways to measure it (King and Maruna 2009; Unnever and Cullen 2009). In this section the aim is to examine some of the measures that have been used to try to identify what has been variously described as punitiveness, punitivism and punitivity (Bosworth 2010; Kury and Shea 2011).

The scale of imprisonment is most commonly cited as a proxy for punitiveness. In some publications this simply takes the form of a head count of prison populations. Other, more detailed, accounts factor prison admissions and length of stay into the equation. As numerous publications have stated, the number of people incarcerated in America has increased fivefold in the past 25 years or so. However, as Figure 6.1 indicates, while there was a 77 per cent increase in the prison population between 1990 and 2000, the increase between 2000 and 2007 was

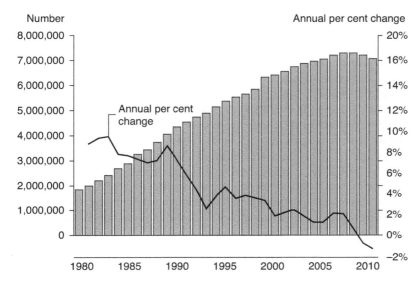

Figure 6.1   The levelling of the prison population in America
Source: Bureau of Justice.

only 4 per cent. The average annual increase from 2000 to 2010 was 1.3 per cent (Bureau of Justice 2012).

Paradoxically, it was during the levelling-off period that much of the literature on punitiveness was produced. Moreover, since 2007 the growth rate for prisons and jails has slowed, suggesting that the levelling of the US prison population is likely to be maintained (Justice Policy Institute 2009). Even in the late 1990s there was evidence that the number of people being sent to prison in the United States was beginning to stabilise (Blumstein and Beck 1999; Trachtenberg 2005).

Moreover, as Joan Petersilia (2003) has pointed out, about one in three new admissions to prison during the 1990s were for parole violation. Approximately 70 per cent of cases were the result of arrest or conviction for a new offence, but the other 30 per cent were for failing to report to the parole officer, absconding, or failing to maintain employment. If parole violators who were non-offenders are removed from the equation, it is apparent that in many American states the number of people in prison remained fairly stable or decreased during the second half of the 1990s. In fact, the number of new court admissions to state prisons increased slightly, from 350,431 in

2000 to 399,251 in 2011, while the number of parole violators admitted to prison was 203,569 in 2000, increasing to 247,851 in 2007 and then decreasing to 200,971 in 2011 (Bureau of Justice 2012).

Even without taking parole violations into account, a number of states have experienced noticeable reductions in prison populations since the turn of the century. During 1999 and 2000, 12 states experienced such a reduction (Mauer 2002; Gormesen 2007; Schiraldi 2003–2004). In 2002, 25 states reduced funding for prisons, and in 2003, 17 states either closed prisons or delayed prison construction (Jacobson 2006). This trend has continued. In 2011, 26 states reduced their prison population – most notably California. It is apparent that the main period of prison growth in America was 1980–1996; the signs are that during the subsequent period, when the punitiveness bandwagon was gaining momentum, prison populations in many parts of America were beginning to level off and in some cases were decreasing. Changes in New York exemplify this trend. Since 2000 the number of people in jails and prisons and on probation or parole has dropped markedly (Austin and Jacobson 2013). Interestingly, although the New York State prison population declined by 17 per cent between 2000 and 2009, sentence lengths and time served increased over the period. However, with the closure of ten prisons in 2011, the state's prison budget began to decrease. A decline in the number of felony arrests in New York City and a consequent decrease in prison admissions appears to lie behind the decreasing prison population in this period.

Natasha Frost (2008) has pointed out that the states with the highest rates of imprisonment are not necessarily those that rank highly on time served. In fact, she notes that there are considerable differences in the use of imprisonment for different crime types as well as variations between states that use longer terms of imprisonment for the relatively few 'serious' offences, while other states give longer sentences across the board. This observation raises questions about deploying the notion of punitiveness as an overarching explanation for changing use of imprisonment. As she notes:

> Although there is a substantial literature devoted to documenting, explaining and theorizing the changing nature of punishment over the past several decades, particularly in and across the United States, few who work in this area take the time to explain precisely what they mean by punitiveness. In the field of social science research where a premium is placed on the explicit conceptualization and operationalization of constructs, authors of studies on variations in punitiveness

have not given sufficient attention to detail in this regard. Scholars engaged in empirical research of this nature have instead typically appealed to a broad, general understanding of punitiveness. Granted, by definition to be punitive is to punish, and therefore, if we are punishing more we are becoming more punitive and vice versa. But this definition of punitiveness as simply 'punishing more' (and typically measured as 'imprisoning more') is too broad to be of much use. (Frost 2008: 278)

Frost suggests that the main reason those who use imprisonment rates to measure punitiveness do so is 'because they are accessible and simple to use'.

Examining the changing nature of punishment and penal policy over the last two decades, we find little evidence of a unilateral move to what might be described as punitiveness. Instead, we find a very mixed range of criminal justice policies, which Pat O'Malley (1999) has described as 'volatile and contradictory'. It would be more accurate to describe these policies as 'bifurcated' rather than simply punitive, but even recognising this does not do justice to the diversity and complexity of crime-control policies in different countries. Also, as David Nelken (2005) has pointed out, there is a need to consider the relation between formal and informal social control mechanisms in different countries if we wish to explore the notion of 'populist punitiveness', since a toughening of formal sanctions in some countries may accompany the simultaneous liberalising of informal sanctions.

It is also the case that probation and parole, described as alternatives to custody or community-based sanctions, are often advocated by penal reformers in place of the 'punitive' sanction of imprisonment. Although they involve placing convicted offenders under some form of state control, probation and parole are seen as more moderate sanctions. In a sense, therefore, the fact that the scale and rate of growth of probation, for example, is significantly greater than the growth of imprisonment over the last two decades suggests that the most significant area of expansion in the US penal system lies not with the archetypal punitive sanction – the prison – as with more moderate sanctions involving community-based penalties (see Figure 6.2).

Another way to study the punitiveness thesis is to examine cross-national data on the use of imprisonment for different offences. Frequently, international league tables are produced to show the countries with the highest rate of incarceration per 100,000 population. Top of the table in 2006 was the United States, with an incarceration

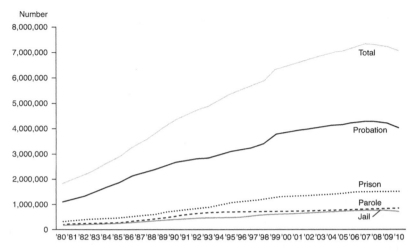

Figure 6.2   Adult correctional population on probation, in jail or in prison, or on parole, 1980–2010

Source: Bureau of Justice Statistics.

rate over 700 per 100,000. England and Wales were relatively high on the list, with 148 per 100,000 population. Towards the bottom are Japan, Ireland, Norway and Finland, with prison populations under 80 per 100,000 population (Walmsley 2006). The repeated message attached to the dissemination of these lists is that countries at or near the top are overly punitive and should seek ways to reduce their prison population. However, such comparisons tend to ignore the varying level and nature of crime. America, for example, has a level of violent crime – even after the crime drop – five or six times higher than that of most European countries. As Ken Pease (1994) has pointed out, countries have markedly different systems for processing and filtering out offenders, and any consideration of punitiveness should take into consideration the time actually served as well as the rate of imprisonment. Thus Pease, writing in the early 1990s, concluded that while England and Wales score highly on the imprisonment rate per 100,000 population, with discretionary release taken into account, the severity of sentencing for all offences except homicide is lower than in several other European countries.

In a more recent cross-national study of imprisonment rates, Alfred Blumstein and his colleagues (2005) make a similar point. Using three indicators of punitiveness – convictions per crime, commitments to prison per conviction, average time served per commitment – they concluded that America is more punitive than other countries, particularly when measured in terms of average time served per conviction. However, Blumstein and his colleagues note there is little consistency in relation to the, arguably limited, measures of punitiveness, with some countries having a low propensity to send people to prison while giving out relatively long prison sentences. In the same vein, it was found that some countries are highly punitive towards some types of crime but non-punitive towards others. This suggests that attitudes to crime and punishment vary from country to country and that the range of attitudes in play cannot be adequately captured by a punitive/non-punitive dichotomy. Clearly, different countries display a different set of responses at different stages of the criminal justice process (Whitman 2003).

Besides imprisonment rates the other widely used point of reference in the punitiveness literature is sentencing. Sentences are seen as getting tougher. The introduction of mandatory sentencing, whether in the form of three-strikes or so-called truth-in-sentencing legislation, is widely seen as encouraging the judiciary to increase sentence lengths, to use immediate custodial options more readily and to reduce the period of remission. These examples of get-tough sentencing, it is often argued, underpin the growth of imprisonment in recent years.

However, recent research on the impact of changes to sentencing policy in the United States has found that these developments involve more rhetoric than reality. In relation to three-strikes legislation, for example, it has been found that many of the states in which this policy was introduced already heavily punished repeat offenders. As James Austin and his colleagues have pointed out:

> The national movement towards three-strikes and you're out legislation has been a symbolic campaign that has had little if any effect on the criminal justice system or public safety. With the noted exception of California, all of the States followed the initial lead of the State of Washington by carefully wording their legislative reforms to ensure that few offenders would be impacted by the law. Contrary to the perceptions of the public and policy makers, there are very few offenders who have a prior conviction for very serious crimes and then repeat the crime. In those rare instances that fit this profile, states already had the capacity to and were sentencing such offenders to very lengthy prison terms. (Austin et al. 1999: 158)

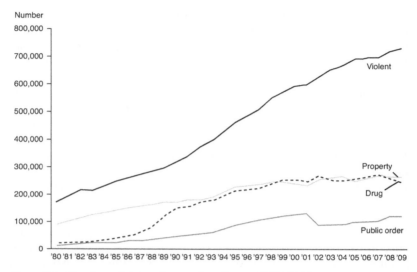

Figure 6.3   Number of state prisoners by offence, 1980–2009
Source: Bureau of Justice Statistics.

It has become evident that sentencers maintain a considerable amount of discretion when passing sentence, even when determinate and mandatory sentences are in force, and that these sentencing styles may well serve to extend rather than restrict the powers of the judiciary. Although there is some evidence that three-strikes laws may have had some impact in relation to drug offences, they apparently had little impact on violent offences. It has also been argued that truth-in-sentencing policies have had little or no impact on incarceration (Sorensen and Steman 2002). More recently many states have modified repressive anti-drug laws and adopted parole and probation reforms.

A number of commentators have placed a great deal of emphasis on the war on drugs, claiming that the preoccupation with getting tough on crack cocaine – the drug of choice for inner-city African Americans – largely accounts for the growth of imprisonment during the 1990s and the increasing level of racial disproportionality in US prisons (Tonry 1995; Mauer 1999). However, as Figure 6.3 indicates, an increased proportion of the prison population since 1990 involves those convicted of violent rather than drug-related offences. In 2010 over half, 53 per cent, of those incarcerated in state and federal prisons were convicted of violent offences (Bureau of Justice 2012). In addition, it has been pointed out that even among the million or so non-violent offenders currently in US prisons, approximately a third have a history of arrest for violent crime (Durose and Murnola 2004). The number of people sent to prison in this period for drug-related offences is admittedly high, but as their sentences are, on average, shorter than given to those convicted of violence, they will tend to make up a smaller proportion of the prison population. As James Jacobs (2001) has argued, liberal criminologists tend to focus on drugs rather than violence because there is less consensus in relation to the use of imprisonment for drug-related offences, with the consequence that the increased use of incarceration appears arbitrary, unjustified and repressive.

In England and Wales evidence has been presented of increasing sentence lengths for different offence categories. This finding is taken as prima facie evidence that sentencers are becoming more punitive (Millie et al. 2003). However, a number of the reasons why sentence lengths and the use of immediate custody are increasing may have little or nothing to do with punitiveness. First is that the number and seriousness of imprisonable cases coming before the courts is increasing. It may well be that the increased length of sentence for some offences that occurred towards the end of the 1990s may have been a function of more serious cases of violence coming before the courts, as the sentencers themselves have claimed, rather than an example of harsher sentences (Millie et al. 2003). Since it is difficult to measure the changing seriousness of offending and because the category of violence is itself so wide, it is hard to assess whether there has been a significant change in the seriousness of cases coming before the courts. However, it is not enough to compare falling crime rates and rising rates of imprisonment and conclude that punitiveness is increasing. This is an example of inverted empiricism. It is necessary to at least examine the rate of attrition at various stages of the criminal justice system, focusing in particular on arrest, conviction, the proportional use of custody and length of time served.

The findings of a study on attrition rates in England and Wales carried out by David Farrington and Darrick Joliffe (2005) present a mixed picture. The custody rate per 1,000 offenders increased in the 1990s for burglary, vehicle theft and assault but decreased for robbery and rape. Average time served increased by about 20 per cent for burglary, vehicle theft and rape, it remained roughly stable for robbery and decreased nearly 30 per cent for assault. In the United States in the 1990s the custody percentage per conviction fell for burglary while the average time served also decreased significantly. For robbery the proportion given custody per conviction declined slightly, and average time served per conviction decreased markedly (Tonry and Farrington 2004).

Patrick Langham (2005), in his examination of crime and punishment trends in the United States between 1981 and 1996, found that the average time served for residential burglary, assault and robbery decreased slightly between 1990 and 1996, while the average time served for rape and homicide increased. Langham concludes that punishment severity changed little over the period 1981–1996, when incarceration rates increased most dramatically in the United States. He suggests that changes in what he calls risk factors – arrest rate, conviction rate, custody rate and total number of days served by offenders before being released – have had the most effect on scale of imprisonment. These cross-national studies indicate, however, that sentencing practice in England, Wales and the United States has become increasingly bifurcated and differentiated in recent years, and therefore it seems inappropriate to characterise sentencing policy simply as getting tough or as an expression of undifferentiated punitiveness.

There are, however, two other related considerations that should be taken into account when looking at sentence lengths and time served. The first is the number of repeat offenders coming before the courts, and the second, the level of recidivism. A significant but rarely explored variable in the sentencing process is the degree of persistence. In relation to the cumulative principle of sentencing, if offenders repeatedly appear in court for the same offence it is predictable that sentence lengths will increase over time (Ashworth 1983; Wasik 2004). According to the cumulative principle, those who repeatedly offend will be punished more severely even if the offence is the same. In England and Wales, for example, the number of offenders coming before the courts with fifteen or more previous convictions increased from 9 to 19 per cent for violence, 12 to 19 per cent for drug offences; 22 to 36 per cent for burglary and 22 to 36 per cent for handling stolen goods between 2000 and 2007 (Ministry of Justice 2008). It was reported in October 2013 that in England and Wales more than 148,000 offenders had fifteen or more previous convictions or cautions (Ford 2013). This is a significant development and requires further investigation, since it suggests that the increase in the use of imprisonment and time served may have little to do with the crime level or the punitiveness of sentences. It may be a function of routinely applying the long-established principle that repeat offenders be punished more severely (Roberts 2003).

A similar line of argument can be developed in relation to recidivism. Even for offenders who have a lower level of court appearances, a return to court after leaving prison is likely to result in a comparatively longer sentence. Despite recent attempts to increase the level of resettlement and reduce the re-entry of ex-prisoners, the continuing high levels of recidivism are, no doubt, having an impact on sentencing practices. In England, Wales and the United States there is evidence that the continuing high levels of recidivism, particularly in relation to violent offenders, almost certainly have had an impact on the use of custody and the period of time served (Cuppleditch and Evans 2005; Langham and Levin 2002).

In relation to sentencing there have been significant changes in the United Kingdom in response to mounting critiques of the justice system on the grounds that it is not cost-effective, not preventative and not efficient. These challenges have led to changes in the scope of the criminal law and criminal procedure, changes in the relationship between state and citizen and changes in the nature of the state itself. They include a greater use of diversion, fixed penalties, summary trials and hybrid civil–criminal procedures, increased incentives to plead guilty and preventive orders (Ashworth and Zedner 2008). These developments have been stimulated by the 'justice gap', a term referring to the perceived inefficiency and uncertainty of the trial process (Crown Prosecution Service 2011). In addition, the publication in 2007 of Baroness Corston's report, which advocates greater use of diversion of women offenders and the establishment of women's centres, has provided a rationale for the creation of a number of pilot projects to divert women from courts and prisons (Easton et al. 2010). Corston's widely accepted claim that the nature of women's offending is significantly different from that of their male counterparts reflects the adoption of a more tolerant attitude to female offending rather than an expression of punitiveness.

Apart from making reference to the growth of imprisonment and changes in sentencing practices, a number of other examples of punitiveness that have been presented have tended to be short lived, sporadic or exaggerated. Zero-tolerance policing, for example, which is associated with the period when Rudolph Giuliani was Mayor of New York, has been phased out. Similarly in the United Kingdom zero-tolerance policing was introduced in one area (Hartlepool) but was abandoned after a couple of years; the police commander, Ray Mallon, was sacked (Stenson 2000). Boot camps were experimented with in America during the 1990s but failed to produce appreciable effects and have been discontinued (Austin 2000). The United Kingdom also experimented with boot camps, but they were quickly closed down before they could become established (Farrington et al. 2002). Anti-social behaviour orders (ASBOs), heralded as an example of a particularly punitive sanction, have also been relatively short lived; the numbers issued have tailed off in the last few years. Also, an ASBO is not a single sanction but a package. It includes preventive and spatial components that are designed to act as both a warning and a punishment (Matthews et al. 2007).

Although ASBOs received the most media and academic attention, there were only 21,508 issued between 2001 and 2011. In England and Wales the most widely used sanction for anti-social behaviour in this period was the Acceptable Behaviour Contract (ABC) – it had no specific statutory basis but involved an informal voluntary agreement between specific individuals and the police and other local agencies – a new form of which has become known as 'contractual governance' (Crawford 2003).

It is the case, however, that there is growing evidence of liberalising tendencies in the crime-control area and that get-tough policies have diminishing support (Listwan et al. 2008). Apart from the demise of zero-tolerance policing and boot camps, there has been declining support for three-strikes legislation. Since 1995 no American state has enacted a three-strikes law. Since then a number of states have passed legislation decreasing the length of sentence for drug and/or low-level offenders (Greene and Schiraldi 2002; Kasindorf 2002). There is renewed focus on rehabilitation in prisons and a move to deinstitutionalise juveniles in some locations. Drug courts and drug diversion strategies have been implemented in Maryland, Arizona and California, and attempts to reduce re-entry have become a priority in many states. The Criminal Justice Reinvestment Act (2010) and the Second Chance Act (2007) seek to address the socio-economic basis of high-crime neighbourhoods and expand re-entry services to all offenders, regardless of charge type (Cadora 2014). There is a growing emphasis on crime prevention and the diversion of offenders away from crime. As Shelley Listwan and her colleagues note:

> In short, it is significant that many jurisdictions are reconsidering the prudence of criminal justice policies that seek to deal with crime through mere discipline, harsh punishment, and rigidly opposed prison sentences. Equally salient, however, is that state and federal legislatures are also introducing and implementing new policies that focus on the rehabilitation and support of offenders. These new progressive policies call into question the common misconception that the United States is strictly a punitive society. (Listwan et al. 2008: 433)

It has been suggested that the main reason for limiting prison growth and developing diversionary and community-based alternatives to custody

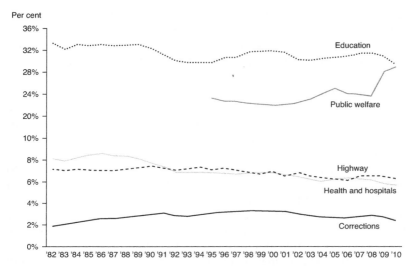

Figure 6.4 State expenditures by function in the United States
Source: Bureau of Justice Statistics.

in America is the increasing fiscal crisis. Although there can be no doubt that most states are under considerable pressure to cut expenditure, the prison population had already levelled off and radical sentencing reforms were already under way in many states prior to the fiscal crisis. Expenditure on corrections has dropped steadily in the United States since the turn of the century. Explaining these policy shifts primarily in terms of fiscal constraints is too simplistic. The fact that a large amount of money is being spent on drug courts and community sentences in a situation in which approximately four million people in America are already under some form of community-based supervision suggests that the motivation to limit prison use is driven by other considerations than saving money (King 2009). The present financial constraints, however, will no doubt provide motivation and justification to continue prison reductions (Scott-Hayward 2009).

In many states there has not been so much a reduction of expenditure as a change of funding patterns, producing a mixed economy of service provision (Harris and McDonald 2000). As Figure 6.4 indicates, while expenditure on corrections has decreased, expenditure on public welfare has increased from approximately 22 per cent of state expenditures in 2000 to 31 per cent in 2010. These figures appear to qualify, if not negate, Loic Wacquant's (2009) claim that the decline in welfare expenditure has pushed up the prison population. Indeed, it is very difficult to find anybody these days who claims that prison works or who advocates prison expansion. Even hard-line conservative criminologists like John Dilulio (1999) are saying enough is enough in relation to the use of imprisonment.

The critical question, however, is not whether we can provide specific examples of punitive or non-punitive policies but whether we can demonstrate a qualitative shift in the nature of punishment over the last decade or so. That is, if claims for the punitiveness thesis are to move beyond a shopping list of specific examples, advocates need to demonstrate that there has been a systematic and concerted shift in recent years towards get-tough policies and that this approach has been dominant. An examination of the counterfactual evidence suggests that over the last decade – the period in which, many writers claim, we have witnessed a surge in punitiveness – the situation appears to be that crime-control policies may, if anything, have become more liberal and more diverse on both sides of the Atlantic.

Changing public attitudes

In opposition to the claim that the public and politicians are becoming more punitive, there is a growing body of evidence that concern with crime is slipping and is becoming less of a political priority for the general public. Indeed, the signs are that as the crime rate drops and attention turns increasingly to wider issues of security and anti-social behaviour, we are moving into a 'pre-crime' society, where the aim is to prevent rather than get tough on crime (Zedner 2007). During the last three US presidential elections, the issue of crime has been conspicuously absent; it has also been much less prominent in the last two UK general elections. At the same time research on US public attitudes reveals that whereas some 37 per cent of the population identified crime as a major issue in 1994, by 2004 only 2 per cent identified it as such (Jacobson 2006). According to Marc Mauer of the Sentencing Project:

> As a result of lowered public concern with crime, the issue has now lost some of its political saliency and usefulness to politicians. This was probably most prominently observed in the 2000 presidential debates, in which, aside from the obligatory defense of the death penalty's supposed deterrent effect by two candidates, there was essentially no discussion at all of crime. (Mauer 2002: 2)

Mauer (2002) argues that sentencing options were once largely limited to incarceration and probation but now a broad range of choice exists in many courtrooms. Community service and restitution programmes are commonplace, and the rapid expansion of drug courts in the 1990s has put into effect a model that demonstrates that court-supervised treatment is often preferable to a period of incarceration. A UK public opinion survey found a widespread belief that prisons do little to reduce crime (Glover 2007). Opposition to the prison system was found to be particularly pronounced amongst women, with almost 60 per cent advocating the use of non-custodial forms of punishment for convicted offenders.

One of the recurring themes in the punitiveness literature is that power has shifted away from established elites and that there has been a general drift towards populism (Garland 2001; Ryan 2003). Another current of criminological thought claims that we are moving rapidly into a risk-orientated criminal justice system and that this form of actuarialism provides the basis for more effective management of marginalised populations (Feeley and Simon 1992). On one level these two claims appear incompatible, since one suggests the distillation of power downwards, towards the general public, while the other suggests that a newly emerging risk-based discourse is providing a repertoire for governance which is largely removed from the language that the general public employs to express views on crime and its control. Thus it might seem that the general development of actuarialism has provided professionals with a new language which both distances the general public while bolstering their professional status. Indeed, as Simon and Feeley (1995) point out, popular discourse about crime remains largely rooted in individualistic moral discourse concerned with the efficacy of punishment, while the discourse of actuarialism provides no compelling moral vision and focuses attention not so much on the individual as on social groups. Actuarial discourse is not designed to provide an understanding of the crime problem as such. Rather, it provides a way of anticipating and managing it. The ascendancy of actuarialism, therefore, does little to engage the general public or provide much in the way of reassurance, since it tends to draw attention to system failures (O'Malley 2004).

Significantly, one of the growing concerns of governments since the 1990s is not so much the shift towards populism as the perceived scepticism and indifference of the general public towards the operation of the criminal justice system (Hutton 2005). The Home Office in England and Wales, for example, developed an ongoing research programme to gauge the level of public confidence in the operation of criminal justice agencies and institutions. The local state has invested considerable effort in developing what is referred to as 'community engagement' (Forrest et al. 2005; Mirrlees-Black 2001). Engaging members of the community in criminal justice events has proved to have very limited success, particularly amongst 'hard-to-reach' groups. Needless to say, the majority of those who do engage with official bodies tend to be those least affected by crime.

Alongside the growth of risk-orientated discourses has been the steady growth of new forms of managerialism tied to performance indicators and the realisation of set targets. New public management (NPM), as it is often referred to, has also established a changing rationale of governance and developed new practices (Cheliotis 2006; McLaughlin and Murji 2001). It appears to offer a more rigorous and focused approach, which provides professionals with a set of working practices that insulates them from public involvement while offering a largely spurious accountability. The performance indicators and targets are set, in most cases, with little or no reference to the public interest. When the public is consulted, the objective of consultation appears to be to reaffirm or legitimise existing policies and practices. Drawing on management styles in the private sector, NPM is linked to the what works agenda and it is claimed that policies are based on hard evidence, not public sentiments (Pitts 2007; Hope 2004). NPM also favours privatisation and the contracting-out of services, emphasising cost effectiveness while creating a growing complex of objectives, evaluation and decision-making criteria that, in general, make public scrutiny and public engagement more difficult. In short, what we have seen since 1990 or so has been not a pronounced shift towards populism but the development of a new configuration of discourses and practices that have further alienated large sections of the public while reaffirming the authority of a new breed of experts, whose decision making is largely removed from public scrutiny.

Conclusion

In conclusion, it has been argued that, first, imprisonment rates are levelling off in the United States, with prison populations and prison expenditure actually decreasing in some states. Second, that there is considerable evidence that crime is slipping down the statistical, social and political agenda. Third, that it is very difficult these days to find politicians or policymakers advocating prison expansion. When politicians announce the building of a new prison, for example, they are normally apologetic. Significantly, the UK Conservative-led neo-liberal government elected in 2007 was on course to reduce the size of the prison estate, and froze plans to build new prisons (Helm, Asthana and Townsend 2010).

The general public has historically had little impact on crime-control policies as policymakers are well insulated from public involvement. There are, however, growing concerns amongst policymakers about public indifference and lack of confidence in the operation of the criminal justice system. At the same time the criminal justice and penal systems have fostered a new body of experts; they may wear jeans and trainers, but they are no less experts. After examining penal trends in different countries, Michael Tonry (2007) concluded:

> Many of the generalizations bandied about in discussions of penal policy in Western countries are not true. If penal populism or populist punitiveness exists at all, it is mostly as reifications in academics' minds of other academics' ideas. (Tonry 2007: 1)

Indeed, the punitiveness debate has mystified rather than clarified recent developments in crime control. Rather than engage in serious investigation of the processes that have pushed up the prison population in certain countries, it has either reduced the changing forms of crime control to the wills, attitudes and interests of policymakers and the general public or, alternatively, sought to explain shifts in the nature of penal policies by reference to a very broad set of determinants – neoliberalism, the level of welfare expenditure, postmodern anxiety and the like – without examining the mediations. The punitivism literature has, however, made a major contribution to the growth of 'so what?' criminology (Currie 2007; Matthews 2009). To this we might add that the empirical reference points used to support the punitiveness thesis have been extremely selective and often short lived. For the most part the complexities of the changing nature of crime control and public attitudes are reduced to a simple punitive/non-punitive dichotomy.

Indicatively, the policy implications of the punitiveness thesis tend to be weak. On the assumption that the main driving force behind recent policy developments has been a widespread punitive intent, the logical consequence has been to call for greater moderation and increased levels of tolerance (Loader 2010). However, since it is hard to find people these days who see themselves as particularly punitive, these pleas will no doubt fall on deaf ears. Thus, rather than provide an analysis of the complex and contradictory processes that have produced the current situation – which might be helpful to policymakers who want to instigate reforms – these accounts descend into voluntarism. The expression 'punitive responses to crime' jars liberal sensibilities, since it is generally seen as an undesirable expression of state power. However, it is arguably the case that in relation to domestic violence, child abuse, tax evasion and the like, increased sanctions would be appropriate.

In short, the populist-punitivism thesis does not provide a very useful or accurate form of explanation. Inadvertently, it can lead to a justification of rather than a reduction in punitive policies since, by making claims that the general public is essentially punitive, it provides moral justification for politicians and policymakers to develop tougher policies. What at first sight appears a critique of punitive policies ultimately provides a justification for such policies.

Thus, the real failure of this debate is that it has diverted attention away from a detailed understanding of the changing forms of crime-control and encouraged the belief that we are dominated by a punitive public and maverick politicians and that there is little scope for change. In many respects this debate represents the limitations of liberal criminology, which has come to dominate academic criminology in recent years. The attraction of the punitiveness thesis is that it appeals to all kinds of liberals. It allows the expression of opposition to harsh or cruel sanctions directed against the poor and marginalised (which satisfies the humanists), it provides a platform for exposing the intellectual or practical problems associated with contemporary forms of punishment (which cheers up the pessimists), and it allows criminologists to expose the apparent ineptitude of politicians and the presumed ignorance of the general public (which satisfies the radicals). This allows them to take the moral high ground and act as educators for a misguided populace. With the general tendency in the liberal camp towards anti-statism as well as anti-punishment, the focus on punitiveness provides a way to pursue these objectives.

If there is something most criminologists agree on, it is that we are in a period of transformation and that the forms of regulation in place during much of the twentieth century are being replaced or at least reconfigured by new control strategies. Where criminologists tend to disagree, however, is in accounting for this change. There is little consensus concerning the nature and direction of change. However, there are signs that the prison population is decreasing in parts of the United States, and there are considerable reservations in the United Kingdom and elsewhere about building more prisons. At the same time we have seen the introduction on both sides of the Atlantic of new sentencing policies, which have moved away from mandatory and determinant sentencing towards adoption of diversionary strategies. In broader terms there appears to be a move towards prevention of crime rather than processing offenders through a cumbersome and expensive criminal justice system, as well as towards what Gilles Deleuze (1995) has described as the 'control society', in which the dominant mode of regulation is continuous and post-disciplinary and involves forms of deinstitutionalisation. This mode of regulation 'corresponds', as Rusche and Kirchheimer (2003) would say, with the changing nature of productive relations associated with post-Fordism and the development of the information society.

7
Governing the Present

Governing through crime?

There is a line of continuity between the claims made by Stuart Hall and his colleagues in their classic *Policing the Crisis* (1978) and Jonathan Simon's widely referenced *Governing through Crime* (2008). Both publications argue that law and order has become a prominent feature of social and political life and an increasingly central part of the state's strategy for governing civil society. Both publications see the growing focus on crime control as a moral panic and argue that a focus on crime, victimisation and fear of crime allows the state to engage in new and extended forms of hegemonic control (Brown 2008). Both publications aim to provide an ostensibly radical attack on claims by the state and of realist and other criminologists that tackling crime and victimisation are an intrinsically positive objective. The difference between the two approaches is, however, that when Hall and his colleagues were writing these claims had a certain validity, while by the time Simon was developing his 'governing through crime' thesis there had been a move away from a law and order society, involving a significant shift in the culture of control.

The war on crime, in combination with the war on drugs, has, Simon argues, created a climate of fear in America and justified an array of restrictive interventions and controls. Despite the billions of dollars spent on crime control, he argues there is no evidence that people are any safer. Instead, he suggests the war on crime has transformed social life and justified more intrusive intervention into families, schools and workplaces – all of which have become increasingly subject to different forms of criminalisation. He boldly claims that:

Governing through crime is making America less democratic and more racially polarised; it is exhausting social capital and repressing our capacity for innovation. For all that, governing through crime does not, and I believe, cannot make us more secure. Indeed it fuels the culture of fear and control that inevitably lowers the threshold of fear as it places greater and greater burdens on ordinary Americans. (Simon 2007: 6)

Thus, the war on crime is seen as largely responsible for transforming post-war America. Simon admits at one point that his thesis is 'polemical and overstated', but can we accept that the war on crime is central to the changing forms of governance in America and has it fuelled racial divisions and undermined democratic relations?

In response to these and related questions, it will be argued that not only is Simon's thesis overstated and one-sided but his explanation of the changing nature of crime control and its impact is misdirected. It is undeniable that a preoccupation with crime control grew from the mid-1960s through the mid-1990s on both sides of the Atlantic, but from the time Simon first coined the term 'governing through crime' in the late 1990s to the publication of his book in 2007, recorded crime not only declined statistically but also significantly decreased as an object of social and political interest (Caplow and Simon 1999).

What is significant about Simon's thesis is that he sees the growing preoccupation with crime in the 1960s onwards in overwhelmingly negative terms. He describes this development as having 'distorted American institutional priorities'. In particular, he claims that the war on crime has reshaped private and social lives and transformed the social meaning of race, thus exacerbating long-standing divisions within American society (Frampton et al. 2008). In addition, the war on crime is blamed for fuelling the development of mass incarceration and for being responsible for the collateral damage that comes from having over two million people – drawn disproportionately from ethnic minorities – in prison.

For Simon, the war on crime has been a disaster, and all forms of crime control, even well-meaning policies, have had negative outcomes. He makes little distinction between desirable and undesirable forms of crime control. In addition, along with David Garland (2001), he sees the growing focus on the victim – which critical criminologists argued for in the 1970s and 1980s – as a largely negative development responsible for mobilising and orchestrating ever more intrusive interventions into our private lives (Christie 1977; Walklate 2007). By casting all forms of crime control as ultimately negative, he gravitates towards a position that denies the validity of victimisation and is sceptical of all forms of state-centred crime-control policies.

While there can be little doubt that mass incarceration and the so-called war on crime have had a significant impact on social and civic life in America, it should be recognised that the neighbourhoods most affected by criminal justice policies are generally those with the highest levels of serious crime and predatory violence (Weaver et al. 2014; Peterson and Krivo 2010). Thus, we need to consider the social and civic effects of not taking crime seriously and of not protecting the poor and the vulnerable. The difficult issue Simon and others fail to address is balancing the effects of criminal justice intervention against widespread victimisation and social security.

Domestic abuse

Let us examine domestic abuse. Simon maintains that the criminalisation of domestic abuse has misfired. The forms of criminalisation and regulation that have been developed do not adequately deal with the complexity of domestic conflict, and in many cases they have served to complicate or exacerbate these issues. Overall, much of the legislation on domestic abuse, he argues, has been ineffective or counterproductive. In addition, the increasing 'governance of the family', as Simon calls it, has resulted in social workers becoming an extended arm of the police by reporting, and ultimately criminalising, domestic abuse.

There is little recognition in Simon's account of the prolonged struggles by feminists and other progressives to transform domestic violence from a private or domestic matter, beyond the reach of criminal law and police intervention, into an issue where women have recourse to the legal process and some level of protection. Legislation may be cumbersome, poorly implemented and in some cases not as effective as reformers had hoped, but this does not mean that this has not been a progressive and worthwhile achievement. In opposition to those liberals who dwell on the limitations and problems of regulating domestic violence, realists and feminists ask how to fashion policy and interventions so as to provide more effective forms of support and protection for victims.

We know that two of the major factors that increase the probability of victimisation are vulnerability and impunity (Sparks 1981; Pease 2007). The aim of intervention should be to reduce vulnerability and increase agency while removing the impunity of offenders. The argument of some liberal feminists that presenting women as victims somehow renders them passive and devoid of agency is misguided. Recognising domestic violence as a legitimate form of victimisation is a major step in addressing and reducing its prevalence. Without victim status there is no formal culpability.

It should be noted that increased intolerance of the abuse of women and children represents a social and cultural shift in many countries in the post-war period, which is a function of the growing emancipation of women and the greater valorisation of the young. This development involves a change of social norms that has, in turn, become codified in law. Without this normative shift, legislation would not have materialised or received widespread public support.

The increase in state regulation of domestic violence can be seen as a function of the 'crisis of the family' and changing gender roles, both inside and outside the domestic sphere (Campbell 1993). The crisis of the family is also linked to the changing nature of communities and patterns of employment, particularly those associated with the feminisation of the labour force. In this changed context, traditional domestic relations have been called into question, and new forms of conflict and tension in the domestic sphere have increased. We can identify similar arguments in relation to anti-racist legislation. Although there are considerable difficulties in mobilising this type of legislation, there can be little doubt that it has served to reduce the level of racial abuse and helped to promote the rights and security of racial minorities both in America and Britain.

The criminalisation of schools

Similar issues arise in relation to Simon's discussion of the 'criminalisation' of schools. According to him, the situation was prompted by reports of youthful violence in the 1960s and 1980s, the association of youth culture with drugs and trafficking and through a growing right-wing movement that depicts public schools as hotbeds of crime. The media, he suggests, have played upon these themes and fuelled fears, while the passing of the Safer Schools Act (1994), the Safe and Drug Free Schools and Communities Act (2002) and similar US legislation has consolidated these fears and drawn public attention to this issue. The Safer Schools Act hardened school discipline and fostered zero-tolerance approaches involving the use of metal detectors, increased surveillance, searches and a range of security measures that cast the school as a high-crime site with a ready supply of victims. In this process, Simon argues, the response has been disproportionate to the threat and has constructed a more direct pathway from the school to the prison for certain groups of young people.

There are three remarkable features of this account. First, there is no empirical assessment of the increasing level of serious incidents that have occurred in many schools in recent decades. Simon dismisses 'objective' assessments of the number of recorded incidents in schools and rejects surveys as unreliable. In this way, the changing nature of the management of school discipline appears arbitrary or unnecessary. Second, he places a great deal of weight on the effects of legislation rather than seeing legislation itself as the outcome of the changing values, sensibilities and interests of a range of actors, including teachers, parents, and the changed personal needs and circumstances of students. Thus criminalisation is not just a response to changes in legislation or government mandates but, as far as criminalisation can be said to be occurring, is a function of a number of determinants. The third feature of Simon's explanation is that it makes no reference to the international nature of these developments. Many countries around the world have had growing concerns about discipline in schools and the perceived problems of violence, drug use, weapon carrying, bullying and the like. The international nature of the concerns suggests that the changes Simon attempts to analyse have a deeper structural, social and cultural basis, which cannot be explained simply in terms of effects of specific legislation or peculiarities of American politics (Baker 2010).

While there are well-known limitations to the crime and victimisation surveys that have been carried out in schools and elsewhere, it is difficult to deny the reality and impact made by a number of shootings in America over the past two decades. There were 93 incidents in which a student murdered someone in school in the years 1992/3–2002/3, of which the Columbine shooting is probably the most dramatic and widely reported (Klein 2006; National Centre for Education Statistics 2007). These shootings, which shocked and concerned teachers, parents and fellow students are, however, only the tip of a very large iceberg of school violence in America. In 2009/10 approximately 90 per cent of middle and high schools in America reported incidents of serious violence, which involves rape, sexual battery, physical attack, fights with a weapon or robbery with a weapon. Some 10 per cent of these schools reported physical attacks with a weapon. In 2003–2004, 2,156 young people were excluded from school in the United States for firearms violations, and 3 per cent of females admitted carrying a weapon to school in the previous thirty days (Neiman and Hill 2011).

In the United Kingdom an online survey carried out in 2005 by the education and teachers-support network found that 45 per cent of teachers reported being threatened with violence; some 20 per cent of those responding said that they had been physically assaulted, and half said that school policies on bad behaviour had not been effectively enforced (Taylor 2005). Between 2007 and 2009 the police were called to deal with just under 3,000 arson attacks on schools across the United Kingdom (Lipsett 2009).

Simon argues that serious incidents are concentrated in schools in deprived inner-city areas. This may be so, but there is also a significant number of serious incidents, including those with weapons, in suburban and middle-class areas. Simon bemoans the fact that crime prevention and securitisation have become widespread features of schools in America. However, the problem is not only that serious violence is not limited to inner-city schools but that there is also little confidence about the prediction and distribution of violence in schools. Consequently, a responsible head teacher, board of governors or PTA is bound to want some degree of protection and safety for the students in their particular school.

What is significant, however, about the growing number of reported incidents of misbehaviour, including violence, in schools is how much of it is dealt with by the schools themselves. In the UK there is a widespread policy of inclusion in schools and considerable efforts are made to deal with issues in-house. The most common way of dealing with serious incidents is through suspension and exclusion. Suspensions are typically one to five days for incidents of fighting, bullying and racial and homophobic abuse, ten to fifteen days for attacking a teacher. Exclusions are normally for carrying a weapon, drug dealing or repeated violence and abuse. It should be noted that exclusion means keeping the pupil out of school for a period of up to thirty days. Thus exclusions are, in effect, long periods of suspension. So-called permanent exclusions normally involve transferring disruptive or violent pupils to another school in the locality. In the United Kingdom approximately 1,000 pupils are suspended every day and in 2008/9 there were 6,500 permanent exclusions (Department of Education 2011).

There is, however, considerable pressure on schools in the UK not to exclude students permanently, and the number of exclusions has decreased in recent years. Given the considerable effort and paperwork involved in permanently excluding pupils, it is likely that schools adopt this measure only in extreme cases. Also, the emphasis on inclusion in schools means that excluded pupils are seen as a sign of failure and consequently there is considerable informal and formal pressure on school managers to deal with issues in-house (Macrae et al. 2003). Metal detectors are rarely used in UK schools and searches are a relatively low-key way to identify those carrying weapons or dealing drugs. The introduction of community police officers in many schools has not had the effect of creating a police state, as some had feared. Rather, it provides relatively informal support for both staff and students. It is remarkable, given how many very serious incidents occur in schools, that there are so few formal arrests and prosecutions of students.

An examination of the changing forms of school regulation in recent decades leaves little doubt that there has been a change of (mis)behaviour on one hand, and a change of response on the other. We should not simply see a change of response as a shift from tolerance, which is good, to intolerance, seen as bad. We need to move away from the liberal notion that intolerance is undesirable and recognise that certain forms of intolerance are necessary to place parameters on acceptable behaviour. Indeed, the changing forms of discipline and security in schools can be seen not as a negative shift towards intolerance but as establishing normative boundaries and forming guidelines for acceptable conduct in a world in which many forms of interpersonal violence – as well as racial and gender abuse – have become socially less acceptable and more difficult to turn a blind eye to. Thus, rather than amount to wholesale criminalisation of schools, the regulation of violent and abusive behaviour is an exemplar of informal controls, involving a range of measures including detention, counselling, psychological testing, anti-bullying strategies, behavioural contracts and restorative justice techniques. All of this is a long way from criminalisation. Rather, it represents the adoption of a diverse range of interventions and sanctions, operating at different levels with different objectives.

As Paul Hirschfield has argued in opposition to Simon's state-controlled, top-down model of the criminalisation of schools, there is a need to understand the interests, motivations and involvement of the governed:

> At the school level, criminalisation is not merely accommodation to an altered level of government constraints, mandates and incentives. Isomorphic institutional changes in schools also follow the diffusion of professional and broader cultural norms and related changes in the perceived needs, behaviours and circumstances of their students. Federal laws like SDFSCA afford states and localities considerable

leeway in defining their own needs, goals and objectives, leaving such issues as metal detectors, drug sweeps, specific zero tolerance provisions and most other program-specific regulations up to local discretion. (Hirschfield 2008: 88)

Hirschfield also points out that most legislative responses to school deviance do not involve codification of new crimes or escalation of penalties. Rather, they involve developing a more formal response to certain activities that are already illegal, such as drug dealing and weapons possession.

There is some indication that the measures adopted in schools have had a positive effect. According to Bureau of Justice statistics (2013), the overall level of victimisation amongst school children aged twelve to eighteen in America decreased from approximately 9 per cent in 1995 to 4 per cent in 2011. In the same period the number of teachers who reported being threatened with an injury also decreased. Similarly, the Youth Violence Project (2011) reported that the rate of serious violent crime in 2007 was less than half that in 1994. The percentage of students who report carrying a weapon to school has gradually decreased since 1993, and reports of feeling afraid have declined in all groups over that period.

Whereas Simon claims that governing through crime has negatively affected the American democratic process, the reality is that crime control and victimisation reduction have played a significant role in encouraging public interest and participation in the political process. The growth of neighbourhood watch, local monitoring committees, mentoring projects, crime-related voluntary organisations, not to mention the jury system, have all served to increase public participation in the criminal justice process (Newman et al. 2004; Matthews et al. 2007).

By failing to differentiate between progressive and regressive forms of criminalisation, Simon's critique moves from a constructive discussion of the undesirable effects of crime control to an untenable and overly negative dismissal of many of the progressive gains that have limited abuse, suffering and victimisation (Ashworth 2000). Thus, the theoretical and political perspective Simon adopts fails to do justice to the complexity of recent developments. His 'governing through crime' thesis, while recognising the way law and order has become a central focus of our lives, fails to fully grasp its significance or implications. In addition, developments have occurred over the last decade or so – during the period Simon was writing *Governing through*

Crime – that further detract from his thesis and suggest that social, political and legal regulation is taking a significantly different direction from the one he suggests. These developments include (a) changes in the social and political significance of crime in contemporary society; (b) a shift towards crime prevention, security and 'pre-crime'; (c) a growing focus on anti-social behaviour, disorder and incivilities; (d) an increased preoccupation with regulating health and lifestyles; and (e) changes in the nature of regulation in and beyond the state.

The changing social and political significance of crime

The most significant development in living memory in relation to crime has been the crime drop. The fact that nearly all forms of recorded crime have decreased significantly in this period in virtually all US states and the United Kingdom suggests a qualitative shift not only in offending behaviour but also in the culture of control (Blumstein and Wallman 2000). Simon makes little reference to this dramatic decrease in most forms of victimisation, instead his argument centres on an apparent increase in the fear of crime. However, the whole focus on the fear of crime and the way it is measured and portrayed has been increasingly questioned by criminologists (Lee 2007). Recent research suggests that the response to criminal victimisation involves a range of emotional responses, including anger and frustration. Fear is far from the most prevalent response to victimisation (Ditton et al. 1999). Moreover, fear of crime need not be seen as an unqualified social ill. Certain forms of fear can be functional, in as much as it serves to increase vigilance and the taking of precautions. The opposite of fear may not be fearlessness but recklessness (Sacco 1993; Jackson and Gray 2010).

A significant indicator of a decreased fear of crime and an increased sense of safety is the transformation that has taken place in New York and London over the past thirty or forty years. Not only are the streets safer and tension reduced, but former no-go areas, like Harlem in New York and Hoxton in London, have been transformed into sought-after areas in which local residents do not feel routinely intimidated or insecure.

Reference is made in the previous chapter to US opinion polls indicating that crime is slipping down the list of public concerns and has featured less and less as an issue in presidential elections (Jacobson 2006). It is ironic, however, that academic criminologists repeatedly blame the media for talking up the crime problem, since they are often guilty of doing exactly the same by conducting surveys, which involve decontextualised and leading questions, that not so much capture or reflect public opinion as construct it (Green 2006).

Similarly, UK public opinion polls suggest that crime has become less of a major concern over the past decade or so. An *Economist*/MORI poll (2010) found that concern decreased 5 per cent between 2003 and 2010. When asked 'What would you say is the most important issue facing Britain today?' only 4 per cent identified crime related issues, while 41 per cent identified the economic situation as their main concern.

The shift towards pre-crime and security

With the advent of the risk society and the growing concern with mitigating hazards has come an increased emphasis, it has been argued, on forestalling risks rather than responding to wrongs. Lucia Zedner (2007), for example, has argued that there is increased emphasis on preventing and anticipating crime and that the responsibility for security falls not only on the state but also on certain agencies, particularly those involved in private security. There has been a shift, Zedner maintains, towards a more wide-ranging and disparate body of practices that constitute a growing focus on security rather than crime control. The aim is to develop preventive interventions that reduce opportunities for transgression and increase surveillance.

These developments are linked to developing forms of actuarialism, which, as Simon himself has noted, involve a shift from traditional forms of crime control to the management of risk (Feeley and Simon 1992). In this process, it has been suggested, the preoccupation with individual offenders is generally replaced by the identification and classification of suspect populations. The focus also shifts towards protection of property and persons and the construction of safe environments away from the preoccupation with crime rates.

For Simon the war on crime is a precursor to the war on terror, with both invoking justifications for increasing state intervention in everyday life. However, forms of anti-terrorist intervention do not fit neatly into the frame of conventional crime prevention since intervention often takes on extralegal forms (Cueller 2008). Criminal law is often seen as an impediment to carrying out anti-terrorist activities, as is evident in the cases of Guantánamo and Abu Graib. There is a tension between the demands of national security and the presumption of innocence before the law, due process and human rights. In many respects the war on terror can be seen as a break with the war on crime, alongside the focus on anti-social behaviour, disorder and incivilities, on one hand, and the shift towards pre-crime strategies linked to actuarialism and the pursuit of security, on the other (McCulloch and Pickering 2009).

Anti-social behaviour, incivilities and disorder

If it can be said that we are gravitating towards a security-oriented, pre-crime society, then the growing preoccupation with anti-social behaviour, incivilities and disorder can be seen as a shift towards subcrime. Importantly, the anti-social behaviour agenda, as it was rolled out in the United Kingdom, was a more or less explicit critique of the functioning of the criminal justice system. This changing focus is used to circumvent and erode established criminal justice principles, notably due process, proportionality and the special protections traditionally afforded to young people (Crawford 2003a). New forms of regulation amount to a challenge to and an assault upon traditional conceptions of criminal justice. Advocates of anti-social behaviour have expressed the view that crime-control mechanisms do not work effectively. The criminal justice system is depicted as outmoded, inefficient and too slow, with talk of a justice gap (the difference between the number of crimes recorded and the number of cases in which the perpetrator is brought to justice). This is increasingly seen in official circles as a sign of the weakness and failure of the criminal justice system (Crown Prosecution Service 2011).

The significance of anti-social behaviour, incivilities and disorder is that, as subcrimes, they do not fall within the purview of criminal law. For the most part they are not incidents with an identifiable victim, such as burglary or an act of violence, but are seen as affecting the quality of life of communities. This has resulted in what Squires and Stephen (2005) refer to as an 'enforcement defect', whereby traditional criminal justice responses that are designed to deal with specific incidents have no mechanism to address the cumulative impact that anti-social behaviour and disorder can have on the community.

What is evident about the regulation of anti-social behaviour is that its focus is not just the offender. Rather, it is designed to enlist the support of parents and family through training and support strategies. Sanctions like anti-social behaviour are not simply get-tough interventions but involve, as in the case of ASBOs, a package of sanctions with a spatial and temporal component designed to act simultaneously as a preventative and punitive measure. They also significantly blur civil and criminal sanctions while going far beyond conventional conceptions of crime to include a focus on civility and manners (Parr 2009). They also bring into play an array of authorities and agencies that can make decisions to take offenders to court or alternatively impose their own particular sanctions. There is also a significant contractual element to anti-social behaviour intervention (Flint and Nixon 2006).

As Flint and Nixon (2006) have argued, a defining element of the new mechanisms that have been developed for controlling anti-social behaviour is the emergence of the neighbourhood as the site in which civility is to be enacted and regulated, resulting in an increasing role for communities to define, survey and report incidents. At the same time the imposition of sanctions is coupled with incentives to promote respect and civility and encourage forms of acceptable behaviour, which is to be achieved partly through extended forms of contractual governance and partly through strategies to encourage subjects to take greater responsibility for their actions within a new framework of rights and obligations and a redefining of the contract between the state and the citizen.

Governing through health and lifestyle

If it was the case that we could talk of governing through crime in the period 1970–1995, so it is that over the last decade or so the focus on crime control has increasingly been overtaken by a focus on lifestyle and health. The primary focus of regulation in advanced capitalism remains the labour market and related issues of credit and financial controls. In a post-Fordist world with its increased job insecurity together with the shift towards a service economy there are greater demands for flexibility and mobility. Consequently, health and lifestyle issues become central concerns of modern life (Schee 2008). The present preoccupation with food consumption, obesity, smoking, drinking and fitness can be seen to some extent as a function of the changing nature of productive relations. The proliferation of television programmes and newspaper articles on diet, health and fitness is testimony to the growing focus on lifestyle and the presentation of self.

Probably the most significant lifestyle development in the past twenty years has been the anti-smoking campaign. Although it has had a legislative component, its driver has been a moral crusade, focusing not only on damage to the smoker's health, but also to that of his or her family and associates. What is significant about this campaign is that the smoking ban on public transport was not enforced by government agencies but by the general public. It is testimony to the initiative's moral weight that once the transport authorities introduced the ban, it was rarely breached. It is also remarkable how anti-smoking developed around the world, with First World countries taking the lead and effecting major changes in smoking habits and attitudes. There is now a noticeable split between advanced Western countries, where smoking is restricted and mostly viewed with disfavour, and developing countries, where smoking remains endemic.

The anti-smoking campaign not only led to increased cigarette prices but also to hard-hitting advertisements identifying the dangers of smoking. Health warnings were placed on tobacco products and awareness campaigns were run in schools. Also, particular populations were targeted – teenagers, young and pregnant mothers. Children were frequently used to bring moral pressure on parents. The sociological and criminological message arising from this campaign is that people can be nudged to change even their most deep-seated habits and that radical changes in lifestyle are possible (Pykett 2012; Reid 2005).

The difference between governing through crime and governing through health and lifestyle is that the former concentrates on the marginalised and the so-called underclass. Governing through health and leisure, on the other hand, focuses on the normal, the everyday and the mundane, not the exceptional. Effective social control, as Foucault argued, involves subjects internalising regulatory strategies, such that they give over their hearts and minds. Thus:

> The emergence of the new public health signals a considerable broadening of the focus of health promotion which has come to take as its object the 'environment' conceived in its broadest sense, spanning the local through to the global level and including social, psychological and physical elements. With the emergence of this broad concept of determining the environment in this new public health, the distinction between healthy and unhealthy populations totally dissolves since everything is potentially a source of 'risk' and everyone can be seen to be 'at risk'. (Peterson 1997: 195)

In the new politics of health everyone has become a potential victim and so may be at risk. Health promoters have been at the forefront of attempts to reorganise social institutions and forge a new conception of the political, seeing themselves as closely allied with social movements that challenge and influence behaviour, attitudes and values. The terms healthy and unhealthy have become the new signifiers of the normal and abnormal and an expression of one's moral worth.

Healthcare is more and more becoming part of the care of the self. Magazine and newspaper articles present healthcare advice from a growing body of experts. Healthcare has also become commercialised and commodified. It is big business. This is not only evident in the growth of drug companies but also in the growth of gyms and fitness programmes. Every new medical breakthrough is treated with respect and admiration as we embrace the ideal of a disease-free society. But the health focus is as much about improving self-image, defying the aging process and beautifying the body as controlling disease. At its extreme it may be about controlling obesity and anorexia/bulimia, but its more mundane purpose is encouraging good dietary habits and lifestyle choices. Cosmetic procedures – facelifts, liposuction, botox treatment and the like – are multiplying. But the most significant aspect of the medicalisation process is the growing responsibility of active citizens to maintain and ensure their health status. Those who act 'irresponsibly'– by smoking or drinking or taking illicit drugs – may disqualify themselves from treatment, which is reserved for 'suitable victims' who take proper control of their lives (Christie 1977). The expectation, often couched in the language of risk, is that individuals are responsible for their own health and need to be knowledgeable, discriminating consumers.

As Anthony Giddens (1992) has noted, 'everyone today in developed countries, apart from the poor, is on a diet'. We can reduce cholesterol levels by eating certain types of margarine. We are expected to count the units of alcohol we consume and reduce our intake of fat, salt and sugar (Nettleton 1997). At the same time medicine is becoming dein-stitutionalised, and the relation between the doctor and the patient is changing. The power of the medical profession is not decreasing – far from it – but alongside the growth of professional power are new forms of self-governance. The individual subject is no longer a concrete individual but an assemblage of risk (Bunton 1997; Haggerty and Ericson 2000).

Simon makes some reference to health, particularly in relation to cancer, and argues that in the war on cancer, unlike the war on crime, prevention is always primary. Whereas in the war on crime, he claims, victims are passive subjects of government, in the war on cancer victims are active subjects who become mobilised to fight. This seems a strange and wholly misguided claim. Cancer patients, particularly those subject to chemotherapy, surgery or radiotherapy – the main treatments – have little control or understanding of the nature of procedures and drugs involved and are, for the most part, relatively passive objects of treatment. In addition, Simon claims that the war on cancer is preferable as a model of war because it emphasises the search for causes. This suggestion shows a blissful lack of awareness of the shift towards preventing crime and the considerable efforts and billions of dollars that have been spent trying to identify crime's causes. Part of the problem is that much of the money spent on research has remained impervious to the differences between social and physical phenomena, and consequently researchers have tried to use the same methods to identify and 'treat' crime as are used in the field of medicine.

The changing nature of governance

Over the past decade or so there has been a growing focus on govern-ance and governmentality and changing forms of state control. Increasing globalisation and the effects of the information society have called into question the role of the nation state. There has also been some suggestion that the relation between state and civil society is in the process of transformation, and that this has had a profound impact on crime control (Garland 1997). A significant feature of this develop-ment, according to John Braithwaite (2008), is that we have moved into a period he describes as 'regulatory capitalism', featuring new systems of 'networked governance'. This involves, he suggests, a shift from Fordism, involving a systematically specialised, broken-down produc-tion system, to a more volatile post-Fordist form of production, which is more engaged in 'steering' than 'rowing', and that increasingly contracts services to shifting collaborative groups (Crawford 2006). He argues that an elaborate system of monitoring and collaboration has developed in which traditional top-down, command-and-control strategies are being replaced by more flexible networks of private–public arrangements that are more participatory, complex and self-regulating (Black 2001).

In opposition to those who believe we are in an era of neoliber-alism, Braithwaite argues that under regulatory capitalism the govern-ance that shapes daily life is more corporate than state. Under this system markets become regulatory mechanisms rather than regula-tion's antithesis. The glut of regulatory agencies has generated new networks of experts, including what Braithwaite refers to as the 'increased regulation of the state by the state'. The attempt to over-come the 'ungovernability' of late capitalism, he suggests, has created an ever more elaborate network of regulatory agencies that develop changing and complex public–private, formal and informal, state and non-state forms of regulation. In this context the largely state-centred hierarchical command-and-control model Simon adopts looks increasingly outdated and inappropriate.

In opposition to this top-down, state-centred hierarchical model of control that places crime, law and punishment in the centre of intervention, there are signs of a growing diversity and flexibility in systems of regulation, which include the possibility of individuals, communities, and non-state agencies actively participating in a search for solutions to specific social problems (Newman et al. 2004). These new forms, it has been suggested, blur lines of accountability and responsibility on one hand and work to increase representation and consultation on the other (Swyngedouw 2005). These increasingly participatory methods of governance and changing forms of state power create new possibilities for engaging in progressive practice.

Although some of this discussion about changing forms of control in and beyond the state is somewhat speculative, the message that seems to emerge from the literature is that traditional command-and-control strategies, which focus on crime, law and punishment, are gradually being superseded by more flexible, 'smarter' forms of regulation, which move beyond the errant individual to develop more engaged, responsibilising strategies that involve choice and recognise the complexity of decision-making behaviour. The aim is to shape and influence behaviour on a continuous basis – not so much through strategies which focus on exclusion and marginalisation as through those which emphasise inclusivity and self-responsibility. These changes in the culture of control may go some way to explaining the crime drop and today's declining focus on crime related issues.

Conclusion

Nothing excites criminologists as much as the arrival of a new catchphrase or slogan. In the past we have been entertained by such phrases as 'broken windows', 'moral panics', 'net widening', 'populist punitiveness' and, most recently, 'governing through crime'. What is remarkable about these phrases is how often they involve a misrepresentation of the processes they are supposed to describe and how uncritically they are inserted into the vocabulary of academic criminology. Once incorporated in this way, the catchphrases take on a certain autonomy and apparent objectivity. Their repeated use is taken as shorthand for explaining what are often complex processes. It is this process of adoption and a willingness to incorporate the terms within academic criminology that may in part explain the lack of critical scrutiny associated with their deployment.

Simon's thesis, it has been suggested, is another example of 'so what?' criminology, an expression of a form of radical liberalism that is ultimately disingenuous and misleading. It is disingenuous in as much as it detracts from the need to take crime and victimisation seriously and that it argues for the removal of the protective and supportive arm of the state. It is misleading to the extent that during the period Simon developed this thesis, crime was becoming less central to the process of regulation and other important developments linked to post-Fordism and the advent of the information society were gaining prominence.

Crime control and the reduction of victimisation remain important objectives. There is growing disillusionment with the operation of the criminal justice system, increasingly seen as cumbersome, anachronistic and expensive. This is reflected in practice by an increasing focus on preventing crime or dealing with offenders through more informal adjudication processes, such as restorative justice and contractual governance. There are signs that rather than govern through crime, as Simon suggests, we are moving into a pre-crime and post-criminal law society, in the sense that the traditional couplet of the individual act and the fixed punishment centred on due process is being replaced by a mode of regulation with a range of diversion and administrative processes involving the erosion of legal safeguards and human rights provisions (Ashworth and Zedner 2008). The longer-term signs are that regulation in general may become more fluid, more continuous and involve complex systems of surveillance and monitoring, which are post-disciplinary in the Foucauldian sense (Deleuze 1995).

Indicatively, in this analysis Simon, like many of his liberal colleagues, makes virtually no reference to changes in economic and productive relations but tends to explain developments primarily in terms of political will. In addition, he does not directly engage the growing literature on changing social and cultural conditions and changing identities. He makes only passing reference to the enormous changes that have taken place in urban life and family and community structures in this period. Examples of change are highly selective and show little engagement with the counterfactual. Consequently, the 'governing through crime' thesis is theoretically and empirically weak and arguably has little or no policy relevance. The overly pessimistic nature of his analysis, coupled with a lack of appreciation of the contradictions and tensions of recent changes, means that in the style of classic liberal critiques he can only call on authorities to be more lenient and tolerant or hope for some form of spontaneous social movement to overturn the 'damage' that has resulted from the war on crime.

To avoid gravitating towards a position that is anti-crime, anti-punishment and anti-state and sinks into pessimism and impossibilism, one needs to engage in serious discussion of the appropriate role of criminal law and crime control in the post-Fordist era and identify those progressive and positive components that provide protection and support for the weak, the vulnerable and the victimised. It should be remembered that even with the recent dramatic recorded decrease, crime has fallen only to the level in the 1980s. There remain millions of people who still suffer each year as victims of crime.

The evidence suggests that the preoccupation with crime control that developed in the 1970s and 1980s is being superseded by forms of regulation that are more diverse and less hierarchical. These developments contain both positive (emancipatory) and negative (repressive) elements. However, they go far beyond 'rounding up the usual suspects' and increasingly involve the regulation of the 'normal' population engaged in the routines of everyday life. In this way control focuses not so much on the exceptional, the marginalised or the deviant as on the mundane activities of work, consumption and leisure.

References

Ackroyd, S. (2004) 'Methodology for Management and Organisation Studies: Some Implications for Critical Realism', in S. Fleetwood and S. Ackroyd (eds), *Critical Realist. Applications in Organisation and Management Studies*. London: Routledge.

Adler, F. (1975) *Sisters in Crime*. New York: McGraw Hill.

Albertazzi, D., Brook, C., and Ross, C. (2009) 'From Parliament to Virtual Piazza? Opposition in Italy in the Age of Berlusconi'. *Bulletin of Italian Politics* 1 (1): 111–123.

Anderson, B., and Davidson, J. (2002) *Trafficking – A Demand-led Problem? A Multi-country Pilot Study, Save the Children*. Sweden.

Archer, M. (1995) *Realist Social Theory: The Morphogenic Approach*. Cambridge: Cambridge University Press.

Archer, M. (2000) *Being Human: The Problem of Agency*. Cambridge: Cambridge University Press.

Archer, M., Bhaskar, R., Collier, A., Lawson, T., and Norrie, A. (1998) *Critical Realism: Essential Readings*. London: Routledge.

Ariely, D. (2009) *Predictably Irrational*. London: Harper Collins.

Ashworth, A. (1983) *Sentencing and Penal Policy*. London: Weidenfeld and Nicholson.

Ashworth, A. (2000) 'Is the Criminal Law a Lost Cause?' *Law Quarterly Review* 116 (2): 225–256.

Ashworth, A., and Zedner, L. (2008) 'Defending the Criminal Law: Reflections on the Changing Character of Crime, Procedure and Sanctions'. *Crime, Law and Philosophy* 2: 21–51.

Austin, J. (2000) *Multisite Evaluation of Boot Camp Programs: Final Report*. Washington, DC: National Institute of Justice.

Austin, J. (2003) 'Why Criminology Is Irrelevant'. *Criminology and Public Policy* 2: 557–564.

Austin, J., and Jacobson, M. (2013) *How New York City Reduced Mass Incarceration: A Model for Change?* Brennan Center for Justice at New York University School of Law.

Austin, J., Clarke, J., Hardyman, P., and Henry, D. (1999) 'The Impact of Three Strikes and You're Out'. *Punishment and Society* 1 (2): 131–162.

Ayres, J. (1999) 'From the Streets to the Internet: The Cyber-Diffusion of Contention'. *Annals* 566 (November): 132–143.

Baker, E. (2010) 'Governing through Crime – The Case of the European Union'. *European Journal of Criminology* 7 (3): 187–213.

Bauman, Z. (1991) *Modernity and Ambivalence*. Cambridge: Polity.

Bauman, Z. (2000) *Liquid Modernity*. Cambridge: Polity.

Bauman, Z. (2011) *Culture in a Liquid Modern World*. Cambridge: Polity.

Beccaria, C. (1963) *Of Crimes and Punishments*. Indianapolis: Bobbs-Merrill (originally published in 1764 as *Dei Delitti e Della Pene*).

Becker, H. (1953) 'Becoming a Marijuana User'. *American Journal of Sociology* 59 (3): 235–242.

Becker, H. (1966) 'Whose Side Are We On?'. *Social Problems* 14 (3): 234–237.

Beckett, K., and Herbert, S. (2008) 'Dealing with Disorder: Social Control in the Post-industrial City'. *Theoretical Criminology* 12 (1): 5–30.

Beitz, C. R. (2001) 'Human Rights as a Common Concern'. *American Political Science Review* 95: 269–282.

Berger, P., and Luckmann, T. (1967) *The Social Construction of Reality*. New York: Doubleday.

Bhaskar, R. (1978) *A Realist Theory of Science*. Hassocks: Harvester.

Bhaskar, R. (1979) *The Possibility of Naturalism*. Hassocks: Harvester.

Bhaskar, R. (1999) *A Realist Theory of Science*. London: Verso.

Bhaskar, R. (2002) *From Science to Emancipation*. London: Sage.

Black, J. (2001) 'De-centering Regulation: The Role of Regulation and Post-regulation in a Regulatory World'. *Current Legal Problems* 54: 103–146.

Blau, J., Moncada, A., and Moncada, A. (2007) 'It Ought to Be a Crime: Criminalizing Human Rights Violations'. *Sociological Forum* 22 (3): 364–371.

Blumstein, A., and Beck, A. J. (1999) 'Population Growth in US Prisons 1980–1996', in M. Tonry and J. Petersilia (eds), *Prisons*. Chicago: University of Chicago Press.

Blumstein, A., and Wallman, J. (2000) *The Crime Drop in America*. Cambridge: Cambridge University Press.

Blumstein, A., Tonry, M., and Van Ness, A. (2005) 'Cross National Measures of Punitiveness', in M. Tonry and D. Farrington (eds), *Crime and Punishment in Western Countries 1986–1999*. Chicago: University of Chicago Press.

Bondeson, U. (2005) 'Levels of Punitiveness in Scandinavia: Description and Explanation', in J. Pratt et al. (eds), *The New Punitiveness: Trends, Theories Perspectives*. Cullompton: Willan.

Bosworth, M. (2010) 'Introduction: Reinventing Penal Parsimony'. *Theoretical Criminology* 14 (3): 251–256.

Bottoms, A. (1995) 'The Philosophy and Politics of Punishment and Sentencing', in C. Clarkson and R. Morgan (eds), *The Politics of Sentencing Reform*. Oxford: Clarendon Press.

Boudon, R. (1998) 'Limitations of Rational Choice Theory'. *American Journal of Sociology* 104 (3): 817–828.

Bourdieu, P. (1977) *Outline of a Theory of Practice*. Cambridge: Cambridge University Press.

Bourdieu, P. (1987) 'What Makes a Class? On the Theoretical and Practical Existence of Groups'. *Berkeley Journal of Sociology* 32: 1–17.

Bourgois, P. (1995) 'The Political Economy of Resistance and Self-Destruction in the Crack Economy: An Ethnographic Perspective'. *Annals of the New York Academy of Sciences* 749: 97.

Bourgois, P. (1996) *In Search of Respect: Selling Crack in El Barrio*. Cambridge: Cambridge University Press.

Bourgois, P. (2000) 'Disciplining Addictions: The Bio-politics of Methadone and Heroin in the United States'. *Culture, Medicine and Psychiatry* 24: 165–195.

Bourgois, P. (2002) 'Understanding Inner-City Poverty: Resistance and Self-Destruction and US Apartheid', in J. MacClancy (ed.), *Exotic No More: Anthropology on the Front Lines*. Chicago: University of Chicago Press.

Bourgois, P. (2002a) 'Anthropology and Epidemiology on Drugs: The Challenges of Cross-Methodological and Theoretical Dialogue'. *International Journal of Drug Policy* 13: 259–269.

Bourgois, P. (2003) 'Crack and the Political Economy of Social Suffering'. *Addiction Research and Theory* 11 (1): 31–37.

Bourgois, P. (2010) 'Useless Suffering: The War on Homeless Drug Addicts', in H. Gusterson and C. Besteman (eds), *The Insecure American*. Berkeley: University of California Press.

Bourgois, P., and Schonberg, J. (2009) *Righteous Dopefiends*. Berkeley: University of California Press.

Bowling, B. (1999) 'The Rise and Fall of New York Murder: Zero Tolerance or Crack's Decline?'. *British Journal of Criminology* 39 (4): 531–554.

Box, S. (1983) *Power, Crime and Mystification*. London: Tavistock.

Braithwaite, J. (1981) 'The Myth of Social Class and Criminality Reconsidered'. *American Sociological Review* 46: 36–57.

Braithwaite, J. (1982) 'Challenging Just Desserts: Punishing White Collar Criminals'. *Journal of Criminal Law and Criminology* 73 (2): 723–763.

Braithwaite, J. (1989) *Crime, Shame and Reintegration*. Cambridge: Cambridge University Press.

Braithwaite, J. (1989) 'Criminological Theory and Organisational Crime'. *Justice Quarterly* 6 (3): 333–358.

Braithwaite, J., and Pettit, P. (1990) *Not Just Deserts: A Republican Theory of Criminal Justice*. Oxford: Clarendon Press.

Braithwaite, J. (2005) *Markets in Vice: Markets in Virtue*. Oxford: Oxford University Press.

Braithwaite, J. (2008) *Regulatory Capitalism: How It Works, Ideas for Making It Work Better*. Cheltenham: Edward Elgar.

Braithwaite, J., and Braithwaite, V. (2001) 'Shame, Shame Management and Regulation', in E. Ahmed, N. Harris, J. Braithwaite and V. Braithwaite (eds), *Shame Management through Reintegration*. Cambridge: Cambridge University Press.

Brotherton, D. (2008) 'Beyond Social Reproduction: Bringing Resistance Back in Gang Theory'. *Theoretical Criminology* 12 (1): 55–78.

Brown, M. (2008) 'Aftermath: Living with the Crisis: From PCT to Governing Through Crime', *Crime, Media, Culture* 4 (1): 123–129.

Brownmiller, S. (1975) *Against Our Will: Men, Women and Rape*. London: Secker and Warburg.

Bunton, R. (1997) 'Popular Health, Advanced Liberalism and Good Housekeeping Magazine', in A. Petersen and R. Bunton (eds), *Foucault, Health and Medicine*. London: Routledge.

Bureau of Justice (2012) *Prisoners in 2011*. NCJ 239808. US Department of Justice.

Bureau of Justice (2013) *Indicators of School Crime and Safety 2012*. US Department of Justice.

Burr, V. (2003) *Social Constructionism*. London: Routledge.

Cadora, E. (2014) 'Civic Lessons: How Certain Schemes to End Mass Incarceration Can Fail'. *The Annals of the American Academy of Political and Social Science* 651: 277–285.

Cain, M. (1990) 'Realist Philosophy and Standpoint Epistemologies or Feminist Criminology as a Successor Science', in L. Gelsthorpe and A. Morris (eds), *Feminist Perspectives in Criminology*. London: Open University Press.

Campbell, B. (1993) *Goliath: Britain's Dangerous Places*. London: Methuen.

Caplow, T., and Simon, J. (1999) 'Understanding Prison Policy and Population Trends', in M. Tonry and J. Petersilia (eds), *Prisons*. Chicago: University of Chicago Press.

Carlen, P. (1992) 'Criminal Women and Criminal Justice: The Limits to and Potential of Feminist and Left Realist Perspectives', in R. Matthews and J. Young (eds), *Issues in Realist Criminology*. London: Sage.

Carlen, P. (2002) 'Carceral Clawback: The Case of Women's Imprisonment in Canada'. *Punishment and Society* 4 (1): 115–121.

Carlen, P. (2011) 'Against Evangelism in Academic Criminology: For Criminology as Scientific Art', in M. Bosworth and C. Hoyle (eds), *What Is Criminology?* Oxford: Oxford University Press.

Carr, E. (1964) *What Is History?* Harmondsworth: Penguin.

Castells, M. (1997) *The Power of Identity, Vol. 11*. Oxford: Blackwell.

Chamard, R. (2010) 'Routine Activities', in E. McLaughlin and T. Newburn (eds), *The Sage Handbook of Criminological Theory*. London: Sage.

Cheliotis, L. (2006) 'Penal Managerialism from Within: Implications for Theory and Research'. *International Journal of Law and Psychiatry* 29: 397–404.

Chesney-Lind, M. (1973) 'Judicial Enforcement of the Female Sex Role: The Family Court and the Female Delinquent'. *Issues in Criminology* 8 (2): 51–69.

Christie, N. (1968) 'Changes in Penal Values'. *Scandinavian Studies in Criminology* 2. Oslo: Universitetsforlaget.

Christie, N. (1977) 'Conflicts as Property'. *British Journal of Criminology* 17: 1–19.

Christie, N. (1986) 'The Ideal Victim', in E. Fattah (ed.), *From Crime Policy to Victim Policy*. London: Macmillan.

Clarke, R. (1997) 'Introduction', in R. Clarke (ed.), *Situational Crime Prevention: Successful Case Studies*. New York: Harrow and Heston.

Clarke, R., and Felson, M. (1993) *Routine Activity and Rational Choice: Advances in Criminological Theory, Vol. 5*. New Brunswick: Transaction.

Clarke, R., and Newman, G. (2006) *Outsmarting the Terrorists*. Westport, CT: Praeger.

Clarke, R. V., and Cornish, D. B. (1985) 'Modeling Offender's Decisions: A Framework for Research and Policy', in M. Tonry and N. Morris (eds), *Crime and Justice: An Annual Review of Research* 6. Chicago: University of Chicago Press.

Cloward, R., and Ohlin, L. (1960) *Delinquency and Opportunity: A Theory of Delinquent Gangs*. New York: Free Press.

Cohen, A. (1955) *Delinquent Boys: The Culture of the Gang*. New York: Free Press.

Cohen, L. E., and Felson, M. (1979) 'Social Change and Crime Rate Trends: A Routine Activity Approach'. *American Sociological Review* 44: 588–608.

Cohen, S. (1979) 'Guilt, Justice and Tolerance: Some Old Concepts for a New Criminology', in D. Downes and P. Rock (eds), *Deviant Interpretations*. London: Martin Robinson.

Cohen, S. (1985) *Visions of Social Control*. Cambridge: Polity.

Cohen, S. (1998) *Against Criminology*. New Brunswick: Transaction Books.

Coleman, J. (1986) *Individual Interests and Collective Action*. Cambridge: Cambridge University Press.

Conklin, J. (2003) *Why Crimes Rates Fell*. Boston: Pearson.

Cook, P. (1991) 'The Technology of Personal Violence', in M. Tonry (ed.), *Crime and Justice* 14. Chicago: University of Chicago Press.

Cornish, D., and Clarke, R. (1986) *The Reasoning Criminal: Rational Choice Perspective on Offending*. New York: Springer-Verlag.

Cornish, D. B. (1993) 'Theories of Action in Criminology: Learning Theory and Rational Choice Approaches', in R. V. Clarke and M. Felson (eds), *Routine Activity and Rational Choice*. New Brunswick: Transaction.

Cornish, D. B., and Clarke, R. V. (1987) 'Understanding Crime Displacement: An Application of Rational Choice Theory'. *Criminology* 25 (4): 933–947.

Corston, J. (2007) *The Corston Report: A Review of Women with Particular Vulnerabilities in the Criminal Justice System*. London: Home Office.

Crawford, A. (2003) 'Contractual Governance and Deviant Behaviour'. *Journal of Law and Society* 30 (4): 479–505.

Crawford, A. (2003a) 'Governing through Anti-Social Behaviour: Regulatory Challenges to Criminal Justice'. *British Journal of Criminology* 49 (61): 810–831.

Crawford, A. (2006) 'Contractual Governance and the Post-regulatory State? Steering, Rowing and Anchoring the Policing of Security'. *Theoretical Criminology* 10 (4): 449–480.

Crawford, A. (2006a) 'Networked Governance and the Post-regulatory State'. *Theoretical Criminology* 10 (4): 449–479.

Crawford, A., Jones, T., Woodhouse, T., and Young, J. (1990) *The Second Islington Crime Survey*. London: Middlesex University.

Cressey, D. (1979) 'Fifty Years of Criminology; From Sociological Theory to Political Control'. *Pacific Sociological Review* 22 (4): 457–480.

Cromby, J., and Nightingale, D. (1999) 'What's Wrong with Social Constructionism', in J. Cromby and D. Nightingale (eds), *Social Constructionist Psychology*. Buckingham: Open University Press.

Crown Prosecution Service (2011) *Narrowing the Justice Gap*, www.cps.gov.uk/publications/justicegap.html.

Cueller, M. (2008) 'The Political Economics of Criminal Justice'. *University of Chicago Law Review* 75: 941–983.

Cullen, F. (2011) 'Beyond Adolescence-Limited Criminology: Choosing Our Future'. *Criminology* 49 (2): 287–330.

Cullen, F., and Gendreau, P. (2001) 'From Nothing Works to What Works: Changing Professional Ideology in the 21st Century'. *Prison Journal* 81 (3): 313–338.

Cullen, F. T., Gendreau, P., Jarjoura, G. R., and Wright, J. P. (1997) 'Crime and the Bell Curve: Lessons from Intelligent Criminology'. *Crime and Delinquency* 43 (4): 387–411.

Cuppleditch, L., and Evans, W. (2005) *Reoffending of Adults: Results from the 2002 Cohort*. Home Office Statistical Bulletin. London: Home Office.

Currie, E. (1974) 'Beyond Criminology: A Review of the New Criminology'. *Issues in Criminology* 9: 133–142.

Currie, E. (1985) *Confronting Crime*. New York: Pantheon Books.

Currie, E. (1989) 'Confronting Crime: Looking toward the Twenty-First Century'. *Justice Quarterly* 6 (1): 5–25.

Currie, E. (2007) 'Against Marginality: Arguments for a Public Criminology'. *Theoretical Criminology* 11 (2): 175–190.

Currie, E. (2010) 'Plain Left Realism: An Appreciation and Thoughts for the Future'. *Crime, Law and Social Change* 54 (2): 111–124.

Davies, N. (2004) 'Scandal of Society's Misfit Dumped in Jail'. *Guardian*, December 6.

Davis, P. (2004) 'Sociology and Policy Science: Just in Time'. *British Journal of Sociology* 55 (3): 447–450.

Deleuze, G. (1995) *Negotiations*. New York: Columbia University Press.

Department of Education (2011) *Permanent and Fixed Period of Exclusions from Schools 2009/10*, www.education.gov.uk/rsgateway/DB/SFR/s001080/index.shtml.

Dilulio, J. (1999) 'Two Million Are Enough'. *Wall Street Journal*, March 12.

Dilworth, C. (1990) 'Empiricism versus Realism: High Points in the Debate during the Past 150 Years'. *Studies in the History, and Philosophy of Science* 21 (3): 431–462.

Ditton, J., Farrall, S., Bannister, J., Gilchrist, S., and Pease K. (1999) 'Reactions to Victimisation: Why Has Anger Been Ignored?'. *Crime Prevention and Community Safety – An International Journal* 1: 37–53.

Dolan, P., Hallsworth, M., Halpern, D., King, D., Metcalfe, R., and Vlaev, I. (2010) *Mind Space: Influencing Behaviour through Public Policy*. London: Cabinet Office, Institute for Government.

Donzelot, J. (1979) *The Policing of Families*. London: Hutchinson.

Doob, A., and Webster, C. (2006) 'Countering Punitiveness: Understanding Stability in Canada's Imprisonment'. *Law and Society Review* 40 (2): 325–368.

Downes, D. (1988) 'The Sociology of Crime Control in Britain'. *British Journal of Criminology* 28 (2): 4–57.

Du Bois, W., and Wright, R. (2002) 'What Is Humanistic Sociology'. *American Sociologist* 33 (4): 5–36.

Dunaway, R. G., Cullen, F. T., Burton, V. S., and Evans, T. D. (2000) 'The Myth of Social Class and Crime Revised: An Examination of Class and Adult Criminality'. *Criminology* 38: 589–632.

Durose, M., and Murnola, C. (2004) *Profile of Non-Violent Offenders Exiting State Prisons*, NCJ 207081. Bureau of Justice Factsheet: Department of Justice.

Easton, H., Silvestri, M., Evans, K., Matthews, R., and Walklate, S. (2010) *Conditional Cautions: Evaluation of the Women's Specific Condition Pilot*. Research Series 14/10. London: Ministry of Justice.

Economist/IPSOS MORI (2010) *Issues Facing Britain*, www.IPSOSMORI.com/researchpublications.

Ekblom, P., and Tilley, N. (2000) 'Going Equipped: Criminology, Situational Crime Prevention and the Resourceful Offender'. *British Journal of Criminology* 40: 376–398.

Elster, J. (1993) 'Some Unresolved Problems in the Theory of Rational Behaviour'. *Acta Sociologica* 36 (3): 179–190.

Ericson, R. (2007) *Crime in an Insecure World*. Cambridge: Polity.

Ericson, R., and Carriere, K. (1994) 'The Fragmentation of Criminology', in D. Nelken (ed.), *The Futures of Criminology*. London: Sage.

Farrall, S., and Bowling, B. (1999) 'Structuration, Human Development and Desistance from Crime'. *British Journal of Criminology* 39 (2): 253–268.

Farrell, G. (2010) 'Situational Crime Prevention and Its Discontents: Rational Choice and Harm Reduction Versus "Cultural Criminology"'. *Social Policy and Administration* 44 (1): 40–66.

Farrington, D., and Joliffe, D. (2005) 'Crime and Punishment in England and Wales 1981–1999', in M. Tonry and D. Farrington (eds), *Crime and Punishment in Western Countries 1980–1999*. Chicago: University of Chicago Press.

Farrington, D., Ditchfield, J., Howard, P., and Joliffe, D. (2002) *Two Intensive Regimes for Young Offenders: A Follow-up Evaluation*. London: Home Office.

Farrington, D., Gottfredson, D., and Sherman, L. (2002) 'The Maryland Scientific Scale Methods', in L. Sherman, D. Farrington, B. Welsh and D. Mackenzie (eds), *Evidence-Based Crime Prevention*. London/New York: Routledge.

Fawcett Society (2004) *Women in the Criminal Justice System*. London: Fawcett Society.

Feeley, M., and Simon, J. (1992) 'The New Penology: Note on the Emerging Strategy of Corrections and Its Implications'. *Criminology* 3: 449–474.

Felson, M. (1994) 'Linking Criminal Choices, Routine Activities, Informal Control, and Criminal Outcomes', in D. B. Cornish and R. Clarke (eds), *The Reasoning Criminal*. New York: Springer-Verlag.

Felson, M., and Poulsen, E. (2003) 'Simple Indicators of Crime by Time of Day'. *International Journal of Forecasting* 19 (4): 595–601.

Ferrell, J. (1996) *Crimes of Style: Urban Graffiti and the Politics of Criminality*. Boston: Northeastern University Press.

Ferrell, J. (1997) 'Criminological Verstehen: Inside the Immediacy of Crime'. *Justice Quarterly* 14 (1): 3–23.

Ferrell, J. (1999) 'Cultural Criminology'. *Annual Review of Sociology* 25: 395–418.

Ferrell, J. (2004) 'Boredom, Crime and Criminology'. *Theoretical Criminology* 8 (3): 287–302.

Ferrell, J. (2007) 'For a Ruthless Cultural Criticism of Everything Existing'. *Crime, Media, Culture* 3 (1): 91–100.

Ferrell, J., and Sanders, C. R. (eds) (1995) *Cultural Criminology*. Boston: Northeastern University Press.

Ferrell, J., Hayward, K., and Young, J. (2008) *Cultural Criminology*. London: Sage.

Ferrell, J., Milovanovic, D., and Lyng, S. (2001) 'Edgework, Media Practices and the Elongation of Meaning: A Theoretical Ethnography of the Bridge Day Event'. *Theoretical Criminology* 5 (1): 177–202.

Fleetwood, S., and Ackroyd, S. (2004) *Critical Realist Applications in Organisation and Management Studies*. London: Routledge.

Flint, J., and Nixon, J. (2006) 'Governing Neighbours: Anti-social Behaviour Orders and New Forms of Regulating Conduct in the UK'. *Urban Studies* 43 (5/6): 939–955.

Ford, R. (2013) 'Thousands of Criminals Have at Least Fifteen Previous Convictions'. *The Times,* October 30.

Forrest, S., Myhill, A., and Tilley, N. (2005) *Practical Lessons for Involving the Community in Crime and Disorder Problem-Solving. Development and Practice Report 43*. London: Home Office.

Foucault, M. (1977) *Discipline and Punish: The Birth of the Prison*. London: Allen Lane.

Foucault, M. (1979) *The History of Sexuality, Vol. 1: An Introduction*. London: Allen Lane.

Foucault, M. (1984) 'What Is an Author?', in P. Rabinow (ed.), *The Foucault Reader*. London: Penguin.

Foucault, M. (1991) 'Governmentality', in G. Burchell, C. Gordon and P. Miller (eds), *The Foucault Effect: Studies in Governmentality*. Hertfordshire: Harvester/ Wheatsheaf.

Foucault, M. (2002) 'The Subject of Power', in J. Faubion (ed.), *Power: Essential Works of Foucault 1954–1984*. London: Penguin.

Foucault, M. (2007) *Security, Territory, Population*. New York: Palgrave Macmillan.

Foucault, M. (2009) 'Alternatives to Prison: Dissemination or Decline of Social Control'. *Theory Culture Society* 26 (6): 12–24.

Frampton, M., Hanley, I., Lopez, I., and Simon J. (2008) *After the War on Crime*. New York: New York University Press.

Fraser, N. (1981) 'Foucault on Modern Power: Empirical Insights and Normative Confusions'. *Praxis International* 3: 272–287.

Fraser, N. (1989) *Unruly Practices: Power, Discourse and Gender in Contemporary Social Theory*. Cambridge: Polity.

Fraser, N. (2003) 'From Discipline to Flexibilization? Rereading Foucault in the Shadow of Globalisation'. *Constellations* 10 (2): 160–171.

Frost, N. (2008) 'The Mismeasure of Punishment: Alternative Measures of Punitiveness and Their (Substantial) Consequences'. *Punishment and Society* 10 (3): 272–298.

Garland, D. (1981) 'The Birth of the Welfare Sanction'. *British Journal of Law and Society* 8 (Summer): 29–45.

Garland, D. (1996) 'The Limits of the Sovereign State: Strategies of Crime Control in Contemporary Society'. *British Journal of Criminology* 36 (4): 445–472.

Garland, D. (1997) 'Governmentality and the Problem of Crime: Foucault, Criminology, Sociology'. *Theoretical Criminology* 1 (2): 173–214.

Garland, D. (1999) 'The Commonplace and the Catastrophic: Interpretations of Crime in Late Modernity'. *Theoretical Criminology* 3 (3): 353–364.

Garland, D. (2001) *Culture of Control*. Oxford: Oxford University Press.

Garland, D. (2002) 'Of Crimes and Criminals: The Development of Criminology in Britain', in M. Maguire, R. Morgan and R. Reiner (eds), *The Oxford Handbook of Criminology* (2nd edn). Oxford: Oxford University Press.

Garland, D. (2006) 'Concepts of Culture in the Sociology of Punishment'. *Theoretical Criminology* 10 (4): 419–448.

Gelsthorpe, L. (1997) 'Feminism and Criminology', in M. Maguire, R. Morgan and R. Reiner (eds), *The Oxford Handbook of Criminology* (2nd edn). Oxford: Oxford University Press.

Giddens, A. (1979) *Central Problems in Social Theory: Action, Structure and Contradiction in Social Analysis*. California: University of California Press.

Glazer, B., and Strauss, A. (1967) *The Discovery of Grounded Theory*. Chicago: Aldine.

Glover, J. (2007) 'More Prisons Are Not the Answer to Punishing Criminals, Says Poll'. *Guardian*, August 28.

Goffman, E. (1968) *Asylums*. New Orleans: Pelican.

Goode, E. (1994) 'Round Up the Usual Suspects: Crime, Deviance and the Limits of Constructionism'. *American Sociologist* (Winter): 90–104.

Gormesen, L. (2007) 'Prison Population Begins to Level'. *Corrections Today*, December.

Gouldner, A. (1962) 'Anti-Minotaur: The Myth of Value Free Sociology'. *Social Problems* 9 (3): 199–213.

Gouldner, A. (1968) 'The Sociologist Partisan'. *American Sociologist* 3 (2): 103–116.

Green, D. (2006) 'Public Opinion versus Public Judgement about Crime: Correcting the "Comedy of Errors"'. *British Journal of Criminology* 46 (1): 131–154.

Green, D. (2009) 'Feeding Wolves: Punitiveness and Culture'. *European Journal of Criminology* 6 (6): 517–535.

Green, D., and Shapiro, I. (1994) *Pathologies of Rational Choice Theory*. New Haven: Yale University Press.

Greenberg, D. (2001) 'Novus Ordo Saeclorum? A Commentary on Downs and Beckett and Western'. *Punishment and Society* 3 (1): 81–93.

Greene, J., and Schiraldi, V. (2002) *Cutting Correctly: New Prisons Policies for Times of Fiscal Crisis*. San Fransico: Centre For Juvenile and Criminal Justice. cjjcj.org/pdf/cut_cor.pdf.

Gutmann, A. (1985) 'Communitarian Critics of Liberalism'. *Philosophy and Public Affairs* 14 (3): 308–322.

Hagan, J., Levi, R., and Dinovitzer, R. (2008) 'The Symbolic Violence of the Crime – Immigrant Nexus: Migrant Mythologies in the Americas'. *Criminology and Public Policy* 17 (1): 95–112.

Haggerty, K. (2008) 'Review of L. Sherman et al. (eds), Evidence-Based Crime Prevention'. *Theoretical Criminology* 12 (1): 116–121.

Haggerty, K., and Ericson, R. (2000) 'The Surveillant Assemblage'. *British Journal of Sociology* 51 (1): 605–622

Hall, S. (1980) *Drifting into Law and Order Society*. London: Cobden Trust.

Hall, S., and Winlow, S. (2007) 'Cultural Criminology and Primitive Accumulation: A Formal Introduction to Strangers Who Should Really Become More Intimate'. *Crime, Media, Culture* 3 (1): 82–90.

Hall, S., Critcher, C., Jefferson, T., Clarke, J., and Roberts, B. (1978) *Policing the Crisis*. London: Macmillan.

Hammersley, M. (1992) *What's Wrong with Ethnography?* London: Routledge.

Hammersley, M., and Atkinson, P. (2007) *Ethnography Principles in Practice*. London: Routledge.

Hancock, L., and Matthews, R. (2001) ' Crime, Community Safety and Toleration', in R. Matthews and J. Pitts (eds), *Crime, Disorder and Community Safety: A New Agenda*. London: Routledge.

Hannah-Moffat, K. (2001) *Punishment in Disguise*. Toronto: University of Toronto Press.

Harcourt, B. (1998) 'Reflections on the Subject: A Critique of the Social Influence Conception of Deterrence, the Broken Windows Theory and Order Maintenance Policing New York Style'. *Michigan Law Review* 97: 21–72.

Harne, L., and Radford, J. (2008) *Tackling Domestic Violence: Theories, Policies and Practice*. New York: McGraw Hill.

Harris, J., and McDonald, C. (2000) 'Post-Fordism, the Welfare State and the Personal Social Services: A Comparison of Australia and Britain'. *British Journal of Social Work* 30: 51–70.

Hay, C. S. (2004) 'Theory, Stylised Heuristic or Self-Fulfilling Prophecy? The Status of Rational Choice Theory in Public Administration', *Public Administration* 82 (1): 39–62.

Haylett, C. (2001) 'Illegitimate Subjects?: Abject Whites, Neoliberal Modernisation and Middle Class Multiculturalism'. *Environment and Planning: Society and Space* 19 (3): 351–370.

Hayward, K. (2004) *City Limits: Crime, Consumer Culture and the Urban Experience.* London: Glasshouse.

Hayward, K. (2007) 'Situational Crime Prevention and Its Discontents: Rational Choice Theory Versus the "Culture of Now"'. *Social Policy & Administration* 41 (3): 232–250.

Hayward, K. (2012) 'A Response to Farrell'. *Social Policy and Administration* 46 (1): 21–34.

Hayward, K., and Presdee, M. (2010) *Framing Crime.* London: Routledge.

Hayward, K., and Young, J. (2004) Cultural Criminology: Some Notes on the Script'. *Theoretical Criminology* 8 (3): 259–285.

Hayward, K., and Young, J. (2012) 'Cultural Criminology'. *Oxford Handbook of Criminology.* Oxford: Oxford University Press.

Held, D. (1989) *Political Theory and the Modern State.* Cambridge: Polity.

Helm, T., Asthana, A., and Townsend M. (2010) 'George Osborne Takes Spending Axe to Prisons and Legal Aid'. *Guardian,* October 16.

Herrnstein, R., and Murray, C. (1994) *The Bell Curve.* New York: Free Press.

Hillyard, P., Pantazis, C., Tombs, S., and Gordon, D. (2004) *Beyond Criminology: Taking Harm Seriously.* London: Pluto Press.

Hindmoor, A. (2010) 'Rational Choice', in D. Marsh and G. Stoker (eds), *Theory and Methods in Political Science* (3rd edn). London: Palgrave Macmillan.

Hirschfield, P. (2008) 'Preparing for Prison: The Criminalization of School Discipline in the USA'. *Theoretical Criminology* 12 (1): 79–102.

Hirschi, T. (1969) *Causes of Delinquency.* Berkeley: University of California Press.

Hobbs, D. (2001) 'Ethnography and the Study of Deviance', in P. Atkinson, A. Coffey, S. Delamont, and J. Lofland (eds), *Handbook of Ethnography.* London: Sage.

Honneth, A. (1995) *The Struggle for Recognition.* Cambridge Mass: MIT Press.

Hope, T. (2004) 'Pretend It Works: Evidence and Governance in the Evaluation of the Reducing Burglary Initiative'. *Criminology and Criminal Justice* 4 (3): 287–308.

Horvath, M., and Brown, J. (2009) *Rape: Challenging Contemporary Thinking.* Cullompton: Willan.

Houston, S. (2001) 'Beyond Social Constructionism: Critical Realism and Social Work'. *British Journal of Social Work* 31: 845–861.

Howard and Griffin (1999)

Hulsman, L. (1986) 'Critical Criminology and the Concept of Crime'. *Contemporary Crisis* 10 (1): 63–80.

Human Rights Watch (2003) *Ill Equipped: US Prisons and Offenders with Mental Illness.* New York: Human Rights Watch.

Hutton, N. (2005) 'Beyond Populist Punitiveness?'. *Punishment and Society* 7 (3) 243–258.

Ignatieff, M. (1981) 'State, Civil Society and Total Institutions: A Critique of Recent Social Histories of Punishment'. *Crime and Justice* 3: 153–192.

Jackson, J., and Gray, E. (2010) 'Functional Fear and Public Insecurities about Crime'. *British Journal of Criminology* 50 (1): 1–22.

Jacobs, J. (2001) 'Facts, Values and Prison Policies: A Commentary on Zimring and Tonry'. *Punishment and Society* 3: 183–188.

Jacobson, M. (2006) 'Reversing the Punitive Turn: The Limits and Promise of Current Research'. *Criminology and Public Policy* 5 (2): 277–284.

Jones, T., Maclean, B., and Young, T. (1986) *The Islington Crime Survey*. Aldershot: Gower.

Jupp, V. (1995) *Methods of Criminological Research*. London: Routledge.

Justice Policy Institute (2009) *Response to FBI Uniform Crime Report*. Washington: Justice Policy Institute.

Kantola, J. (2006) 'Feminism', in C. Hay, M. Lister and D. Marsh (eds), *The State: Theories and Issues*. London: Palgrave Macmillan.

Karmen, A. (2000) *The New York Murder Mystery: The True Story behind the Crime Crash of the 1990s*. New York University Press.

Kasindorf, M. (2002) 'Three Strikes Laws Falls Out of Favour: Harsh Sentences, Questionable Results, Dim Measures' Appeal. *USA Today*, February 28.

Katz, J. (1988) *The Seductions of Crime: Moral and Sensual Attractions of Doing Evil*. New York: Basic Books.

Kelling, G. L. (2001) '"Broken Windows" and the Culture Wars: A Response to Selected Critiques', in R. Matthews and J. Pitts (eds), *Crime, Disorder and Community Safety*. London: Routledge.

Kelly, L. (2005) 'You Can Find Anything You Want: A Critical Reflection of Research on Trafficking in Persons Within and Into Europe'. *International Migration* 43 (1–2): 235–269.

King, A., and Maruna, S. (2009) 'Is a Conservative Just a Liberal Who Has Been Mugged? Exploring the Origins of Punitive Views'. *Punishment and Society* 11 (2): 147–169.

King, T. R. (2009) *The State of Sentencing 2008: Developments in Policy and Practice*. Washington, DC: Sentencing Project.

Kinsey, R., Lea, J., and Young, J. (1986) *Losing the Fight against Crime*. Oxford: Blackwell Press.

Kiser, E., and Hechter, M. (1998) 'The Debate on Historical Sociology: Rational Choice Theory and Its Critics'. *American Journal of Sociology* 104 (3): 785–816.

Klein, J. (2006) 'An Invisible Problem: Everyday Violence Against Girls in Schools'. *Theoretical Criminology* 10 (2): 147–178.

Kuper, A. (1999) *Culture: The Anthropologist's Account*. Harvard: Harvard University Press.

Kury, H., and Shea, E. (2011) *Punivity: International Developments*. Bochum: Universitatverlag Dr. Brockmeyer.

Kydd, A., and Walter, B. (2006) 'The Strategies of Terrorism'. *International Security* 31 (1): 49–80.

Lamb, S. (1999) *New Versions of Victims: Feminists' Struggle with the Concept*. New York: New York University Press.

Langham, P. (2005) 'Crime and Punishment in the United States 1981–1989', in M. Tonry and D. Farrington (eds), *Crime and Punishment in Western Countries*. Chicago: University of Chicago Press.

Langham, P., and Levin, D. (2002) *Recidivism of Prisoners Released in 1994*, Bureau of Justice Special Report, US Department of Justice.

Lappi-Seppälä, T. (2007) 'Trust, Welfare and Political Economy'. *Crime and Justice: An Annual Review of Research* 35.

Laub, J. (2004) 'The Life Course of Criminology in the United States'. *Criminology* 42 (1): 1–26.

Laub, J., and Sampson R. (2001) 'Understanding Desistance from Crime', in M. Tonry (ed.), *Crime and Justice, Vol. 28.* Chicago: University of Chicago Press.

Layder, D. (1993) *New Strategies in Social Research.* Cambridge: Polity.

Lea, J. (1992) 'The Analysis of Crime', in J. Young and R. Matthews (eds) *Rethinking Criminology: The Realist Debate.* London: Sage.

Lea, J. (1998) 'Post-Fordism and Criminality', in N. Jewson and S. MacGregor (eds), *Transforming Cities: Contested Governance and New Spatial Divisions.* New York: Routledge.

Lea, J., and Young, J. (1984) *What Is to Be Done about Law and Order? Crisis in the Eighties.* Harmondsworth: Penguin.

LeBel, T., Burnett, R., Maruna, S., and Bushway, S. (2008) 'The "Chicken and Egg" of Subjective and Social Factors in Desistance from Crime'. *European Journal of Criminology* 5: 131–159.

Lee, M. (2007) *Inventing the Fear of Crime: Criminology and the Politics of Fear.* Cullompton: Willan.

Lemert, E. (1962) 'Paranoia and the Dynamics of Exclusion'. *Sociometry* 25 (1): 2–20.

Lemke, T. (2003) 'Comment on Nancy Fraser: Rereading Foucault in the Shadow of Globalisation'. *Constellations* 10 (2): 172–179.

Leonard, E. (1983) *Women, Crime and Society.* London: Longman.

Levi, M. (2002) 'Suite Justice or Sweet Charity? Some Explorations of Shaming and Incapacitating Business Fraudsters'. *Punishment and Society* 4 (2): 147–163.

Levitt, S., and Dubner, S. (2006) *Freakonomics.* London: Penguin.

Levitt, S., and Dubner, S. (2009) *Super Freakonomics.* London: Penguin.

Lilly, R., Cullen, F., and Ball, R. (2011) *Criminological Theory: Contexts and Consequences* (5th edn). London: Sage.

Lipsett, A. (2009) 'Nearly 3,000 School Arson Attacks in Two Years'. *Guardian*, May 2.

Listwan, S., Jonson, C., Cullen, F., and Latessa, E. (2008) 'Cracks in the Penal Harm Movement: Evidence From the Field'. *Criminology and Public Policy* 7 (3): 423–465.

Loader, I. (2010) 'For Penal Moderation: Notes Towards a Public Philosophy of Punishment'. *Theoretical Criminology* 14 (3): 349–368.

Lukes, S. (2005) *Power: A Radical View* (2nd edn). New York: Palgrave Macmillan.

Lyng, S. (1990) 'Edgework: A Social Psychological Analysis of Voluntary Risk Taking'. *American Journal of Sociology* 95 (4): 851–886.

MacKinnon, C. (1997) 'Rape: On Coercion and Consent', in K. Conboy, N. Medina and S. Stanbury (eds), *Writing on the Body: Female Embodiment and Feminist Theory.* Columbia: Columbia University Press.

Macrae, S., Maguire, M., and Melbourne, L. (2003) 'Social Exclusion: Exclusion from School'. *International Journal of Inclusive Education* 7 (2): 89–101.

Manicas, P. (2006) *A Realist Philosophy of Social Science.* Cambridge: Cambridge University Press.

Martinovic, M. (2002) *The Punitiveness of Electronically Monitored Community Based Programs.* Paper presented the Probation and Community Corrections: Making the Community Safer Conference. Perth, Australia. September.

Martinson, R. (1974) 'What Works? Questions and Answers about Prison Reform'. *Public Interest* 35: 22–45.

Maruna, S. (2000) *Making Good: How Ex-Convicts Reform and Rebuild Their Lives.* Washington: American Psychological Association.

Maslow, A. (1970) *Motivation and Personality.* New York: Harper and Row.

Mathieson, T. (1974) *The Politics of Abolition.* London: Martin Robertson.

Matthews, R. (1987) 'Taking Realist Criminology Seriously'. *Crime, Law and Social Change* 11 (4): 371–401.

Matthews, R. (1992) 'Replacing Broken Windows', in R. Matthews and J. Young (eds), *Issues in Realist Criminology.* London: Sage.

Matthews, R. (1998) *Informal Justice?* London: Sage.

Matthews, R. (2001) *Armed Robbery.* Cullompton: Willan.

Matthews, R. (2002) 'Crime and Control in Late Modernity'. *Theoretical Criminology* 6 (2): 217–226.

Matthews, R. (2003) 'Rethinking Penal Policy: Towards a Systems Based Approach', in R. Matthews and J. Young (eds), *The New Politics of Crime and Punishment.* Cullompton: Willan.

Matthews, R. (2005) 'The Myth of Punitiveness'. *Theoretical Criminology* 9 (2): 175–201.

Matthews, R. (2008) *Prostitution, Politics and Policy.* London: Routledge.

Matthews, R. (2009) 'Beyond "So What?" Criminology: Rediscovering Realism'. *Theoretical Criminology* 13 (3): 341–362.

Matthews, R. (2009a) *Doing Time: An Introduction to the Sociology of Imprisonment* (2nd edn). London: Palgrave Macmillan.

Matthews, R. (2010) 'Realist Criminology Revisited', in E. McLaughlin and T. Newburn (eds), *The Sage Handbook of Criminological Theory.* London: Sage.

Matthews, R. (2010a) 'The Construction of "So What?". Criminology: A Realist Analysis'. *Crime, Law and Social Change* 54 (2): 125–140.

Matthews, R., Easton, H., Briggs, D., and Pease, K. (2007) *Assessing the Use and Impact of Anti-Social Behaviour Orders.* Bristol: Policy Press.

Matthews, R., Hancock, L., and Briggs, D. (2001a) *Jurors Perceptions and Understanding of the Court Process.* On-line publication. London: Home Office.

Matza, D., and Sykes, G. (1961) 'Juvenile Delinquency and Subterranean Values'. *American Sociology Review* 26: 713–719.

Mauer, M. (1999) *Race to Incarcerate.* Washington: Sentencing Project.

Mauer, M. (2002) 'State Sentencing Reforms: Is the "Get Tough" Era Coming to a Close?'. *Federal Sentencing Reporter* 15 (1): 50–52.

Maxwell, J. (2012) *A Realist Approach for Qualitative Research.* Los Angeles: Sage.

McCulloch, J., and Pickering, S. (2009) 'Pre-crime and Counter-Terrorism: Imagining Future Crime in the "Wars on Terror"'. *British Journal of Criminology* 51 (4): 707–738.

McIntosh, M. (1968) 'The Homosexual Role'. *Social Problems* 6 (20): 182–192.

McLaughlin, E., and Murji, K. (2001) 'Lost Connections and New Directions: Neo-Liberalism, New Public Managerialism and the Modernisation of the British Police', in K. Stenson and R. Sullivan (eds), *Crime, Risk and Justice.* Cullompton: Willan.

McNay, L. (1992) *Foucault and Feminism: Power, Gender, and the Self.* Boston: Northeastern University Press.

Mead, I. (1986) *Beyond Entitlements: The Social Obligations of Citizenship*. New York: Free Press.

Melossi, D. (2001) 'The Cultural Embededness of Social Control: Reflections of the Comparison of Italian and North American Cultures Concerning Punishment'. *Theoretical Criminology* 45 (4): 403–424.

Merquior, J. (1985) *Foucault*. Illinois: Fontana Press.

Merton, R. (1938) 'Social Structure and Anomie'. *American Sociological Review* 3: 672–682.

Meyer, J., and O'Malley, P. (2005) 'Missing the Punitive Turn? Canadian Criminal Justice "Balance" and Penal Modernism', in J. Pratt, D. Brown, M. Brown, S. Hallsworth and W. Morrison (eds), *The New Punitiveness: Trends, Theories, Perspectives*. Cullompton: Willan.

Miller, P., and Rose, N. (2008) *Governing the Present*. Cambridge: Polity Press.

Millie, A., Jacobson, J., and Hough, M. (2003) 'Understanding the Growth of the Prison Population in England and Wales'. *Criminal Justice* 3 (4): 369–387.

Mills, C. W. (1959) *The Sociological Imagination*. Oxford: Oxford University Press.

Mingers, J. (2004) 'Future Directions in Management Science Modelling: Critical Realism and Multimethodology', in S. Fleetwood and S. Ackroyd (eds), *Critical Realist Applications in Organisation and Management Studies*. London: Routledge.

Ministry of Justice (2008) *Offender Management Caseload Statistics*. London: HMSO.

Mirrlees-Black, C. (2001) *Confidence in the Criminal Justice System: Findings from the 2000 British Crime Survey*. Research Findings 137. London: Home Office.

Mooney, J. (2000) *Gender, Violence and the Social Order*. London: Palgrave Macmillan.

Moore, D., and Hannah-Moffat, K. (2005) 'The Liberal Veil: Revisiting Canadian Penality', in J. Pratt, D. Brown, M. Brown, S. Hallsworth and W. Morrison (eds), *The New Punitiveness: Trends, Theories, Perspectives*. Cullompton: Willan.

Muncie, J. (1996) 'The Construction and Deconstruction of Crime', in J. Muncie and E. McLaughlin (eds), *The Problem of Crime*. London: Sage.

Munro, V., and Kelly, L. (2009) 'A Vicious Cycle? Attrition and Conviction Patterns in Contemporary Rape Cases in England and Wales', in M. Horvath and J. Brown (eds), *Rape: Challenging Contemporary Thinking*. Cullompton: Willan.

Murray, C. (1996) *Charles Murray and the Underclass: The Developing Debate*. London: IEA Health and Welfare Unit.

Murray, C. (1997) *Does Prison Work?* London: IEA Health and Welfare Unit.

Myhill, A., and Allen, J. (2002) *Rape and Sexual Assault of Women: Findings from the British Crime Survey*. London: Home Office Research and Statistics Directorate.

Neiman, S., and Hill, M. (2011) *Crime, Violence, Discipline and Safety in US Public Schools*. US Department of Education.

Nelken, D. (2005) 'When Is a Society Non-punitive? The Italian Case', in J. Pratt, D. Brown, M. Brown, S. Hallsworth and W. Morrison (eds), *The New Punitiveness: Trends, Theories, Perspectives*. Cullompton: Willan.

Nettleton, S. (1997) 'Governing Risky Self: How to Become Healthy and Wise?', in A. Petersen and R. Bunton (eds), *Foucault, Health and Medicine*. London: Routledge.

Newman, J., Barnes, M., Sullivan, H., and Knops, A. (2004) 'Public Participation and Collaborative Governance'. *Journal of Social Policy* 33 (2): 203–233.

Norrie, A. (1986) *Crime, Reason and History: A Critical Introduction to the Criminal Law*. London: Weidenfeld and Nicholson.

Norrie, A. (1994) 'Practical Reasoning and Criminal. Responsibility: A Jurisprudential Approach', in D. B. Cornish and R. Clarke (eds), *The Reasoning Criminal*. New York: Springer-Verlag.

O'Brien, M. (2005) 'What Is Cultural about Cultural Criminology?'. *British Journal of Criminology* 45: 599–612.

O'Brien, M., and Penna, S. (2007) 'Critical Criminology: Chaos or Continuity?'. *Criminal Justice Review* 32 (3): 246–255.

O'Brien, P. (1982) *The Promise of Punishment: Prisons in Nineteenth Century*. France: Princetown University Press.

O'Malley, P. (1996) 'Post-Social Criminologies. Some Implications of Current Political Trends for Criminological Theory and Practice'. *Current Issues in Criminal Justice* 8 (1): 26–38.

O'Malley, P. (1999) 'Volatile and Contradictory Punishment'. *Theoretical Criminology* 3 (2): 175–196.

O'Malley, P. (2004) *Risk Uncertainty and Government*. London: Glasshouse Press.

Parr, S. (2009) 'Confronting the Reality of Anti-Social Behaviour'. *Theoretical Criminology* 13 (3): 363–381.

Patterson, O. (2006) 'A Poverty of the Mind'. *New York Times*, March 26: 1–3.

Pavlich, G. (1999) 'Criticism and Criminology: In Search of Legitimacy'. *Theoretical Criminology* 3 (1): 29–52.

Pawson, R. (2006) *Evidence-Based Policy: A Realist Perspective*. London: Sage.

Pawson, R. (2013) *The Science of Evaluation: A Realist Manifesto*. London: Sage.

Pawson, R., and Tilley, N. (1997) *Realist Evaluation*. London: Sage.

Pearce, F., and Tombs, S. (1992) 'Realism and Corporate Crime', in R. Matthews and J. Young (eds), *Issues in Realist Criminology*. London: Sage.

Pease, K. (1994) 'Cross National Imprisonment Rates', in R. King and M. Maguire (eds), *Prisons in Context*. Oxford: Clarendon.

Pease, K. (2007) 'Victims and Victimisation', in S. Shoham, O. Beck and M. Kent (eds), *International Handbook of Penology and Criminal Justice*. CRC Press.

Pepinsky, H., and Quinney, R. (1991) *Criminology as Peacemaking*. Bloomington: Indiana University Press.

Peterson, A. (1997) 'Risk, Governance and the New Public Health', in A. Petersen and R. Bunton (eds), *Foucault, Health and Medicine*. London: Routledge.

Petersilia, J. (2003) *When Prisoners Come Home: Parole and Prisoner Reentry*. Oxford: Oxford University Press.

Peterson, R., and Krivo, L. (2010) *Divergent Social Worlds: Neighborhood Crime and the Racial – Spatial Divide*. New York: Russell Sage Foundation.

Piacentini, L. (2005) 'Cultural Talk and Other Intimate Acquaintances with Russian Prisons'. *Crime, Media, Culture* 1 (2): 189–208.

Piper, C., and Easton, S. (2006) 'What's Sentencing Got to Do With It? Understanding the Prison Crisis'. *Contemporary Issues in Law* 8 (4): 356–376.

Pires, A., and Acosta, F. (1994) 'What's Real in Realism? What's Construction in Constructionism? The Case of Criminology'. *Journal of Human Justice* 5 (2): 6–33.

Pitts, J. (2007) 'Who Cares What Works?' *Youth and Policy* 95.

Pitts, J. (2008) *Reluctant Gangsters: The Changing Face of Youth Crime*. Cullompton: Willan.

Pitts, J. (2013) 'The Third Time as Farce: What Ever Happened to the Penal State?', in P. Squires and J. Lea (eds), *Criminalisation and Advanced Marginality: Critically Exploring the Work of Loic Wacquant*. Bristol: Policy Press.

Player, E., and Jenkins, M. (1994) *Prisons After Woolf: Reform through Riot*. London: Routledge.

Plummer, K. (2001) *Documents of Life: An Invitation to a Critical Humanism*. London: Sage.

Porpora, D. (1998) 'Four Concepts of Social Structure', in M. Archer, R. Bhaskar, A. Collier, T. Lawson, and A. Norrie (eds), *Critical Realism: Essential Readings*. London: Routledge.

Porter, S. (1993) 'Critical Realist Ethnography: The Case of Racism and Professionalism in a Medical Setting'. *Sociology* 27 (4): 591–609.

Pratt, J. (1998) *Governing the Dangerous: Dangerousness Law and Social Change*. Sydney: Federation Press.

Pratt, J. (2006) 'Beyond Evangelical Criminology', in I. Aertson, T. Daems and L. Robert (eds), *Institutionalizing Restorative Justice*. Cullompton: Willan.

Pratt, J. (2007) *Penal Populism*. London: Routledge.

Pratt, J. (2008) 'Scandinavian Exceptionalism in an Era of Penal Excess: Part 11: Does Scandinavian Exceptionalism Have a Future?'. *British Journal of Criminology* 48 (3): 275–292.

Pratt, J., Brown D., Brown, M., Hallsworth, S., and Morrison, W. (2005) *The New Punitiveness: Trends Theories, Perspectives*. Cullompton: Willan.

Presdee, M. (2000) *Cultural Criminology and the Carnival of Crime*. London: Routledge.

Pykett, J. (2012) 'The New Maternal State: The Gendered Politics of Governing through Behavioural Change'. *Antipode* 44 (1): 217–238.

Ray, L., and Sayer, A. (1999) *Culture and Economy after the Cultural Turn*. London: Sage.

Raymond, J., and Hughes, D. (2001) *Sex Trafficking of Women in the United States*. Coalition Against Trafficking in Women, http://wwwpdfportal.com/sextraffus_60699.pdf.

Reid, R. (2005) *Globalising Tobacco Control*. Indiana: Indiana University Press.

Reiman, J. (2004) *The Rich Get Richer and the Poor Get Prison*. Boston: Allyn and Bacon.

Roberts, J. (2003) 'Public Opinion and Mandatory Sentencing: A Review of International Findings'. *Criminal Justice and Behaviour* 36: 483–508.

Robinson, G. (2008) 'Late Modern Rehabilitation'. *Punishment and Society* 10: 429–445.

Rock, P. (1988) 'The Present State of Criminology in Britain'. *British Journal of Criminology* 28 (2): 58–69.

Rogers, C. (2012) *On Becoming a Person: A Therapist's View of Psychotherapy*. Houghton: Miffin Harcourt.

Rose, N. (1999) 'Government and Control'. *British Journal of Criminology* 40 (2): 324–339.

Rose, N. (2007) *The Politics of Life Itself*. Princeton, New Jersey: Princeton University Press.

Roshier, B. (1989) *Controlling Crime: The Classical Perspective in Criminology*. Milton Keynes: Open University Press.

Rusche, G., and Kirchheimer, O. (2003) *Punishment and Social Structure*. New Jersey: Transaction.

Ryan, M. (2003) *Penal Policy and Political Culture*. Winchester: Waterside Press.

Sacco, V. (1993) 'Social Support and the Fear of Crime'. *Canadian Journal of Criminology* 35: 187–196.

Sampson, R. (2006) '"Open Doors Don't Invite Criminals": Is Increased Immigration behind the Drop in Crime?'. *New York Times*, March 11: 27–28.

Sampson, R., and Laub, J. (1993) *Crime in the Making: Pathways and Turning Points through Life*. Cambridge MA: Harvard University Press.

Sampson, R., and Raudenbush, S. (1999) 'Systematic Social Observation in Public Spaces: A New Look at Disorder in Urban Neighbourhoods'. *American Journal of Sociology* 105 (3): 603–651.

Sandel, M. (1982) *Liberalism and the Limits to Justice*. Cambridge: Cambridge University Press.

Sayer, A. (1991) 'Behind the Locality Debate: Deconstructing Geographies Dualisms'. *Environment and Planning* 23: 283–308.

Sayer, A. (1992) *Methods in Social Science: A Realist Approach*. London: Routledge.

Sayer, A. (1997) 'Critical Realism and the Limits of Critical Social Science'. *Journal for the Theory of Social Behaviour* 27 (4): 473–488.

Sayer, A. (2000) *Realism and Social Science*. London: Sage.

Sayer, A. (2005) *The Moral Significance of Class*. Cambridge: Cambridge University Press.

Sayer, A. (2009) 'Who's Afraid of Critical Social Science?'. *Current Sociology* 57 (6): 767–786.

Sayer, A. (2010) *Methods in Social Science: A Realist Approach* (2nd edn). London: Routledge.

Sayer, A. (2011) *Why Things Matter to People: Social Science, Values and Ethical Life*. Cambridge: Cambridge University Press.

Scarpitti, F. (1985) 'The Recent History of the American Society of Criminology'. *Criminologist*, November: 1–3.

Schee, C. (2008) 'The Politics of Health as a School-Sponsored Ethic: Foucault, Neoliberalism and the Unhealthy Employee'. *Educational Policy* 22: 854–874.

Schiraldi, V. (2003–2004) 'Digging Out: As US States Begin to Reduce Prison Use, Can America Turn the Corner on Its Imprisonment Binge?'. *Pacific Law Review* 24: 563–579.

Schwendinger, H., and Schwendinger, J. (1975) 'On the American Society of Criminology'. *Crime and Social Justice* (Spring/Summer) (11): 2–5.

Scott-Hayward, C. (2009) *The Fiscal Crisis in Corrections: Rethinking Policies and Practices*. New York: Vera Institute of Justice.

Sen, A. (2004) 'Elements of a Theory of Human Rights'. *Philosophy and Public Affairs* 32 (4): 315–356.

Sherman, L., Farrington, D., Welsh, B., and MacKenzie, D. (2002) *Evidence Based Crime Prevention*. London: Routledge.

Silver, A. (1967) 'The Demand for Order in Civil Society', in D. Bordua (ed.), *The Police*. New York: Wiley.

Silvestri, M., and Crowther-Dowey, C. (2008) *Gender and Crime*. London: Sage.

Simon, J. (2007) *Governing through Crime: How the War on Crime Transformed American Democracy and Created a Culture of Terror*. New York: Oxford University Press.

Simon, J. (2009) *Governing through Crime*. New York: Oxford University Press.

Simon, J., and Feeley, M. (1995) 'True Crime: The New Penology and Public Discourse on Crime', in T. Blomberg and S. Cohen (eds), *Punishment and Social Control*. Berlin: de Gruyter.

Skeggs, B. (2001) 'Feminist Ethnography', in P. Atkinson, S. Delamonte, A. Coffey, and J. Lofland (eds), *Handbook of Ethnography*. London: Sage.

Sloan-Hewitt, M., and Kelling, G. (1990) 'Subway Graffiti in New York City: "Getting up" vs. "Meanin It and Cleanin It"', in R. Clarke (ed.), *Situational Crime Prevention: Successful Case Studies*. New York: Harrow and Heston.

Smart, C. (1976) *Women, Crime and Criminology: A Feminist Critique*. London: Routledge and Kegan Paul.

Smart, C. (1990) 'Feminist Approaches to Criminology or Postmodern Woman Meets Atavistic Man?', in L. Gelsthorpe and A. Morris (eds), *Feminist Perspectives in Criminology*. Milton Keynes: Open University Press.

Somers, M. (1998) '"We're No Angels": Realism, Rational Choice, and Relationality in Social Science'. *American Journal of Sociology* 104 (3): 722–784.

Sorensen, J., and Steman, D. (2002) 'The Effect of State Sentencing Policies on Incarceration Rates'. *Crime and Delinquency* 48 (3): 456–475.

Sparks, R. (1981) 'Multiple Victimisation: Evidence, Theory and Future Research'. *Journal of Criminal Law and Criminology* 72 (2): 762–778.

Squires, P., and Stephen, D. (2005) *Rougher Justice: Anti-Social Behaviour and Young People*. Cullompton: Willan.

Stenson, K. (2000) 'Someday our Prince Will Come: Zero Tolerance Policing in Britain', in T. Hope and R. Sparks (eds), *Crime, Risk and Insecurity*. London: Routledge.

Sutherland, E. (1949) 'Is "White Collar Crime" Crime?'. *American Sociological Review* 10 (2): 132–139.

Sutherland, E. and Cressey, D. (1960) *Principles of Criminology*. Philadelphia: Lippencott.

Swyngedouw, E. (2005) 'Governance Innovation and the Citizen: The Janus Face of Governance-Beyond-the-State'. *Urban Studies* 42 (11): 1991–2006.

Sykes, G. (1974) 'The Rise of Critical Criminology'. *Journal of Criminal Law and Criminology* 65 (2): 206–213.

Szasz, T. (1970) *The Manufacture of Madness*. New York: Harper and Row.

Taylor, I. (1982) Law and Order: Arguments for Socialism. London: Macmillan.

Taylor, I., Walton, P., and Young, J. (1973) *The New Criminology*. London: Routledge.

Taylor, I., Walton, P., and Young, J. (1975) *Critical Criminology*. London: Routledge.

Taylor, I., Walton, P., and Young, J. (2013) *The New Criminology* (2nd edn). London: Routledge.

Taylor, M. (2005) 'Survey Shows Extent of Classroom Abuse'. *Guardian*, March 21.

Thaler, R., and Sunstein, C. (2008) *Nudge: Improving Decision about Health, Wealth and Happiness*. London: Penguin.

Thompson, E. (1975) *Whigs and Hunters: The Origin of the Black Act*. London: Allen Lane.

Tilley, N. (2001) 'Evaluation and Evidence-Led Crime Reduction Policy and Practice', in R. Matthews and J. Pitts (eds), *Crime, Disorder and Community Safety*. London: Routledge.

Tilley, N. (2002) 'Crime Prevention in Britain 1975–2010: Breaking Out, Breaking In and Breaking Down', in G. Hughes, E. McLaughlin and J. Muncie (eds), *Crime Prevention and Community Safety: New Directions*. London: Sage.

Tonry, M. (1995) *Malign Neglect: Race, Crime and Punishment in America*. New York: Oxford University Press.

Tonry, M. (2001) *Penal Reform in Overcrowded Times*. New York: Oxford University Press.

Tonry, M. (2007) 'Determinants of Penal Policy', in M. Tonry (ed.), *Crime and Justice: An Annual Review of Research, Vol. 36*. Chicago: University of Chicago Press.

Tonry, M., and Farrington, D. (2004) *Crime and Punishment in Western Countries 1980–1999*. Chicago: University of Chicago Press.

Trachtenberg, B. (2005) 'State Sentencing Policy and New Prison Admissions'. *University of Michigan Journal of Law Reform* 38 (2): 479–430.

Trasler, G. (1986) 'Situational Crime Control and Rational Choice: A Critique', in K. Heal and G. Laycock (eds), *Situational Crime Prevention: From Theory to Practice*. London: HMSO.

Travis, A. (2007) 'Top Judge Attacks Trapdoor to Prison'. *Guardian*, May 3.

Tsoukas, H. (1989) 'The Validity of Idiographic Research Explanations'. *Academy of Management Review* 14 (4): 551–561.

Unnever, J., and Cullen, F. (2009) 'Empathetic Identification and Punitiveness: A Middle Range Theory of Individual Differences'. *Theoretical Criminology* 13 (3): 283–311.

Van Aelst, P., and Walgrave, S. (2002) 'New Media, New Movements? The Role of the Internet in Shaping the Anti-Globalisation Movement'. *Information, Communication and Society* 5 (4): 465–493.

Vaughan, B. (2007) 'The Internal Narrative of Desistance'. *British Journal of Criminology* 47 (3): 390–404.

Wacquant, L. (2000) 'The New "Peculiar Institution": On the Prison as Surrogate Ghetto'. *Theoretical Criminology* 4 (3): 377–389.

Wacquant, L. (2001) 'Deadly Symbiosis: When Ghetto and Prisons Merge'. *Punishment and Society* 3 (1): 45–134.

Wacquant, L. (2005) 'The Great Penal Leap Backward: Incarceration in America from Nixon to Clinton', in J. Pratt, D. Brown, M. Brown, S. Hallsworth, and W. Morrison (eds), *The New Punitiveness: Trends, Theories, Perspectives*. Cullompton: Willan.

Wacquant, L. (2009) *Punishing Then Poor: The Neoliberal Government of Social Insecurity*. Durham, North Carolina: Duke University Press.

Waddington, D., and King, M. (2009) 'Identifying Common Causes of UK and French Riots Occurring since the 1980s'. *Howard Journal* 48 (3): 245–256.

Walklate, S. (2007) *Handbook of Victims and Victimology*. Cullompton: Willan.

Walters, R. (2003) 'New Modes of Governance and the Commodification of Criminological Knowledge'. *Social and Legal Studies* 12 (1): 5–26.

Wasik, M. (2004) 'What Guides Sentencing Decisions', in A. Bottoms, S. Rex and G. Robinson (eds), *Alternatives to Prison: Options for an Insecure Society*. Cullompton: Willan.

Weaver, V., Hacker, J., and Wildeman, C. (2014) 'Detaining Democracy? Criminal Justice and American Civic Life'. *The Annals of the American Academy of Political and Social Science* 651 (1): 6–21.

Weber, M. (1949) *The Methodology of the Social Sciences*. New York: Free Press.
Weber, M. (1968) *Economy and Society*. Berkeley: University of California Press.
Webber, C. (2007) 'Background, Foreground, Foresight: The Third Dimensional of Cultural Criminology?'. *Crime, Media, Culture* 3 (2): 139–157.
Weeks, J. (2007) *The World We Have Won*. Oxford: Routledge.
Weitzer, R. (2007) 'The Social Construction of Sex Trafficking: Ideology and the Institutionalization of a Moral Crusade'. *Politics and Society* 35: 447–475.
White, R. (2010) 'A Green Criminology Perspective', in E. McLaughlin and T. Newburn (eds), *The Sage Handbook of Criminological Theory*. London: Sage.
Whitman, J. (2003) *Harsh Justice: Criminal Justice and the Widening Divide between America and Europe*. Oxford: Oxford University Press.
Willan Walmsley, R. (2006) *World Prison Population List* (7th edn). International Centre for Prison Studies, London: Kings College.
Willis, P. (1977) *Learning to Labour: How Working Class Kids Get Working Class Jobs*. New York: Columbia University Press.
Willis, P. (2000) *The Ethnographic Imaginations*. Cambridge: Polity.
Wilson, J. (1983) *Thinking about Crime*. New York: Basic Books.
Wilson, J. (2011) 'Hard Times, Fewer Crimes'. *Wall Street Journal*, May 28: 28–29.
Wilson, J., and Kelling, G. (1982) 'The Police and Neighbourhood Safety: Broken Windows'. *Atlantic Monthly* 127: 29–38.
Wright, R. T., and Decker, S. H. (1997) *Armed Robberies in Action: Stickups and Street Culture*. Boston: Northeastern University Press.
Young, J. (1975) 'Working-class Criminology', in I. Taylor, P. Walton and J. Young (eds), *Critical Criminology*. London: Routledge
Young, J. (1986) 'The Failure of Criminology: The Need for a Radical Realism', in R. Matthews and J. Young (eds), *Confronting Crime*. London: Sage.
Young, J. (1988) 'Radical Criminology in Britain: The Emergence of a Competing Paradigm'. *British Journal of Criminology* 28 (2): 159–183.
Young, J. (1992) 'Ten Points of Realism', in J. Young and R. Matthews (eds), *Rethinking Criminology: The Realist Debate*. London: Sage.
Young, J. (1994) 'Incessant Chatter: Recent Paradigms in Criminology', in M. Maguire, R. Morgan and R. Reiner (eds), *The Oxford Handbook of Criminology*. Oxford: Oxford University Press.
Young, J. (1997) 'Left Realist Criminology: Radical in Its Analysis, Realist in Its Policy', in M. Maguire, R. Morgan and R. Reiner (eds), *The Oxford Handbook of Criminology* (2nd edn). Oxford: Oxford University Press.
Young, J. (1998) 'Risk of Crime and Fear of Crime: A Realist Critique of Survey Based Assumptions', in M. Maguire and J. Pointing (eds), *Victims of Crime: A New Deal?* Milton Keynes: Open University Press.
Young, J. (2003) 'Merton with Energy, Katz with Structure: The Sociology of Vindictiveness and the Criminology of Transgression'. *Theoretical Criminology* 7 (3): 389–413.
Young, J. (2004) 'Voodoo Criminology and the Numbers Game', in J. Ferrell, K. Hayward, W. Morrison and M. Presdee (eds), *Cultural Criminology Unleashed*. London: Glasshouse Press.
Young, J. (2007) *The Vertigo of Late Modernity*. Thousand Oaks, CA: Sage.
Young, J. (2011) *The Criminological Imagination*. Cambridge: Polity.

Youth Violence Project (2011) *National Statistics*, http://youthviolence.edschool. virginia.edu/violenceinschools/national-statistics.html.

Zedner, L. (2002) 'Dangers of Dystopias in Penal Theory'. *Oxford Journal of Legal Studies* 22 (2): 341–366.

Zedner, L. (2007) 'Pre-Crime and Post-Criminology?'. *Theoretical Criminology* 11 (2): 261–282.

Zedner, L. (2009) *Security*. London: Routledge.

Zedner, L. (2011) 'Putting Crime Back on the Criminological Agenda', in M. Bosworth and C. Hoyle (eds), *What Is Criminology?* Oxford: Oxford University Press.

Zimring, F. (2007) *The Great American Crime Decline*. New York: Oxford University Press.

Index

abolitionists, 25
abstraction, 29, 68
administrative criminology,
    12–14, 26
adolescent-limited criminology, 5
American Society of Criminology,
    3, 4
anti-social behaviour, 17, 129,
    147–149
Archer, M., 31, 39–41
Ariely, D., 85

Bauman, Z., 47, 94
Becker, H., 5
Berger, P., 35
Bhaskar, R., 40
Blumstein, A., 124
Bourdieu, P., 111
Boudon, R., 80
Bourgois, P., 111–115
Braithwaite, J., 34, 115, 152
British Crime Survey, 13
broken windows thesis, 16–17

Cain, M., 11
Carlen, P., 11, 26
causality, 58–60, 89, 109
Clarke, R., 12, 73–75, 77,
    78–80, 81, 84
communitarianism, 19
Conklin, J., 89
conservative criminology, 15–18, 26
cookbook criminology, 53–54
Cornish, D., 73–75, 81
Corston, B., 129
Crawford, A., 43
crime
    categories of, 30–31
    construction of, 34–36, 37
    and social class, 33
crime drop, 48, 87–88, 101, 106
critical criminology, 5–8, 94
Cullen, F., 3–4

cultural criminology
    contribution of, 94
    critique of, 84
    defence of, 103–111
    realist response, 97–103
    see also realism
Currie, E., 8

desistance, 40
domestic violence, 10
Donzelot, J., 45
Downes, D., 4
drug wars, 113, 126
Dubner, S., 88–89

edgework, 95
Elster, J., 83
empiricism, 55–58
    abstract, 55–56
    functional, 56
    inverted, 57
ethnography, 63–64, 113–114
    defense of, 63
    instant, 101
    liquid, 101
    photo, 113
European Society for the
    Study of Deviance and
    Social Control, 2

Farrell, G., 84–85
Farrington, D., 127
fear of crime, 146
Felson, M., 75–76, 77
feminist criminology,
    9–12, 129
Ferrell, J., 96, 100, 103
Foucault, M., 2, 11, 19,
    34, 44–45, 150
Fraser, N., 46, 99
freakonomics, 87–88
freedom, 18–19
Frost, N., 122

Printed and bound by CPI Group (UK) Ltd, Croydon, CR0 4YY